Ordering the Baptismal Priesthood

Ordering the Baptismal Priesthood

Theologies of Lay and Ordained Ministry

Edited by Susan K. Wood, S.C.L.

Michael Downey
Zeni Fox
Richard R. Gaillardetz
Aurelie A. Hagstrom
Kenan B. Osborne, O.F.M.
David N. Power, O.M.I.
Thomas P. Rausch, S.J.
Elissa Rinere, C.P.
R. Kevin Seasoltz, O.S.B.
Susan K. Wood, S.C.L.

LITURGICAL PRESS
Collegeville, Minnesota

www.litpress.org

Cover design by David Manahan, O.S.B. Illustration from Art Today, Inc.

Translations of all conciliar texts are taken from *Vatican Council II: Constitutions, Decrees, Declarations,* A Completely Revised Translation in Inclusive Language, ed. Austin Flannery, O.P. (Northport, N.Y./Dublin: Costello Publishing Co. and Dominican Publications, 1996).

1   2   3   4   5   6   7   8   9

Library of Congress Cataloging in Publication Data

Ordering the baptismal priesthood : theologies of lay and ordained ministry / edited by
  Susan K. Wood ; Michael Downey ... [et al.].
    p.   cm.
  Includes bibliographical references and index.
  ISBN 0-8146-2941-5 (alk. paper)
    1. Priesthood. 2. Jesus Christ—Priesthood. 3. Pastoral theology—Catholic Church.
  I. Wood, Susan K. II. Downey, Michael.

BX 1912.O73 2003
262'.142—dc21

2003047609

Contents

Introduction

The Collegeville Ministry Seminar

Susan K. Wood, S.C.L.

For several centuries before Vatican II, the ordained priesthood was understood to be not only the central but also the exclusive locus of ministry in the Roman Catholic Church. The priesthood operated in the sacred order while the laity were to work in the secular world as an extension of the priestly function. These separate roles were most dramatically evident in the liturgy, where the priest was understood—by priest and laity alike—to be the active agent representing Christ, performing sacred rituals and handling sacred objects. The laity were understood to be essentially passive recipients of the grace dispensed by the priests. This theology and the cultural life associated with it gave priests a strong sense of identity. Unfortunately, it also contributed to an impoverishment of the identity of all of the baptized as full participants in the life of the Body of Christ. It prevented the baptized from living out their full responsibilities to minister in the Church.

The Second Vatican Council called for a theological and liturgical renewal emphasizing the Church as communion rather than as institution. The council called for a vision of the Church as sacramental rather than juridical, a shift in perspective that requires a reconsideration of the theology of ministry. This entails a fundamental change in the understanding of how sacred and secular realms relate to one another. It calls the laity out of passivity into active participation in the ministry of the Church, a call inherent in their baptism and in the example of Jesus of Nazareth. The result has been the blossoming of lay ministry evident in virtually any Catholic parish in the United States.

The demographics of Catholic life in the United States also signals changed ministerial relationships. The decreasing number of priests has reached crisis proportions in a number of areas in the United States, particularly in the Midwest. Nationwide, in the year 2000 there were as few as 22,394 active diocesan priests to serve 19,181 parishes.[1] The number of parishes represents about a 25 percent increase over the last half of the twentieth century, with the Catholic population growing 106 percent since 1950.[2] Parishes today are about a third larger than they were in the 1950s, averaging 3,085 parishioners, although they are served by fewer priests.[3] Well over one-third of all parishes exceed 2,500 registered parishioners.[4]

Parishes without a resident pastor have increased from 500 in 1960 to about 2,500 in 2000.[5] Approximately 17 percent of all parishes are administered by a non-resident pastor or entrusted to someone other than a priest.[6] Nearly one-third of all parishes in the Upper Plains Region (VIII) are without a resident pastor. In areas of the most severe shortage, pairing and clustering are becoming more common, and often two or three rural parishes now are served by a single pastor.

The need for effective pastoral leadership is heightened by the concurrent increase in the number of U.S. Catholics, now 59,181,907. At the same time, weekly attendance at Sunday Mass for Catholics is estimated to be 31.9 to 33.5 percent—a number far lower than in the 1960s. Pastoral leaders must not only be sufficient in number, but must also provide a credible witness to a Christian faith no longer accepted as the religious and social norm. They must be able to delegate responsibility and draw forth the talents and commitment of parishioners and other members of the staff.

Lay ministers are increasingly meeting the ever-growing and diversified pastoral needs experienced in parish and diocesan life today. The number of parishes employing lay ministers grew from 54 percent in 1992 to nearly 63 percent in 1997.[7] Lay ecclesial ministers make up about 20 percent of the ecclesial workforce of church personnel nationwide.[8] In upcoming decades, the Roman Catholic Church in the United States will increasingly need the service of excellent lay ministers. Lay ministers' knowledge of the theological tradition and the witness they give to a life in Christ will be critical to the vitality of parish communities. However, lack of recognition of the role of the lay minister, lack of job security, and unjust levels of financial compensation are deterrents to some who might otherwise respond to the call to ministry. A number of rural pastors who find it financially difficult to hire credentialed lay ministers question the necessity of masters-level study for lay ministers. It is a sign of great hope in the Catholic Church that, despite these obstacles, so many individuals embrace the vocation of lay ministry.

There are profound conflicts over the theology and practice of ministry in the Roman Catholic Church. Lay and ordained ministers often feel threatened by each other in ways and for reasons that neither fully understand. The affirmation of lay ministry rooted in baptism has left many priests and potential priests questioning their identity in the Church. Some lay ministers resent what they see as prerogatives and privileges accorded to the ordained. While some members of the Church are attempting to reclaim an identity for the ordained based on hierarchical and juridical powers, others are rejecting the very notion of the distinctive ministry of the ordained. Both lines of thinking betray the vision of Vatican II and of the formative traditions of the Church. It will be impossible for Catholic institutions to educate future generations of students if the current polarization surrounding ministry is not resolved.

Ministry in the Roman Catholic Church calls for collaboration between lay and ordained because both are both incorporated into the life of Christ at baptism and called to mutual responsibility in the Church. Such collaboration does not polarize lay and ordained forms of ministry, but engages both in a cooperative service to the Church that transcends the tensions Catholics experience today. In order for this to occur, there must be a clear articulation of a contemporary theology of ministry that supports and affirms collaboration. Neither a theology of ordained ministry nor a theology of lay ministry can be developed in isolation from each other.

Pastoral practice in the Church often runs ahead of theological reflection. Needs arise; people fill them. The need for this reflection is even more acute due to the development of ministries since Vatican II. This expansion has been occasioned both by the implementation of the Rite of Christian Initiation of Adults, which makes the entire parish a community of Christian formation, and the teaching of Vatican II that the apostolate of the laity is proper to them by virtue of their baptism. Specialized ministries have arisen out of the community to serve this expanded understanding of the Christian community.

Ordained ministry also arises out of baptism, even though the Second Vatican Council stated that the common priesthood of the faithful and the ministerial or hierarchical priesthood differ essentially and not only in degree.[9] The two priesthoods are interrelated because "each in its own way shares in the one priesthood of Christ."[10] Ordination is simply not possible apart from baptism, for it arises from and for the Church constituted by the prayer in the name of the Father, Son, and Spirit and by submission to the baptismal waters symbolizing the death and resurrection of Christ and rebirth in the Spirit. Consequently, both lay and ordained ministry represent an ordering of the baptismal priesthood of all the faithful. We now need to pause and engage in sustained theological reflection on current pastoral needs and practices of ministry.

To articulate a contemporary theology of lay and ordained ministry, Saint John's University in Collegeville, Minnesota, received a grant from the Lilly Foundation to sponsor a research seminar, the "Collegeville Ministry Seminar," in August 2001. Ten theologians—Michael Downey, Zeni Fox, Richard R. Gaillardetz, Aurelie Hagstrom, Kenan Osborne, O.F.M., David Power, O.M.I., Thomas P. Rausch S.J., Elissa Rinere, C.P., R. Kevin Seasoltz, O.S.B., and Susan K. Wood, S.C.L.—gathered for eight days in August 2001 to discuss prepared position papers on various aspects of lay and ordained ministry. The second half of the seminar consisted of an exercise in constructive theology which resulted in seven points of convergence contributing to a theology of ordered ministries. This volume represents the results of the Collegeville Ministry Seminar.

NOTES

1. Bryan T. Froehle and Mary L. Gautier, *Catholicism USA: A Portrait of the Catholic Church in the United States*, Center for Applied Research in the Apostolate (Maryknoll, N.Y.: Orbis Books, 2000) 113, 49.

2. Ibid., 49–50.

3. Ibid., 59, 50.

4. Ibid., 62.

5. Ibid., 121.

6. Ibid., 60.

7. Ibid., 154.

8. Ibid., 157.

9. *Lumen Gentium* 10.

10. Ibid.

MINISTRY AND MINISTRIES

Ministerial Identity

A Question of Common Foundations

MICHAEL DOWNEY

The diminishing numbers of priestly and religious vocations has stirred in us an awareness of a broadly-based, more participatory exercise of ministry as well as a fuller appreciation of the fact that it is in the nature of the Church as the Body of Christ to be blessed with many gifts, ministries, and offices. While some insist on correcting the "vocations crisis," others recognize in these changes rich fruits of the Second Vatican Council, a sign of God's deep love for the Church, and a challenge to a more creative and effective ordering of the gifts and the energy within the Body of Christ. We live at a moment of great opportunity in the Church, not least of all because the manifold gifts of the Body are flourishing, at times in unexpected ways.

In times of great transition, or in periods of perceived crisis, there is a tendency to safeguard and strengthen identity—be it personal, corporate, or national—by way of contrast to the other, or others. Within the Church there are numerous efforts to safeguard and strengthen the identity and distinctiveness of this or that ministry, be it ordained or non-ordained, in contradistinction to other exercises of ministry. One such effort is expressed in the all-too-familiar warnings against the "clericalization of the laity" and the "laicization of the clergy." Due, perhaps, to a deeply ingrained North American pragmatism, efforts to settle the question of the distinctiveness of ordained ministry in contrast to the common ministry of the baptized more often than not are focused on the matter of what one does. Faced with what is thought to be a blurring of the clergy/lay distinction, the ordained are often left wondering about their proper place in the sacramental rites, while lay ministers, or lay ecclesial ministers, often blessed with gifts of leadership and service, seek to identify the skills proper to the exercise of their ministry. Far too often, exercises of all forms of ministry today are rooted in secular models of leadership, with their penchant for "doing," "skills," and "outcomes," and are insufficiently informed by the vocation to effectiveness in the Church's mission shaped by the riches of our theological and spiritual traditions.

These two governing concerns in understanding ministry today—(1) identity by contrast to the others and (2) the focus on ministerial skills—were clearly in evidence at two gatherings in which I was invited to participate. At the first gathering I was asked to speak to the presidents/rectors and deans of Roman Catholic seminaries and theologates who had gathered in Chicago in October 2000 for the annual meeting of the Midwestern Association of Theological Schools. My assigned topic, "Strengthening Priestly Identity and Developing Pastoral Skills," was to be addressed in light of the conference theme, "Forming an Enduring Priestly Identity in a Changing Church." The titles themselves are expressive of the very problem that needs to be overcome.

I sought to do precisely this by highlighting the contours of *As I Have Done for You: A Pastoral Letter on Ministry*, jointly authored by Roger Cardinal Mahony and the priests of the Archdiocese of Los Angeles, attending to the key elements of the theology of ministry, specifically ordained ministry, at the heart of the letter.[1] In the pastoral letter there is an understanding of ministry in which *knowing* has priority over *doing*, and so I sought to invite the presidents/rectors and deans away from an overly pragmatic view of ministry both in preparation for ministry as well as in its exercise. It was, and remains, my conviction that the most important "skill" of the minister is *to know*, to cultivate a whole way of being, a habit of knowing and loving the tradition so that it can be effectively passed on and others might live fruitfully within it. This means that being schooled in theological and spiritual traditions is required, not merely desirable.

Several months after the meeting of the Midwestern Association of Theological Schools, I participated in the first National Symposium on the Spiritual Formation of Lay Ecclesial Ministers held in Indianapolis. I was invited for the purpose of commenting, from the perspective of one who studies and teaches in the field of Christian spirituality, on the findings of a Lilly-funded team of sociologists headed by James Davidson of Purdue University who had made some preliminary investigations into the spirituality of what they had loosely identified as the lay ecclesial minister.[2]

If the governing concern of the seminary and theologate presidents/ rectors and deans was to identify what distinguishes the ordained ministry from the common ministry of the baptized, the governing concern of Davidson and his team was to hammer out a distinctive spirituality of the lay ecclesial minister by way of sharp contrast to the spirituality of the ordained, vowed religious, and the laity in general. My own view, expressed at the symposium in response to the findings of the Davidson team, is that we would do much better to explore the common matrix[3] of ministry rather than insist on nailing down those elements that distinguish one group of ministers in the Church from the others, even if it means that we run the risk of what some fear is a blurring of the clergy/ lay distinction at this time of transition.

My impression in the aftermath of these two gatherings lingers: The organizers of both had become so preoccupied with what is unique to a specific vocation/ministry, identifying one in sharp contrast to the other, that whatever might be had in common by way of theological and spiritual foundations is obscured as a result. It came as a great consolation to learn that many of the participants in the National Symposium on the Spiritual Formation of Lay Ecclesial Ministers were uneasy with many of the Davidson team's premises, and articulated their conviction that the attention must be shifted to the common theological and spiritual foundations for ministries ordained and nonordained. While most participants voiced agreement with some of the assumptions of Davidson's study, they clearly disagreed with two key assumptions that shaped most of the study and determined the team's findings: (1) the spirituality of the layperson is different from that of the clergy and professed religious; (2) the spirituality of the lay ecclesial minister is different from that of the laity in general.

My purpose in this essay is to work in exactly the opposite direction from Davidson's starting point. My assumptions are that all ministry is rooted in baptism by which we are given a share in the mission of Word and Spirit, that all in the Church are called to one and the same holiness, and that each and every ministry, ordained and nonordained, is to be anchored in a common ecclesiological spirituality. The distinctiveness of this or that ministry is properly understood only in light of the common foundation of all ministry in baptism. All ministers, ordained and non-ordained, are first and finally members of God's Holy People, who are consecrated for mission and whose mission is consecration of the world through Christ in the gift of the Spirit to the glory of God the Father.

I shall proceed in four steps. First, I shall offer several vignettes that depict some of the tensions and transitions in ministry in the Church today. Second, I shall hold up two "snapshots" that capture the pragmatism and preoccupation with skills so prevalent in the exercise of ministry today. Third, and most important, I shall lay the foundations for an understanding of all ministry in the baptismal call to holiness through participation in the mission of Word and Spirit, a mission whose effectiveness is strengthened and safeguarded when all members of the Body live from a common ecclesiological spirituality. Fourth, recognizing the problems with the term "lay ecclesial ministry," I shall give some indication of the distinctiveness of this type of lay ministry as well as of the ministry of the presbyter, in a way that does not obfuscate but rather clarifies the whole Body's consecration for mission and mission of consecration.

I. TENSIONS AND TRANSITIONS

The vignettes that follow are similar to some of those provided in *As I Have Done for You*. In their pastoral letter, Cardinal Mahony and the priests of the Archdiocese of Los Angeles begin by articulating a collaborative and inclusive understanding of ministry. They then provide a series of exercises aimed at assisting parish groups and other ecclesial bodies in taking stock of the real changes that are now facing, and will continue to face, the Archdiocese of Los Angeles. Vignettes such as these are part of that exercise and are aimed at helping us to see and understand movements already under way and to recognize the need for yet more changes in our ministerial structures. Seeing and understanding the ministerial needs of a changing Church call for concrete planning for the future. The wide reception of the pastoral letter in dioceses throughout the United States and abroad is one small indication that the ministerial challenges facing the Church of Los Angeles are widely shared.

- A forty-nine-year-old sister has been the director of religious education in her parish for ten years. Over the last year, tensions between her and the pastor have been mounting. These tensions are brought to a head when a third-year seminarian, twenty-seven years old, is assigned to help out in the parish as part of his seminary formation. He is introduced to the parish community during the Sunday Masses. The pastor is "all aglow with excitement and enthusiasm," referring to the seminarian as "the hope for the future of the Church." The DRE feels resentful because the pastor has made a "big scene," "falling all over the seminarian." "The pastor acts like the only ones doing ministry are himself and this 'wet behind the ears' seminarian," she claims. "I cover for him day in and day out. So do all the other lay ministers on the staff. Each of us does more than he does." The sister, a formally trained minister, says she feels like hired help. She does not feel appreciated. Do you have any advice for her? For the pastor?

- A young couple is preparing for marriage. They expect to visit with a priest periodically in the course of the preparation. In the initial contact, the priest instructs the couple to work henceforward with the parish marriage preparation team, comprised of married couples and led by the lay pastoral associate. The couple express their disappointment at not having one-on-one contact with the priest and decide to go to another parish for "personal attention." If you were the lay pastoral associate, what would you say to the young couple?

- A senior pastor feels that he cannot retire because there is no priest to replace him as pastor. Despite his age, deteriorating health, and long years of service, he decides to stay on as pastor out of a sense of responsibility to his people. What other options are at his disposal?

- A laywoman feels called to lay ecclesial ministry. She has no interest in theology or even spirituality. She wants to enroll in a program to provide her with administrative and management skills. She insists: "I am a *lay* minister. Leave theology to the priests and theologians. I just want to serve the people of my parish." Should the parish support her "call" to "ministry"?

• The functions of ministry continue to evolve today as they have in the past. In the Church of the future, it is conceivable that lay ministers may regularly preside at burial services, witness marriages, and baptize. If the priest is identified primarily with what he does, this identity is potentially threatened with changes in activity. Since some of what the priest does is becoming more and more interchangeable with what laypeople do, this may result in an identity crisis for the priest. A sixty-two-year-old priest approaches his bishop and expresses his frustration this way:

> Now that just about anybody can do just about anything in the Church, why would anyone want to be a priest?

> With the Second Vatican Council's affirmation of the importance of the laity, and with its understanding that the fullness of the sacrament of holy orders resides in the bishop(s), the importance of the priesthood has gotten lost in the shuffle.

> The priest's "job description," saying Mass and hearing confessions, gets so little attention because of the administrative burdens of a parish priest, and because of the expectation that he "empower the laity."

> My "job description" has changed too much already. I am afraid that I will be unable to negotiate yet more changes that lie ahead.

What would you say to this priest if you were his bishop?

It is instructive to note that, in these vignettes, the governing concerns are with the distinctiveness of ministerial identity closely tethered to what one does. This is particularly true of the last vignette, in which a senior priest expresses his objection that the tasks once associated with his "job description" are no longer exclusive, or proper, to him. What should also be noted, however, is that such a concern cuts across generations, so that it all too often happens that many seminarians and younger priests today readily identify themselves as "doers" and "hands on" ministers, linking their distinctive identity to what they do. What is more, this emphasis on doing cuts across clerical/lay lines, so that many of the lay ministers emerging in the Church also find themselves in pragmatic overdrive, concentrating much of their energy on developing marketable skills which are thought to be uniquely theirs. In both cases, what is lacking is a recognition of the importance of ministry as a way of being, of knowing and loving and living within the tradition, and inviting others to live within it, so that they too might share in the mission of Word and Spirit.

II. DOERS UNTO DEATH

As noted above, candidates for ordination too often facilely identify themselves as "doers" or "hands on" sacramental ministers, leaving what is thought to be the more speculative, theological work to the theologians. This is no less true of some lay ministers, whose energies are often given to developing leadership skills and to assuring their own place in the sacramental rites. There is an emergent sense, perhaps over the last fifteen years or more, that it is unrealistic or impractical to consider that ongoing theological education and formation, the cultivation of the *habitus theologicus*, is part and parcel of the life of one given to ministry in the Church. Theology is thought to be speculative, "ivory tower," while the minister is thought to be the "people's person," a compassionate heart, a listening ear, a "doer." In my view, this position is untenable and its consequences, both remote and immediate, are disastrous.

The dynamic of the displacement of the theological, reflective, indeed contemplative dimension of ministry may be seen in two snapshots from my first few years as a seminary professor. It is important to note, however, that similar convictions are often expressed in different ways by lay ministers, as I learned early on in my work in preparing laypeople for ministry in the Church.

- While in his final year of preparation for ordination, a seminarian returned from his period of internship in a parish. A man in his mid-forties, gregarious and ostensibly emotionally mature,

with a strong sense of social responsibility and a good sense of
the needs of the Church, he enthusiastically announced upon
his return—to his classmates, to the lower classmen, as well as
to the faculty—what he had gained from his internship. Above
all else, he had learned from the pastor of his internship parish,
a model pastor for many in the diocese, the secret to effective
priestly ministry: "The people don't care what you know; they
just want to know that you care."

• The second snapshot has as its central figure a Mexican-American,
fifty-eight years old, recently ordained for the Archdiocese of
Los Angeles. In September following his ordination, he returned
to Saint John's Seminary for the "Class Mass" concelebrated
with his three ordination classmates. At the dinner following the
Class Mass he was asked to share with all the seminarians there
gathered what he had learned in his first several months of ordained ministry. He narrated the details of a harrowing daily
schedule, of an overwhelming number of crises—from burying
infants to stopping on the freeway as victims of car accidents
were pried from the wreckage. And more. And still more. Crisis
after crisis. Stories of all that he had done in his first several
months as a priest. But never once was there a hint of his ministry of preaching or presiding at the Eucharist. Never one word
of prayer, or of leading others in prayer. And not one word of
leading others in the way of probing the meaning of the Scriptures, or of leading them in the ways of holiness. Amidst this
litany of horrors, the newly ordained communicated what was
his important message to the seminarians: "And *nothing* you
learn in the seminary can possibly prepare you for what you will
be doing as a priest." So much for the ministry of seminary pro-
fessors, spiritual directors, and formators!

These two brief snapshots give a glimpse of an understanding of the
identity of the priest that corresponds to the "Servant Leader" model of
the priest identified by Donald Cozzens.[4] Much of the controversy
about Cozzens's treatment of the personal integrity of priests has
clouded one of the central theses of his work. He juxtaposes two images
of the priest: "Servant Leader" and "Tender of the Word." Since the

Second Vatican Council, the former has all but eclipsed the latter. In my view, it has also eclipsed other helpful understandings of the priesthood as well. Cozzens seems to favor an understanding of priesthood in which there is more room for the reflective, indeed the contemplative, dispositions needed if one is to be a Tender of the Word. He concludes his work, subtitled "A Reflection on the Priest's Crisis of Soul," by treating briefly the "intellectual crisis" facing priests, urging priests to develop a deeper knowledge of Scripture, theology, literature, the arts.[5] This crisis is no less true of lay ministers in the Church. Its solution lies in the recovery of a more reflective and contemplative understanding of all ministry, in which power and doing are displaced as the governing concerns for understanding ministry and its exercise.

Cozzens points out the many advantages of the Servant Leader model, but above all the ability of this model to serve as a corrective to the sacral/cultic model of pre-conciliar days. With this I am, by and large, in agreement. But I wonder if Cozzens sufficiently recognizes that the predominance of the Servant Leader model of priesthood may have had the negative effect of furthering a functional approach to ordained ministry, of the priest as what might be called the "doer unto death." The way forward, as in any understanding of diverse models, lies in the integration of the best elements in each. For our purposes, the priest of the future might best be understood as a Servant Leader who is at one and the same time Tender of the Word. The related challenge, of course, is to chart out the implications of both these models for an understanding of lay ministry as well, in such a way that both ministries are understood as rooted in baptism, in service of the mission of the Church, strengthened and safeguarded in the common sources of an ecclesiological spirituality.

III. BAPTISM: PARTICIPATION IN THE MISSION
OF WORD AND SPIRIT

By our baptism, we bear the name Christian. Whatever our way or walk in life, whatever our calling, our particular vocation, it is in service of our common call given as a gift in baptism. And the one call is this: to participate in the mission of the Word and the Spirit and, by so doing, to share in the very life of God.

Who is this God? God's name above and beyond all naming is love. God is love (1 John 4:8). What is love? Love is the life that pours itself forth—as gift. The gift of God's life, which is love, is constantly, everywhere and always, even in this time and place, here and now, pouring forth as gift.

The *Word* is God's love made visible, tangible, audible. Word is God's love seen, touched, heard. Our call, that of every one of us, ministers ordained and nonordained, is to continue to render love visible, tangible, audible, so that God is seen and touched and heard in the midst of a broken world. Our one call is to cultivate, to nurture, to sustain all manifestations of love—through preaching, teaching, catechesis, and sacramental celebration, but also in art, literature, works of mercy, tending the sick, and promoting a more just society and a Church that more effectively mirrors the reign of God.

The *Spirit* is God's love creating, animating, bonding. Spirit is God's very life toward us, for us, with us, and yes, within us. Our call is to participate in all creative, animating, bonding, and unifying expressions of divine love, becoming a sign of reconciliation, of peace in the midst of a world so deeply divided. By the gift of the Spirit, God dwells within us and gives us again and again, and yet again, firm faith to walk in the light of Christ, abundant hope to move forward in the face of every obstacle, and love's flourishing so that we might share in the divine life—even now.

The Spirit has been given in baptism, and sealed and strengthened in confirmation. The fruits of the Spirit are the gift to every one of the baptized: love, joy, peace, patience, kindness, generosity, faithfulness, gentleness, self-control. Against these there is no law (Gal 5:22-26). How are these to be cultivated in the day in and day out of our lives? How are these fruits, the seeds of which are given in baptism, nurtured and sustained? How do we live together during these dark days in the communion of the Spirit, participating more fully in the mission of Word and Spirit, becoming a sign of reconciliation and peace? Answering these questions provides occasion to chart out the contours of an ecclesiological spirituality which is the basis for any discussion of ministries ordained or nonordained in the Church today. Such a spirituality, rooted in the gift of baptism, is (1) biblical, (2) liturgical, and (3) imbued with a sense of responsibility springing from membership in God's Holy People.

On the Solemnity of the Epiphany, January 6, 2001, John Paul II promulgated an apostolic letter entitled "At the Beginning of the New Millennium," in which he takes stock of the Jubilee celebrations of the year 2000 as well as the challenges that yet await us. There is a remarkable convergence between the three dimensions of an ecclesiological spirituality rooted in the primacy of baptism and the key elements of the vision of John Paul II for the future of the Church. In speaking of the "program" for the third millennium, John Paul writes: "I wish to indicate certain pastoral priorities: holiness, prayer, Sunday Eucharist... listening to the Word."[6]

It is my contention that the inordinate attention being given in some circles to the uniqueness and distinctiveness of this or that ministry, be it ordained or nonordained, as well as the pragmatic overdrive operative in the exercise of most ministry today, can be overcome only by a return to our common foundations: an ecclesiological spirituality which is all of ours by baptism. How is this to be cultivated, nurtured, and sustained? By (1) being washed in the Word; (2) living what we say and do at liturgy; and (3) understanding ourselves as first and finally members of God's Holy People. Taking seriously these elements of a baptismal spirituality is what is required if we are to be readied for the Spirit's flourishing in our midst. It is also what is demanded if we are to face ministerial challenges and reshape ministerial structures so that the Church might more effectively realize its mission of making manifest the magnitude of God's love in the Church and in the world.

1. Washed in the Word

Because of the renewal of Church life and practice prompted by the Second Vatican Council, Roman Catholics have grown in an appreciation of the importance of Sacred Scripture. But there is yet much more to be done. Many still tend to think of the Word of God as secondary to the sacraments. Caesarius of Arles (d. 542) affirms the importance of reverence for the Word in this well-known passage:

Brothers and Sisters, here is a question for you: which to you seems the greater, the Word of God or the Body of Christ? If you want to give the right answer you will reply that God's Word is not less than Christ's Body. Therefore, just as we take

care when we receive the Body of Christ so that no part of it
falls to the ground so, likewise, should we insure that the
Word of God which is given to us is not lost to our souls because we are speaking or thinking about something different.
One who listens negligently to God's Word is just as guilty as
one who, through carelessness, allows Christ's Body to fall to
the ground.[7]

This deep appreciation of the Word of God in Sacred Scripture is
cultivated beginning on Monday morning with a focus on the following
Sunday's scripture readings, especially the gospel. Christian life is life
with the Word, embracing the Word and being embraced by it, day by
day, week by week, season by season.

How to be washed in the Word? It requires time, if only five minutes in the morning, given to sacred reading. This is a way of reading
quite different from grabbing useful information from the morning
newspaper, different from the way a "consumer" takes in data from the
Internet. This is a slow, careful pondering God's Word in the pages of
the Bible. It is a method for prayerful reading and a guide to living. It is
a means of descending to the level of the heart and finding God through
the simple act of reading. Binding prayer to Scripture is a way of pray-
ing that prepares us for contemplation—being able to find God in all
things. In this approach, just one line or one simple word is selected and
then revisited over and over again throughout the day:

In the tender compassion of our God
the dawn from on high shall break upon us. (Luke 1:78)

This line, or just one word from the line, becomes like a signpost we
follow throughout the day, a marker from one day to the next. The
words of the poetic, contemplative bishop Robert F. Morneau point the
way:

Markings

On the Mississippi—mark twain!
If heading toward Oz—the yellow brick road!
When the British come—one if by land, two . . .

What are the markings for your soul?
Are the longitudes and latitudes true co-ordinates?
And when you do get lost—what then?

I look to Polaris, and head due north!
I listen for the wind of the Spirit—Joy—and dance!
I lean into God's word and find a lamp unto my feet.[8]

A baptismal spirituality is a whole way of life wherein we learn to lean into the Word of God, to find a lamp unto our feet, so that we can behold the gift that is always and everywhere being offered. It is a whole way of life by which we become a living doxology, so that all we say and do becomes an act of praise to the Father, through Christ, by the presence and power of the Holy Spirit given in baptism. This is consecrated living. Prayerful living. A way of being held in the knowledge that all that I am and all that I have is first and finally gift. Prayer is a way of living with, in, and from that gift. All the time. Ministry that springs from any motive other than this is misguided.

And this will most assuredly be the case unless we take time to allow ourselves to be washed in the Word. Just a few words. Or a line. One that lingers all day long: "The dawn from on high." "Breaking in upon us." "Compassion." We are being washed in the Word. In its ebb and flow. But we must take time. Make time. Time management is the discipline to be acquired if we are to let the Word "drop down" into our deepmost parts. It is a simple discipline: selecting one phrase, one line, one word, spending time with it, and going back to it through the day. Then we will find that it comes back to us and embraces us: "The tender compassion of our God."

The immediate response, of course, is that no one has time. But we may have more time than we think! How long is our commute to work? Twenty minutes? Forty minutes? An hour? And when we are commuting to and from work, are we cursing the drivers, or blessing the Lord? What do we listen to in the car during the morning and evening commute? Circumlocutious chatter on a talk show? Mind numbing, dashboard thumping lyrics of gangsta rap—albeit of the softer variety? Or something that soothes the spirit, clears the head, so that the mind and heart might discern the presence of the living God, even while we are traveling at sixty miles an hour in the land of eternal traffic. Then there are the seemingly never-ending minutes as we wait for the elevator, or stand in the cafete-

ria line for twenty minutes of that precious fifty-minute "lunch hour."
And the hurried efforts to pump gas into what seems like a bottomless
tank, the apparently interminable delay at the grocery checkout line, the
eternity of waiting for the results of a medical test.

As we spend time with the Word, letting it sink into our marrow, we
grow in reverence. This fundamental attitude of reverence is then
brought to others, to creation, to our work, to our relationships, to the
sacramental life of the Church. It is the condition for the possibility of
effectiveness in mission.

Of reverence, Anne Lamott, a novelist from the San Francisco Bay
Area, writes:

> Let's think of reverence as awe, as presence in and openness to
> the world. The alternative is that we stultify, we shut down
> ... Try walking around with a child who is going, "Wow, wow,
> Look at the dirty dog! Look at the burned-down house! Look at
> that red sky!" And the child points and you look and you see
> and you start going, "Wow! Look at that huge crazy hedge!
> Look at the teeny little baby! Look at the scary dark cloud!"
>
> I think this is how we are supposed to be in the world—
> present and in awe.[9]

Sacred reading helps us cultivate a sense of awe or reverence in the
face of God's gift. All that we have and are is gift, God's gift, to be welcomed the way a little child welcomes a gift, with awe.

Sacred reading is aimed at helping us to receive a gift—the gift of
God's love as the life that pours itself forth. The life and love of God
are constantly coming as gift, a gift to be received. But receiving a gift
takes discipline. We must learn how to hear God, how to receive, before
we respond.

If there is one prime disposition, a single attitude to be cultivated in
our day by ministers in the Church, it is *active receptivity.* The challenge that awaits us if we are to overcome "turf wars" and hyperactivity
is to move from an understanding of ministry as power and doing to an
understanding of ministry rooted in narrative and gift. The first step for
all ministers in the Church is to pray by lingering with and pondering
over the question: What have I been given so that I might pass it on?
Ministry is not so much our doing as it is a response to what has been

given for the effectiveness of the mission of the Word and Spirit, making manifest the magnitude of God's love in our own time and place. Effectiveness in this mission requires not yet another repertoire of skills, judged to be appropriate to either ordained or lay ministry, but a deeper receptivity to the Spirit's gifts as we move forward together in mission. It requires a greater measure of confidence and hope so that we might live freely with, in, and from the gift, passing it on to others without burden or cost.

2. Living What Is Said and Done in Liturgy

In the waters of baptism, by the anointing in the Spirit in confirmation, and through the ongoing celebration of the Eucharist, we are brought into a way of life rooted in worship and service. Living for the glory of God the Father, through Christ, in the Spirit, which is the very heart of the Christian life, is a life of worship and of service, whatever our particular ministry in the Church or our service to the larger human family might be. For all, the question is this: Is worship really at the center of my life, and do I see service as a source of spirituality? Or, do I think of spirituality as something associated with the "interior life," or with a particular devotion, or a prayer technique? Do I consider the spiritual life as something to be nourished and sustained primarily by devotional literature, such as the writings of Thomas Merton, Henri Nouwen, or Simone Weil?

Do I truly see worship and service as ways of being and building the Body of Christ? And do I recognize that all we do and say are ways of becoming a living doxology, becoming transfigured into a living act of praise to the Father, through Christ, in the communion of the Spirit? Living a life rooted in worship and service entails living what we say and do in liturgy, and understanding ourselves as first and finally members of God's people.

It may be helpful to consider that it is in the sacramental life of the Church that we express and receive our identity as the Body of Christ in this time and place. In each of the sacraments we are expressing how we hope to make good on the one and only life we have to live, and at the same time receiving the gift of God's life which enables us to live in such a way. My remarks here will be limited to the sacraments of baptism, confirmation, and Eucharist, for these are the sacraments by which we become members of the Body and receive the gift of the Body of Christ given and giving, week by week, or day by day.

Baptism. In baptism we are initiated into a way of life rooted in the covenant. This covenant is itself rooted in the love of God given in Christ and the ongoing gift of the Spirit, the life of God pouring itself forth in gift here and now. Our lives are shaped by an awareness of responsibility more than obligation, a responsibility springing from our membership in God's Holy People. We commit ourselves to being and building the Body of Christ in the Church and in the world, so that both will be transformed by love.

Confirmation. In the sacrament of anointing in the Spirit, we pledge to live according to the Spirit, rather than the flesh. What does this entail? It entails living together as one Body in the Spirit. How do we know if we are doing this? We know by the fruits of the Spirit—love, joy, peace, patience, kindness, generosity, faithfulness, gentleness, self-control (Gal 5:22-23). We claim that, in contrast to the way of "the flesh" and the ways of "the world," this way of living truly constitutes "the good life." And we take comfort in the words of Saint Paul: "Against these, there is no law" (Gal 5:23).

Eucharist. The Eucharist is the heart and soul of Catholic life. The eucharistic mystery has been described in various ways throughout Christian history, but, at the most basic level, the Eucharist is a meal. It is a meal of communion and justice. In this meal we eat and we drink with all present at the Lord's table. This is a sharing in the very Body and Blood of the Lord. This eating and drinking bonds us together as members of one Body. Sharing in the Body and Blood of the Lord expresses our willingness to share, not just with those who gather at the table of the Lord, but with all those who make up the human family.

The Eucharist is a meal of communion. It unites us in the very life of God—Father, Son, and Spirit who exist in relationship to one another in a way that is altogether equal, mutual, and interdependent. By sharing in the divine life, we are given the grace to build a world of rightly-ordered relationships rooted in equality, mutuality, and interdependence, thus mirroring the divine life of the Trinity in which we share through the Eucharist.

And the Eucharist is a meal of justice. Justice is not an idea, but an activity. We know what justice is by looking at the life and actions of the just person. The just person does not give exactly the same thing or amount to everyone. Rather, the just person seeks to create a world in which all may grow, especially the poor, the weak, the wounded, the last, littlest, and least.

In the sacrament of the Eucharist, all who are gathered at the table of the Lord express their willingness to share, to work toward equality, mutuality, and interdependence in human relationships, and to build a world in which all may grow. To celebrate the Eucharist, fully, consciously, and actively, is to recognize this as the way to make good on the life we have been given as a gift.

3. Understanding Ourselves as Members of God's Holy People

All ministers, ordained and nonordained, are first and finally members of God's people. All are baptized. The grace of baptism and confirmation by which we are made Christian is not shaken by ordination.

By baptism, we are incorporated into the People of God, the Body of Christ. All, not just some, are called to live the fullness of the Christian life through witness, worship, and service. This is our common call. In this lies our consecration for mission and our mission of consecration. Every ministry, every service, is to be understood in terms of the fundamental Christian call to strengthen the People of God, to be and build the Body of Christ as a sacrament of the magnitude of God's love in and for the world through:

Witness. We do this in many ways—by teaching, catechizing, proclaiming the Word, prophetic utterance, faithfulness in illness, challenging structures and systems that depersonalize and dehumanize, constant prayer, hoping when there seems to be no reason to hope.

Worship. We do this through full, conscious, and active participation in the sacramental worship of the Church, but also through all those activities of our lives by which God is praised and glorified.

Service. We serve in many ways, but, above all, by attending to the material needs of those in our families, neighborhoods, parishes, and communities.

Whatever the call, whatever the gift, it is to be exercised, shared for the purpose of witness, worship, and service by which we live out this ecclesiological spirituality whose origin and foundation lies in baptism.

IV. MINISTERIAL ICONICITY:
MAKING MANIFEST THE THREE IN ONE LOVE

It is within the context of a common call given in baptism that we may speak of the distinctiveness of ministries, ordained and non-ordained. All ministry is a response to the grace first given in baptism, a participation in the mission of Word and Spirit by which the magnitude of God's love is made manifest in the Church and the world. By our participation in this mission, we share in the very life of God, the divine life, the trinitarian life.

The three in one love, Father, Son, and Spirit, exist in a relationship that is altogether equal, mutual, interdependent.[10] The proper exercise of ministry makes manifest the trinitarian life, the God whose very being is to be in relationship: Father, Son, Spirit—toward us, for us, with us, in us.

The three who are distinct are equal to one another. It follows that whatever distinction of ministries, those who exercise them are fundamentally equal one to another because of the grace, dignity, and invitation to holiness received in our shared baptism. In the same way that the Son is not less than the Father, and the Spirit not less than the Son, so too no ministry in the Church is to be judged less essential or expendable if the Body and all its members—member for member—are to flourish. The three in one love exist in relationship that is mutual and interdependent, so that each is vital to the divine life. If the Son were not, then God would not be God. And the same may be said of the Father and the Spirit. In the Christian dispensation, God is not a solitary individual or an independent agent, but a communion of three in one love. The fullness of the divine life is the full flourishing of persons, human and divine, in perfect loving relation. Ministry in the Church is in service of the full flourishing of persons in loving relation through which the divine life is made manifest.

From this vantage, the life of the minister is a *way of being* in which the principal category for self-understanding is *relationship.* Ministerial identity may be discerned within the context of relationships: with the Body of Christ, the Church; with Christ himself through the gift of the Holy Spirit; with other ministers; with the bishop. It is an identity grounded in relationship with others, more than in what the minister does. It is a relational identity that can be cultivated, nurtured, and sustained only by constant pondering of the Word of God in Scripture; by ongoing participation in the sacramental worship of the Church —which amounts to much more than knowing our proper role in the sacramental rites; and by understanding oneself first and finally as a member of God's people.

The distinctiveness of diverse ministries might then be understood in terms of iconicity. In Christian spiritual traditions, an icon does not so much represent or stand for another, invisible reality, but rather discloses, manifests, or conveys that reality in and through itself. It is in this sense that we might speak of ministerial iconicity, because in the diverse ministries of the Church something of the nature of the whole Church and its mission is disclosed.

While acknowledging the many problems that accompany the usage of the term "lay ecclesial ministry," it is nonetheless crucial to recognize the emergence of laypeople whose lives are devoted to ministry, those who have made an explicit commitment to service of the Body of Christ. Rather than focusing discussion of their distinctiveness in the Church in terms of full-time, recognized, authorized service, or in terms of leadership, I want to suggest that the question of the ministerial identity of these lay ministers is best understood in terms of their being an *icon of the Church ad-vent-ing.* The flourishing of gifts among the laity, in unprecedented numbers and in unforeseen ways, serves as a reminder that the Church is always coming to be, participating in the mission of Word and Spirit in a particular time and place. The Church at this moment may be likened to the disciples on the road to Emmaus (Luke 24:13-35). Like them, we continue to speak with one another about all that God has been doing in our midst. Like them, we are on the road, *in via,* in the midst of a journey, and, like them, we have expectations that may not have been met. As we re-examine and perhaps let go of some of our tightly held expectations of the Church and of ministry, we come to realize that the gift of Christ's presence, the power of the Spirit, is ours to receive. The Lord is in our midst, no less than on the road to Emmaus, as the Church is yet coming to be in its fullness.

Lay ministers in the Church today are those who are given to accompanying other disciples on the road. As companions on the journey, they may teach and guide, listen and console, but they always do so alongside, and shoulder to shoulder with, the community of the baptized. Their lives are a constant reminder of the nature of the Church as

a Body of Hope, a community always and everywhere open to possibility that can come only as a gift. As *icon of the Church ad-vent-ing,*
these lay ministers invite the Church to renewed and deeper faith in the
Spirit's guidance, to profound gratitude for the Spirit's gifts, and to an
ever-widening hope for a future as yet unknown.

It is from this same relational ground that the distinctiveness of the
ordained ministry also becomes clearer. My remarks here are limited to
the ministry of presbyter, or priest, whose ordination makes of him a
sign of ecclesial communion.[11]

When the intellectual and contemplative dimensions of the priestly
ministry are not displaced from or thought to be tangential to that ministry, but rather are cultivated, the priest becomes more deeply related to
the concerns of human life, history, the world, and the Church, more
fully immersed in the life of his people. Being schooled in the ways of
theological thinking and developing habits of critical reflection are not
simply things that one does as a means of preparation for ordained ministry. Nor is the cultivation of the contemplative dimension of the
priestly vocation "monastic." Neither is it something that can be rele-
gated to a small portion of the schedule, before getting on to the "stuff"
of the priest's day: "lights, locks, and leaks"—and today, litigation; the
seemingly endless round of meetings; the many duties and tasks that
must be accomplished. Prayerful reflection is to be a constant in the life
of the priest, if not a whole way of life, as it is for those who are, by vocation, called to a life of prayer in the strict and formal sense.

The tension between the contemplative and the "priest-as-doer" is
not a problem that can be easily written off as a result of the "vocations
shortage." In the last century, one of the towering figures in Catholic
theology, Karl Rahner, who wrote extensively on the nature of the
priesthood, addressed this tension in terms of the essential compatibility
of the priestly and the poetic.[12] Like the priest, the poet is not necessarily one who is removed or withdrawn from the life of the world, de-
tached from the pressing needs and exigencies of the day. There is a
kind of poetry, theology, and priestly ministry that is shaped by being
immersed in the life of a people, by embracing the life, hopes, and
struggles of a people and being embraced by them. Such priests speak
from the heart of a people, *to* the heart of a people.

I am suggesting that the priest can and should know what is properly his to know by virtue of his vocation, preparation, and ongoing for-

mation. Priests can know intellectually *and* emotionally, affectively as well as effectively, how to evangelize, to catechize, to preach, to pray, to celebrate, to discern, and, above all, to draw all the baptized together into communion and mutual service. But this will occur only if the priest is steeped in the same ecclesiological spirituality that nourishes and sustains all the baptized. Strengthening priestly identity demands that the ordained minister allow his heart to pause and ponder in the presence of reality: God's presence in human life, history, the world, and the Church. This might allow him to emerge once again as the *icon of the community's pondering heart.*

Gathered at the table of word and sacrament together with all those on the road to what is yet coming to be, the ordained opens with them the Scriptures and breaks the Bread. There the Body is enlightened, enlivened, guided, and healed, to take up again the mission of Word and Spirit, rendering love visible, tangible, audible, in our own time and place, strengthened so that we might participate in Love's creative, animating bonding in the midst of a broken world and an increasingly divided Church. As *icon of the community's pondering heart,* the priest's most important ministry is opening the Scriptures and breaking the Bread in a way that allows all present, by the gift first given in baptism, *to behold* the Body of Christ and the gift/ing of the Spirit in their midst, so that each one—member for member—might more effectively bear witness in word and deed to the magnitude of God's love always and everywhere on offer.

CONCLUSION

It is my contention that ministerial identity cannot be nurtured and sustained when focused on what the priest does, or on what makes his ministry different from the common call of the baptized. Further, it is my contention that recent efforts to define the identity and/or spirituality of lay ecclesial ministers by focusing on their "doings," or "practices," as in the Lilly-funded Davidson team's research instrument, in sharp contrast to the ministerial doings and spiritual practices of the ordained and of vowed religious, are misguided. In order to meet the shifting needs of a rapidly changing Church, what is required is that ministers ordained and nonordained recover an appreciation of the common foundations of their identity in Word, worship, and a sense of being first and finally members of God's Holy People, altogether and all together gifted so that they might more effectively participate in the mission of the Church to make manifest the magnitude of God's love.

NOTES

1. Roger Cardinal Mahony and the Priests of the Archdiocese of Los Angeles, *As I Have Done for You: A Pastoral Letter on Ministry* (Chicago: Liturgy Training Publications, 2000).

2. The following general description of the lay ecclesial minister, a description based on years of consultation and research, emerges from *Lay Ecclesial Ministry: The State of the Questions,* A Report of the National Conference of Catholic Bishops' Subcommittee on Lay Ministry (Washington, D.C.: National Conference of Catholic Bishops, 1999): Lay ecclesial ministry refers to a vocation of full-time church service in response to the needs of each local community. Within the context of the common call to service which is given to all the baptized, "lay ecclesial ministry" refers to professionally trained or otherwise properly prepared women and men, including vowed religious, who are in positions of service and leadership in the Church. This is a unique vocation in the Church, a call to service *in the name of the Church.* "Lay ecclesial ministry" does not describe one kind of service or work, but refers to the ministries of committed persons, women and men, married or single, which are exercised in a stable, public, recognized, and authorized way. This is church ministry in the strict and formal sense. It emerges from a personal call, requires appropriate formation, and is undertaken with both the support and the authorization of competent church authority.

By contrast, the Davidson team's study of lay ecclesial ministers included anyone and everyone in any way involved in ministry in the Church, with the exception of the ordained and vowed religious. Yet it is clear from *Lay Ecclesial Ministry: The State of the Questions* that the term is not meant to describe any layperson involved in church ministry, and does, in fact, describe the ministry of some vowed religious.

3. Kenan B. Osborne, *Ministry: Lay Ministry in the Roman Catholic Church* (New York/Mahwah, N.J.: Paulist Press, 1993) 530 ff.

4. Donald Cozzens, *The Changing Face of the Priesthood: A Reflection on the Priest's Crisis of Soul* (Collegeville, Minn.: The Liturgical Press, 2000).

5. Ibid., 139–141.

6. John Paul II, apostolic letter *Novo Millennio Ineunte,* "At the Beginning of the New Millennium" (January 6, 2001) 29.

7. Sermon 300.2 among the sermons of Saint Augustine, *Patrologia Latina* 39, col. 2319.

8. Robert F. Morneau, "Markings," *Fathoming Bethlehem* (New York: Cross-road, 1997) 104–105.

9. Anne Lamott, *Bird By Bird: Some Instructions on the Writing Life* (New York: Anchor Books, 1994) 100.

10. Here I follow Catherine Mowry LaCugna, *God For Us: The Trinity and Christian Life* (San Francisco: Harper, 1991). In *Altogether Gift: A Trinitarian Spirituality* (Maryknoll, N.Y.: Orbis Books, 2000) I have attempted to express the doctrine of the Trinity and its practical implications for Christian life and spirituality in terms of God as Giver, Given, and Gift/ing.

11. For fuller treatment of the notion of the priest as a sign of ecclesial communion, see Susan K. Wood, *Sacramental Orders* (Collegeville, Minn.: The Liturgical Press, 2000).

12. Karl Rahner, "Priest and Poet," in *Theological Investigations,* vol. 3 (New York: Crossroad, 1974) 294–317.

The Ecclesiological Foundations of Ministry within an Ordered Communion

RICHARD R. GAILLARDETZ

The last thirty-five years have seen a flourishing of a new reality in the Catholic Church that few could have anticipated as the Second Vatican Council came to a close. This reality, generally referred to as "lay ministry," has leapt ahead of theological reflection, raising a host of questions regarding the definition of lay ministry, its scope and limits, and its relationship both to ordained ministry and to the activities in which all the Christian faithful fulfill their baptismal call. These questions are reflected in the struggle to find a nomenclature adequate to this new situation: Should we speak of "lay ministry," "the lay apostolate," "lay ecclesial ministry," "nonordained ministry," or perhaps "the ministry of the baptized"? This particular question might seem fairly insignificant, a mere matter of titles, but in fact our nomenclature generally reflects an operative view of the Church. Here I will propose the beginnings of an ecclesiological foundation for ministry that might guide us as we consider the significance and place of these new ministries.

A NEW ECCLESIOLOGICAL VISION
EMERGING OUT OF VATICAN II

While the Second Vatican Council made important advances in our understanding of the Church, it was not able to articulate a complete, internally coherent ecclesiology. Rather, in important if at times halting and uncertain steps, the council sketched out the way toward a postconciliar ecclesiology. Three features of the council's emergent ecclesiology might be fruitful for developing the ecclesiological foundations for a theology of ministry in the Church: (1) the priority of the baptismal call of the *Christifideles*, (2) the Church's call to mission in the world, and (3) the Church as an ordered communion.

1. The Priority of the Baptismal Call of the *Christifideles*

One of the most important initiatives of the Second Vatican Council was its attempt to find new foundations for its consideration of the Church. The preparatory draft document on the Church given to the bishops at the opening of the council was little more than a synthesis of the ecclesiology that had been operative throughout much of the first half of the twentieth century. As Bishop de Smedt of Bruges observed in a famous conciliar intervention, this ecclesiological perspective suffered from clericalism, triumphalism, and juridicism.[1] It presupposed that the Church was, as Pope Pius X put it, an "unequal society" comprised of two ranks, the clergy and the laity.[2]

With the rejection of the ecclesiology reflected in that document, the council set upon a new course. The Dogmatic Constitution on the Church, *Lumen Gentium (LG),* offered a new framework for situating any and all distinctions in the Church. That new framework or, as Kenan Osborne refers to it, "common matrix," was made evident in the well-known decision to place the chapter on the Church as people of God prior to the chapter on the hierarchy in the *De Ecclesia* schema. In that chapter, the council members "were focusing on the common matrix, the fundamental equality and dignity of each and every follower of Jesus."[3] This matrix is further reinforced by the council's frequent use of the term *Christifideles* to refer to all the baptized and by its appeal to the priesthood of all believers. Before there are ordained and nonordained, clergy and lay, all church members are the Christian faithful, the baptized, called to a common discipleship in Christ. Indeed, the council's theological affirmation of the equal dignity of all the baptized readily suggests a view of the Church as the "community of disciples," although the council did not itself make use of this metaphor.[4] In baptism we are initiated into Christ's body the Church and, in a sense, discover ourselves fully, our truest identity, in the life of the Church. At the same time, by baptism into Christ's body, the

Church, we are drawn by the power of the Holy Spirit into participation in the triune life of God.

All Christians, by baptism, are called in discipleship to follow the way of Jesus of Nazareth, to grow in holiness, and to help further the reign of God. This commitment, far from being one among many human commitments that one might undertake, is in itself more than a religion. As the early Christians understood it, this commitment brought one into a new form of existence, a new understanding of the human vocation.

The Second Vatican Council augmented its rich treatment of the common matrix of Christian baptism and discipleship with an uneven yet still significant use of the biblical notion of charism. It is a development that was strongly advocated by Cardinal Suenens, who gave a very influential speech on the subject on October 22, 1963.[5] This more pneumatological line of thought is evident in the first chapter of *Lumen Gentium,* which considers the place of charisms in the context of the whole people of God's participation in the life of the Church.[6]

> The Spirit dwells in the church and in the hearts of the faithful, as in a temple, prays and bears witness in them that they are his adopted children. He guides the church in the way of all truth and, uniting it in fellowship and ministry, bestows upon it different hierarchic and charismatic gifts, and in this way directs it and adorns it with his fruits. (*LG* 4)

The theme is picked up again in the second chapter.

> Moreover, it is not only through the sacraments and the ministries that the holy Spirit makes the people holy, leads them and enriches them with his virtues. Allotting his gifts "at will to each individual," he also distributes special graces among the faithful of every rank *(inter omnis ordinis fideles).* By these gifts, he makes them fit and ready to undertake various tasks and offices for the renewal and building up of the church. (*LG* 12)

While the terminology employed is not altogether consistent, nevertheless there is a fundamental assertion that charisms are given to all the faithful "for the renewal and building up of the church." There are clear

Pauline resonances here, as charisms are not presented as private gifts or talents but gifts of the Holy Spirit offered *to and for* the Church *through* the individual believer (cf. 1 Cor 12).

Apostolicam Actuositatem (AA), the Decree on the Apostolate of the Laity, returns to this topic, but with an important broadening of perspective.[7] In this document, charisms are offered by the Holy Spirit for both Church *and world*:

> From the reception of these charisms, even the most ordinary ones, there follow for all christian believers the right and duty to use them in the church and in the world for the good of humanity and the development of the church, to use them in the freedom of the holy Spirit who "chooses where to blow," and at the same time in communion with the sisters and brothers in Christ, and with the pastors especially. (*AA* 3)

Here baptismal charisms are properly correlated to the building up of the Church *and* the furtherance of the Church's mission in the world.

2. The Church in Mission

Our baptism into the Church means, most fundamentally, that we are baptized into the Church's mission. This mission is no mere extrinsic task imposed upon the Church from without; it is the very *raison d'être* of the Church. Indeed, the Church's mission derives from its trinitarian origins. Salvation history reveals to us a God who sends forth the Word and Spirit in mission as the very expression and fulfillment of God's love for the world. God's Word, spoken into human history from the beginning of creation and made effective by the power of the Spirit, in the fullness of time became incarnate as Jesus of Nazareth. The origins of the Church, in turn, are inextricably linked to Jesus' gathering a community of followers who, after his death and resurrection, were empowered by his Spirit to continue his mission to serve, proclaim, and realize the coming reign of God. In *Gaudium et Spes (GS),* the Pastoral Constitution on the Church in the Modern World, the council writes: "Proceeding from the love of the eternal Father, the church was founded by Christ in time and gathered into one by the holy Spirit" (no. 40).

The affirmation of the missiological character of the whole Church was one of the most important teachings of the Second Vatican Council. Although the council's desire to affirm a positive theology of the laity led it to attribute to the laity a particular apostolate for the transformation of the world, there are other instances where the council affirmed that it was in fact the mission of the whole Church to transform the world in the service of the coming reign of God. So, for example, while there are several texts that speak of the laity as called to be a leaven in the world, in the Pastoral Constitution on the Church in the Modern World it is the whole Church which "is to be a leaven and, as it were, the soul of human society in its renewal by Christ and transformation into the family of God" (*GS* 40). Later in that same section of the document the council members spoke of the mission of the Church to heal and elevate the dignity of the human person, to strengthen human society, and to help humanity discover the deeper meaning of their daily lives. "The church, then, believes that *through each of its members and its community as a whole* it can help to make the human family and its history still more human" (*GS* 40, emphasis mine).

I believe the pastoral constitution offered an emerging insight that it is the whole Church that exists in mission in the world. This suggests that the attitudes and actions of all members of the Church, including the clergy and consecrated religious, have social and political import and thus, in their own way, contribute to the furtherance of the Church's mission to the world. It is certainly the case that not all Christians will participate in the Church's mission in the same manner, but none are exempt from the demands of their baptism to participate in this mission. The Italian theologian, Bruno Forte, insists that

> the relationship with temporal realities is proper to all the baptized, though in a variety of forms, joined more to personal charisms than to static contrasts between laity, hierarchy and religious state...No one is neutral toward the historical circumstances in which he or she is living, and an alleged neutrality can easily become a voluntary or involuntary mask for ideologies and special interests...It is the entire community that has to confront the secular world, being marked by that world in its being and in its action. The entire People of God must be characterized by a positive relationship with the secular dimension.[8]

This firm orientation of all the baptized as those bound together in a common mission is a most necessary foundation for any consideration of church ministry. It serves as a vital corrective against any tendency to allow practical distinctions between the church *ad intra* and the church *ad extra* to turn into a dichotomizing separation. All church ministry is fundamentally oriented toward the Church's mission to the world in the service of God's reign.

3. The Church as an Ordered Communion

Both the 1985 extraordinary synod and Pope John Paul II have referred to the notion of communion as one of the most fundamental to be developed at the Second Vatican Council.[9] Yet, in many ways, of the three ecclesiological principles I have explored here, this is the one least explicitly developed by the council. Still, one can detect an emerging ecclesiology of communion in important conciliar texts. It is most evident in the council's effort to give the Church a firm foundation in the triune life of God. Drawing on St. Cyprian, the council writes that the Church "is seen to be 'a people made one by the unity of the Father and the Son and the holy Spirit'" (*LG* 4). The innermost reality of the Church, its participation in the triune life of God, shifts from background to foreground.[10] The Church's reality must be understood in the light of God's saving work through Christ and in the Spirit. The Church shares in the mystery of God to the extent that it participates in God's saving work on behalf of humankind. Through Christ and by the power of the Spirit we are invited to become adopted sons and daughters of God. The Church is not an autonomous entity; rather, its very existence depends on its relationship to God through Christ and in the Spirit.

The Council's Recovery of the Biblical Understanding of Koinonia

The council drew its understanding of communion from the biblical and patristic concept of *koinonia* or *communio*. This concept played a particularly prominent role in the ecclesiology of St. Paul. His more organic view of the Church suggested not just complementarity and diversity but also *coexistence* within the Church.[11] For Paul, life in Christ meant life in the body of Christ, the Church (cf. 1 Cor 12; Rom 12). There was no such thing as an individual believer understood apart from the life of the Church, for the Church was no mere aggregate of

individuals. Rather, by baptism into the Christian community one participated in a new reality, one was a new creation. Individual believers
did not *make* a church; initiation into the Church through faith and baptism *made* the believer. Faith and baptism introduced the individual into
a new mode of existence.

The council incorporated this biblical view of communion in the
first chapter of *Lumen Gentium*. Attending to the vertical dimension, the
council affirms that it is through the mediation of Christ's Church, by
the power of the Spirit, that we are drawn into the triune life of God.

> This is the Spirit of life, the fountain of water springing up to
> eternal life, through whom the Father gives life to human be-
> ings dead in sin...The Spirit dwells in the church and in the
> hearts of the faithful, as in a temple, prays and bears witness in
> them that they are his adopted children...By the power of the
> Gospel he rejuvenates the church, constantly renewing it and
> leading it to perfect union with its spouse. (*LG* 4)

In that same paragraph we find attention to the horizontal dimension:
"He [the Spirit] guides the church in the way of all truth" and unites "it
in fellowship and ministry." In the Church, believers experience most
profoundly the life of communion into which all humanity is invited.

It is as a union of the vertical and horizontal dimensions that we can
understand ecclesial communion as a sacrament of salvation:

> All those, who in faith look towards Jesus, the author of salva-
> tion and the source of unity and peace, God has gathered to-
> gether and established as the church, that it may be for each and
> everyone the visible sacrament of this saving unity. In order to
> extend to all regions of the earth, it enters into human history,
> though it transcends at once all times and all boundaries be-
> tween peoples. (*LG* 9)

This ecclesial communion is further developed in the council's recovery
of the eucharistic foundations of the Church. The celebration of the Eucharist effects a communion among those believers gathered at each eucharistic celebration as all are united in the breaking of the bread.
Echoing St. Paul (cf. 1 Cor 10:16-17), the council writes that "in the

sacrament of the Eucharistic bread, the unity of believers, who form one body in Christ, is both expressed and achieved" (*LG* 3). This is reaffirmed in number 11: "Then, strengthened by the body of Christ in the Eucharistic communion, they manifest in a concrete way that unity of the people of God which this most holy sacrament aptly signifies and admirably realizes." In the eucharistic *synaxis*, the Christian community proclaims in word and celebrates in ritual and symbol its most profound reality, its truest identity as a people whose lives are being conformed to that of Christ by the celebration of the paschal mystery.

The Church as a Communion of Eucharistic Communions

The nature of the Church as communion is not limited to the *communio* that exists among the members of a particular eucharistic community. By the late second century, the notion of communion was extended to describe that spiritual bond which existed among all local eucharistic communities. There was a common conviction that all eucharistic communities abided together in shared ecclesial communion.[12] For the early Church, the sacrament of the Eucharist brought about not only the communion of those gathered at each altar, but the communion of all local churches. This followed from the emerging eucharistic theology of the time. Wherever the Eucharist was celebrated, the body of Christ was actualized in a sacramental fashion.

Vatican II recalled this extended understanding of ecclesial communion in its treatment of the ministry of the bishop and the relationship between the local churches and the universal Church: "Individual bishops are the visible source and foundation of unity in their own particular churches, which are modelled on the universal church; it is in and from these that the one unique catholic church exists" (*LG* 23). This text, along with others, reflects a move away from that pre-conciliar, universalist ecclesiology which viewed the diocese as little more than an administrative subset of the universal Church. Vatican II represented an at least tentative return to an ecclesiology in which the one universal Church is manifested in the communion of local churches.

The Pneumatological Foundations of an Ecclesiology of Communion

The full reality of this ecclesial communion goes beyond sociological analysis, for it is a communion animated by the Holy Spirit. It is the Spirit that transformed the church of Pentecost from an aggregate group of individuals into a spiritual communion. John Zizioulas, the influential Greek Orthodox theologian and now metropolitan of Pergamon, has noted the West's ecclesiological tendency to focus on the Church's historical institution by Christ rather than on its *constitution* by the Spirit. He writes: "Institution is something presented to us as a fact, more or less a *fait-accompli*."[13] The result is a static conception of the Church that has little place for change or development. When one considers not only the Church's institution by Christ but its *constitution* by the Spirit, new facets of the Church's innermost reality appear. "Constitution is something that involves us in its very being, something we accept freely, because we take part in its very emergence."[14] In the Spirit's constitution of the Church, we must admit an ongoing, dynamic presence of the Spirit continuing to mold and shape the Church through the exercise of human freedom.

The "Ordering" of the Church

A much contested phrase used five times (*LG* 21, 22; *Christus Dominus* 4, 5; *Presbyterorum Ordinis* 7) in council documents is that of "hierarchical communion" (*communio hierarchica*).[15] It seems to have been employed as a safeguard against the danger that notions of communion might degenerate into secular understandings of liberal democratic polity. Yet the qualifier "hierarchical" can serve an important purpose if we purge it of those pyramidal conceptions it gained in the thirteenth century, when medieval ecclesiology employed the neo-platonic cosmology of the late fifth- or early sixth-century figure, Pseudo-Dionysius the Areopagite, as a structuring principle for the Church. *"Hierarchia,"* a term first coined by Pseudo-Dionysius, became in the thirteenth century an ontological schema for viewing the Church as a descending ladder of states of being and truth, with the fullness of power *(plenitudo potestatis)* given to the pope and shared in diminishing degrees with the lower levels of church life.[16] This "hierarchology" has remained with the Church, in varying degrees, up to the present.

There is an alternative view of the term "hierarchy" in reference to the Church, however, and that is to return to its literal sense of "sacred order" (the Gk. adjective *"hier,"* meaning "sacred," with the Greek noun *"arche,"* meaning "origin," "principle" or "rule").[17] This leads to the key affirmation that the Church of Jesus Christ, animated by the Spirit, is now and has always been subject to church ordering as it receives its life from the God who, in Christian faith, is ordered in eternal self-giving as a triune communion of persons. At the same time, there must be the recognition that the specific character of that ordering has changed dramatically throughout the Church's history. This "ordering" of the Church is manifested on numerous levels.

The most fundamental ordering of the Church occurs at baptism. Baptism does not just make one a different kind of individual; it draws the person into a profound ecclesial relationship within the life of the Church as a follower or disciple of Jesus sent in mission to the world. When we consider the sacraments of initiation as a unity, then we recognize that initiation carries with it its own anointing, "laying on of hands," and entrance into eucharistic communion. To be initiated into the Church is to take one's place, one's *"ordo,"* within the community, the place of the baptized. As Zizioulas puts it, "there is no such thing as non-ordained persons in the church."[18] To be baptized is to be "ordained" into a very specific ecclesial relationship along with all who profess the lordship of Jesus Christ.

The relationship established in Christian initiation unfolds in three dimensions. Vertically, if you will, we are baptized into communion with God in Christ by the power of the Spirit. Yet this relation is inseparable from our horizontal relationship with all our brothers and sisters in baptism who constitute together a communion of believers. These two dimensions of the ecclesial relation established in Christian initiation (baptism/chrismation/Eucharist) must be conjoined with a third dimension, the movement outward toward the world as sent in mission. This three-dimensional ecclesial relation established by Christian initiation offers us our primal identity as Christian believers and it can never be abandoned, even as we may be called into some new ecclesial relationship.

In addition to that most basic of ecclesial orderings established in Christian initiation, the presence in the Church today of numerous institutes of religious life, secular institutes, and societies of apostolic life, along with the emergence of the "new movements" (e.g., Focolare, the Neo-Catechumenal Way, the St. Egidio community, Communion and Liberation, Opus Dei) suggests that church order provides a diversity of concrete ways of giving evangelical witness to the Gospel. Alongside this ordering of evangelical witness there exists within the Church an ordering of ministries as well. It is this ministerial ordering that we will need to consider in further detail in the next section of this essay.

THE MINISTERIAL ORDERING OF THE PEOPLE OF GOD

In this treatment of Christian ministry I propose a middle ground between the pre-conciliar identification of ministry with holy orders and the
more contemporary tendency to consider any and all Christian activity as
ministry.[19] Ordered church ministry is a reality broader than the ministry
of the ordained (though inclusive of it) and narrower than Christian discipleship. Ordered ministry refers to any and all ministries that, once formally undertaken, draw one into a new ecclesial relationship within the
life of the Church; in undertaking an ordered ministry, one is ecclesially
re-positioned.

Ministry as "Ecclesial Re-Positioning"

The ecclesial re-positioning involved in the entrance into ministry
will (or should) involve, in some measure, all of the following: (a) a
personal call, (b) ecclesial discernment and recognition of a genuine
charism, (c) formation appropriate to the demands of the ministry, (d)
some authorization by community leadership, and (e) some ritualization
as a prayer for the assistance of the Holy Spirit and a sending forth on
behalf of the community. Let us consider these in turn.

Ministry generally begins with the manifestation of some charism for
the building up of the Church in mission. Of course, all Christians possess
charisms to be exercised in their daily life. These charisms may appear
quite ordinary (making them no less vital), such as the charism of parenting[20] or imbuing the atmosphere of one's workplace with the values of the
Gospel. At other times, these charisms may take on a more dramatic and
even public character, as in the evangelical witness of Dorothy Day. The
exercise of these charisms, however dramatic, does not call for undertaking any new ecclesial relationship for the sake of the Church and its mission beyond that constituted by baptismal initiation. However, there are
other charisms, the manifestation of which does suggest the suitability of
entering into a new, public, ecclesial relationship within the Church.

What distinguishes these many ordered ministries from the more
basic activity of all the baptized in fulfillment of their baptismal call?
For a Christian activity to qualify as an ordered ministry, it would seem
that ministry must be related to a sense of some distinctive public rela-

tionship within the community. The public character of this ministry is evident in the way in which we tend to hold such ministers to a higher moral standard. We recognize the possibility that their moral failings, because of their public character, might be a cause of scandal.

Consider the case of the person who in sharing her faith with family and friends manifests great passion and insight. Members of her local community recognize this charism for sharing the faith, a charism already being exercised in her life, and so call her to exercise this charism in a public ministry of the Church as a catechist. In some cases an individual may sense the presence of this charism as a personal call to service and offer herself or himself to the Church. At other times it is the community itself, in its processes of ecclesial discernment, that will first recognize the presence of a given charism and call that person into ordered ministry. In any case, ministry begins with the recognition by the individual and/or the community of an already existing charism. The failure to recognize that evidence of a charism must *precede* one's entrance into an ordered church ministry has done great harm to the life of the Church. Particularly as regards the ordained, the Church has too frequently suffered from the inadequate ministrations of well-meaning priests and deacons called to ministry because of their personal holiness or eagerness to serve but without evidence of a recognizable charism for the ministry they have undertaken.

Karl Rahner's theology of grace provides a helpful insight into this. Rahner insists that "sacraments of consecration" (e.g., baptism, confirmation, penance, orders) always presuppose a grace *always already present* but now sacramentally manifested in the believer in a new way. He writes:

> What really happens in such a sacrament of consecration is the historical manifestation and the sociologically concretizing specification in the dimension of the visible Church of a holiness and consecratedness which has always existed inescapably in that person in the form of an offer in virtue of God's salvific will.[21]

With respect to ministry, Rahner suggests that adult baptism itself offers an analogy.

> To deal with this question we must not start out from the model
> of infant baptism but must think of individual sacramental
> events in space and time as they occur in and with adults. But it
> is obvious here with reference to baptism and penance that
> these sacraments, even for traditional theology, without detri-
> ment to their efficacy, come upon a person who has already ac-
> cepted in freedom the grace always offered to him and is
> justified.[22]

If we understand a personal charism as a tangible manifestation of
grace, then the call to ordered ministry involves the recognition of a
prior graced disposition to exercise a given ministry.

Having called a baptized believer into a new ministerial relationship in service of the Church and its mission, it will be necessary for the
Church to offer the necessary formation. For some ministries (e.g., extraordinary minister of the Eucharist), this may require little more than a
training weekend. For those preparing for presbyteral ministry, it may
require years of seminary formation. In any case, successful formation
leads to some form of church authorization. Finally, there is the recognition that all ministries are exercises of charisms on behalf of the community and therefore deserve the prayer and sending forth from the
community in some ritual form, whether it be sacramental ordination,
installation, or commissioning. The distinction between these three will
be explored below.

Recovering a Relational Ontology of Ministry

The relational interpretation of ministry has been developed most
provocatively by John Zizioulas in his treatment of ordained ministry.
His approach has the merit of looking beyond Scholasticism, with its
tendency to consider the minister in isolation from the community, to
the patristic tradition. There we find a thoroughly relational perspective in which ordination was concerned with the concrete Christian
community. Through the ritual action associated with ordination, the
ordinati were brought into a new relationship within the community;
ordination called one into a new ministerial relation and, in light of that
new relation, conferred the power necessary for the fulfillment of that
ministry.

Absolute ordinations, the practice of ordaining an individual apart from a call to serve a local church, were prohibited in the early centuries of Christianity. Ministry did not exist as a power or reality in its own right, but only as linked to pastoral service. The relational character of ordained ministry was confirmed in the eucharistic context in which all ordinations were to take place. Ordination did not make sense except as conducted within the liturgical life of the Church. Zizioulas draws on the wisdom of this earlier tradition and suggests that the theological significance of ordination lies neither in the conferral of sacramental powers on the individual being ordained (a standard scholastic approach within Catholicism) nor in the delegation of authority from the community to the individual (a perspective common to many Protestant traditions). Rather, ordination brings the one being ordained into a fundamentally new ecclesial relationship, beyond that established by Christian initiation. Moreover, this new ecclesial relationship, established through sacramental ordination, cannot imply the renunciation of the relation established in Christian initiation. The demands of baptism continue for the ordained. What results from sacramental ordination is a twofold relation. St. Augustine articulated this quite well in one of his sermons:

> What I should be for you fills me with anguish; what I can be with you is my consolation; because for you I am a bishop, but with you a Christian. The first points to my duty, the second to grace. The first shows the danger, the other salvation.[23]

Note that the prepositions "for" and "with" signify the dual relations established by ordination and baptism. Both Christian initiation and ordination can be considered adequately only from within this relational ecclesiology of communion.

James Puglisi's careful study of the ancient ordination rituals of the Western Church confirms our analysis. In the conclusion of the first volume of his study he writes:

> Throughout this study we have seen that the process of ordination includes a complex of actions and roles which inaugurate new, personal, and enduring relationships between the new minister, his Christian brethren and God. Moreover, in the early

church the ordained ministry was seen in the context of a sacramental and Trinitarian ecclesiology in which ordination is presented as one of the communal, liturgical, and juridical actions
through which the Church is built up.[24]

In the second millennium the operative theology evident in later ordination rituals suggests an important shift as "eventually, the meaning of
ordained ministry was disjoined from its concrete and communal ecclesial context, finally becoming autonomous: the minister could perform
certain actions outside of any ecclesial context, and these actions could
be considered valid."[25]

This shift in the understanding of ordination and ordained ministry
in the second millennium was metaphysically underwritten with what
we might refer to as a "substance ontology" that attended primarily to
those changes effected in a particular individual (whether through baptism or ordination). Many Western treatments of sacramental character
have succumbed to the limitations of such a substance ontology, namely
that it makes ontological claims on the individual abstracted from his or
her relational existence. The alternative need not be a rejection of ontology itself; it can be, rather, a shift to a "relational ontology" in which attention is drawn not to the isolated individual, but to the person-
in-relation. Here the ontological change brought about by baptism, and
the sacramental character thereby conferred, can be appreciated adequately only with respect to the ecclesial relationship constituted by
baptism. In keeping with traditional Catholic theological reflection, we
can affirm the ontological effects of sacramental ordination. However,
any such "ontological change" is grounded not in the conferral of powers on an individual but on the reconfiguration of the person into a new
ecclesial relation.

There is, of course, a sense in which we can speak legitimately of the
conferral of ministerial power at ordination. But it is not the conferral of
power that makes the ordained minister; rather, it is the reconfiguration of
the person into a new ministerial relationship that requires that empowerment by the Holy Spirit necessary for the fulfillment of that ministry. The
new "empowerment" is a function of the new ministerial relationship.
Karl Rahner observes, for example, that the most fundamental (but not
sole) identity of the priest is to be a pastor. "He must, then, have all the
powers which necessarily belong to such a leader of a Church in a partic-

ular locality in the light of the theological nature of the Church as such."[26] The powers follow from his particular ecclesial relationship.

Every authentic ecclesial action exercised within an authentic ecclesial relationship is effective only because it is empowered by the Spirit. An ecclesiology of communion does not place the christological and pneumatological in opposition, but rather attends to both from a more developed trinitarian perspective. The Church is indeed the Body of Christ, but it is so only because it is constituted as such by the Holy Spirit who animates the Church and "gifts" it in service of its edification and in view of its mission to the world. This more pneumatologically informed ecclesiology demands a fundamental reconsideration of the nature and exercise of power in the Church.

It is easy to forget that "power" is itself an analogous concept that can be used in many different senses. Within the life of the Church, power can be defined as *the capacity to fulfill one's baptismal call and engage in effective action in service of the Church's life and mission.* Ministerial power is intelligible only as a subset or specification of ecclesial power. Effective Christian action demands that we act out of a particular relationship within the Church. To be a member of the Christian community, to live in *communio,* is in itself to be "empowered" for daily Christian living and for service of the Church's mission. This is the exercise of ecclesial power in its most fundamental sense. The power we receive through baptism/chrismation enables us to fulfill our calling as disciples of Jesus. We are empowered to share the good news of Jesus Christ, to pursue holiness, to love our neighbor, to care for the least, to work for justice, and to build up the body of Christ through the exercise of our particular gifts in service of the Church.

The Spirit's empowerment of all the baptized in service of the Church's mission is the only adequate starting point for any theology of *ministerial* power. Any new empowerment, beyond that oriented toward our common discipleship, must be strictly a function of our entrance into some new ecclesial relation. Power cannot be considered apart from a concrete ecclesial relationship.

Ordered Ministries beyond Ordination

To sum up the position I have developed to this point, the Church is an ordered communion and as such is not merely the aggregate of autonomous individuals who happen to form a group or community. The Church is constituted as a communion of persons-in-relation. Both sacramental initiation into the Church and sacramental ordination are concerned with specifying particular ecclesial relationships within this communion.

Is the ministerial ordering of the community to be limited by those orderings constituted in Christian initiation and sacramental ordination? This seems to be the case for Zizioulas. However, a consideration of early Church life suggests a real diversity of ministries within the life of the Church. In the early Church, the privileged role of the bishop lay in his unique ministry of *episkope,* the pastoral oversight of a eucharistic community in which the bishop functioned as the chief judge and witness to the apostolic faith, the servant of the unity of that community, and the agent for bringing that community into communion with other eucharistic communities. By the third century, the presbyter gradually was given a share in this ministry of oversight, though limited to oversight over a particular community. Indeed, in time, the presbyter would eclipse the bishop as the principal agent of pastoral leadership over a local community. However, both in the case of the bishop and later the presbyter, eucharistic presidency followed from their *de facto* pastoral leadership over a community. Their ecclesial relationship to the local church was decisive. The empowerment for sacramental ministry was offered in view of their ecclesial relationship as leaders of the community.

The diaconate was, of course, a different case entirely, because the deacon was not ordained to pastoral leadership of a eucharistic community but rather to public service of that community as an assistant to the bishop. While this involved no empowerment for sacramental ministry beyond that possible, in principle, for all the baptized (that is, those sacramental ministries that have no essential relationship to presidency over a eucharistic community), the deacon's ministerial relationship to the community did change as he became the iconic public embodiment of Christ the servant.

It is true that by the end of the second century the ministries of bishop, presbyter, and deacon were distinguished from other ministries. However, up through the Middle Ages one continues to find evidence of other "orders" within the life of the Church: readers, virgins, widows, catechumens, penitents, etc. What these groups shared was "a distinctive place in the church's public gathering, especially its worship."[27] In the

Middle Ages, as the basic distinction between the clergy and the laity became more pronounced, the above mentioned "orders" were eclipsed by a hierarchically configured set of ministerial orders. These orders, minor and major, were structured as a *cursus honorum* in which the minister was expected to ascend the ranks, culminating in ordination to the priesthood. In the church of Rome this *cursus honorum* took the following form: porter, lector, exorcist, acolyte (the minor orders), followed by sub-deacon, deacon, presbyter and bishop (the major orders).[28] Originally these minor orders referred to real responsibilities in the life of the Church. As Winfried Haunerland observes, there was a

> more ancient insistence that everyone who was to be ordained a presbyter had previously to prove himself through successful efforts in other ministries—this ultimately yielded to the formal demand that the presbyter must go through all the levels of orders but without at all showing experience and dedication by actually exercising any of those ministries connected to the minor orders.[29]

While a contemporary ecclesiology of communion must reject the ascending hierarchy of orders presupposed in the Middle Ages (and still common in many circles today), it may be fruitful to return to the notion that within the life of the Church ministerial ordering need not be limited by sacramental ordination. Even the briefest appraisal of our contemporary church situation, particularly here in the United States, suggests that there are many Christians who are engaged in ministries that place them in a distinctive relationship within the life of the Church. From parish catechists to diocesan directors of Christian formation, from parishioners who bring communion to the sick on behalf of their community to full-time campus ministers and hospital chaplains, there is today a diverse ordering of ministries that extends the ecclesial order already evident in the ministries of deacon, presbyter, and bishop.

The significance of nonordained ministries exercised in the Church has been granted in contemporary church documents. Yet the current tendency to refer to these nonordained ministries as "lay ministry" and/or "lay ecclesial ministry," while representing an advance, needs to be reconsidered from the perspective we have developed here. The term "lay" is only with difficulty shorn of its past historical associations with

a kind of ecclesial passivity. To define a ministry as "lay" is almost re-
flexively to define it by what it is not, a ministry proper to the ordained.
While the bishops at Vatican II worked mightily to develop a positive
theology of the laity, the fruit of their work can better be read, I believe,
as a positive theology of *all the baptized*, the *Christifideles*, as followers
of Jesus and members of the people of God.[30] Since the time of the
council, laudable attempts have been made to develop a positive theology of "lay ministries," and/or "lay ecclesial ministries." I suggest that
qualifying ministry as "lay" tends to vitiate the construction of such a
theology.

Finally, it is difficult to recognize the significance of the qualifier
"ecclesial" in the term, "lay ecclesial ministry," as it would appear that
all ministry in the Church has an essentially ecclesial referent. Is it possible to develop a nomenclature for the exercise of ministry by those
who are not ordained that is more theologically coherent? I believe the
larger ecclesiological perspective offered in this essay, with its stress on
the Church as an ordered communion, provides such an opportunity by
speaking not only of ordained ministries but also of installed ministries
and commissioned ministries.[31]

Installed Ministries

In *Ministeria Quaedam,* Pope Paul VI extended the scope of ministry in the Church beyond those subject to sacramental ordination. In
that document he suppressed all minor orders, did away with the sub-
diaconate, and created two new "installed ministries" that were to have
a permanent status and were open to baptized males.[32] He specifically
created these two ministries, lector and acolyte, subject to a formal ritual installation. On the one hand, the descriptions offered for these ministries were quite rich, going far beyond the limited liturgical exercise
often associated with them in the United States. On the other hand, the
selection of "lector" and "acolyte" as installed ministries was less a response to the real needs and actual ministerial forms of the Church
today and more a "repristination of offices from the ancient church."[33]
This important papal initiative was further compromised when Pope
Paul continued to require those pursuing ordination to the diaconate
and/or presbyterate to first be installed to the ministries of lector and
acolyte, thereby continuing a residual *cursus honorum* and allowing
only males to be installed to these two ministries. Still, the Pope did

propose that episcopal conferences could petition for the addition of other public ministries. The American bishops have made little use of these installed ministries (except for individuals pursuing ordination).

In spite of the obvious limitations evident in the proposal of *Ministeria Quaedam,* this initiative had in mind the possibility of formal church ministries that (1) would be exercised by the baptized independent of the process of preparing for ordained ministry, (2) were more or less stable (a canonical condition for a ministry to qualify as an ecclesiastical office), (3) required extended ministerial formation, and (4) were subject to ritual authorization in the form of an installation ritual. The intention, it would appear, was to establish stable ministries not unlike the "lay ecclesial ministries" that have been the subject of so much discussion in the United States.[34]

The reinvigoration of Pope Paul's initiative would require a call for a new installed ministry or ministries (e.g., pastoral associate), open to men and women, that correspond to the situation of the many baptized currently exercising formal church ministries that are fairly stable, demand significant ministerial formation, and deserve just financial remuneration.[35] Within a church becoming ever more diverse, there is much to commend the regionalization of such ministries. In North America these ministries might include directors of Christian formation, youth ministers, family life ministers, RCIA directors, and liturgists, among others. In Indonesia, there is a real ministry of exorcism being engaged; in Latin America there are the *delegados de la palabra,* and in Africa there is the concrete leadership of local communities consigned to the lay ministers referred to as *bokambi.*[36] Were these de facto ministries to be made subject to installation on a regional basis in the fashion apparently envisioned by Pope Paul VI, the nomenclature of "lay ecclesial ministry," currently used with respect to those laypeople exercising significant, stable ministries in the Church, might give way to the more helpful term, "installed ministries."

The formalization of these ministries as installed ministries is not merely a matter of institutionalization; it is also an attempt to restore the liturgical dimension of any and all ecclesial re-positioning. A ritual of ministerial installation, though not strictly speaking a participation in sacramental ordination, would not for that reason be empty of meaning. As Haunerland notes, a ritual of installation would still be "a participation in the sacramental, basic form of the church."[37] Moreover, such a ritual, following the analogy of sacramental ordination, would serve to formalize the minister's new ecclesial relation within the community, and would include a ritual of communal "sending" and an epicletic prayer for the assistance and empowerment of the Holy Spirit. Thomas O'Meara has insisted that the employment of some ritual of installation affirms that "ministry begins normally with public and liturgical recognition."[38] Marcel Metzger's study of the ancient document, *Apostolic Constitutions,* led him to conclude that in the early Church virtually all ministries were subject to some kind of ordination or blessing.[39] A full recognition of the significance of installed ministries as ordered ministries in the Church would seem to demand an appropriate ritualization.

Commissioned Ministries

Beyond those ministries that demand significant ministerial formation and a high degree of stability (ordained and installed ministries), there are still other ordered ministries, the undertaking of which places one in a new ecclesial relationship. These might include the ministry of parish catechists, liturgical ministries for proclaiming God's Word (lector), leading the community in sung prayer (cantor), distributing communion to those present at the eucharistic assembly and those absent due to infirmity (special ministers of the Eucharist), and providing for liturgical hospitality and order (ushers, greeters). Such ministries imply a new degree of accountability and require a specialized formation and some formal authorization that distinguishes them from the exercise of other baptismal charisms evident, for example, in parenting or daily Christian witness. At the same time, these ministries will generally be governed at a more local level. The determination of the specific requirements for formation, the particular form the ritualization of the ministry will take (liturgical commissioning), and so on will generally occur at the level of the parish or the diocese.

It is possible to conceive of these three sets of ordered ministries in terms of their place in the life of the universal Church. Over the centuries, the three ordained ministries of deacon, presbyter, and bishop have become foundational ministries exercised throughout the universal Church. The reservation of sacramental ordination for these three ministries reflects their foundational character. Beyond these ministries, we can recognize installed ministries particular to certain regional churches and subject to the legislation of regional and/or national episcopal conferences. Finally, there would be commissioned ministries, the legislation of which would largely be reserved to dioceses and parishes.

CONCLUSION

In this essay I have tried to establish some ecclesiological foundations in service of a theology of ministry that might do justice to the great flourishing of new ministries we are experiencing in the Church today. I believe that too many theological responses to this new reality mistakenly begin with the distinction between cleric and layperson. The starting point proposed here for a theology of ministry is not holy orders, but the community of the baptized called to share a common mission to proclaim, serve, and realize the coming reign of God. This community fulfills its mission as an ordered communion founded on the mission of Christ and constituted by the gifting of the Spirit. As a Church, Christians are called into relationship (1) with one another, (2) with God in Christ by the Spirit, and (3) with the world as sent in mission. This set of primal relationships is established by our baptism and lived out in Christian faith. Any further ordering within the Church beyond that established by baptism exists strictly in service of this primary relationality. Such a perspective calls into question any ecclesiological schema dependent on a strict separation of the intra-ecclesial and extra-ecclesial, sacred and secular, clerical and lay. All the baptized participate in that ordered communion which is the Church sent in mission. All ordered church ministry exists in service of the building up of this Church in mission.

The theological articulation of that which is distinctive to the various ordered ministries in the Church goes beyond the scope of this article. To some extent this will be addressed in other essays included in this volume. The ecclesiological foundations proposed here do relativize without completely obviating the distinctions which must necessarily exist among the various ministerial orders *(ordines)*. Certainly our tradition has singled out, over time, three ecclesial relationships of service to the baptized that are ecclesially configured through sacramental ordination. The ministries of bishop, presbyter, and deacon have changed dramatically in their signification over the centuries.[40] They can be distinguished from other ministerial relationships, at least in part, by their unique participation in an apostolic office, that is, an office oriented toward the exercise of *episkope* or ecclesial oversight in the preservation of the apostolic faith and ecclesial communion.[41] Yet a central presupposition of the perspective sketched out in this essay is that sacramental ordination does not exhaust the ministerial ordering of the people of God. There are other ministries or orders, entrance into which also constitutes a new ecclesial relationship subject to ecclesial discernment, formation, authorization, and ritualization.

The focus on "ordered ministries" recognizes a certain fluidity in the differentiation of ministries in the Church. The specific ordering of ministries has changed dramatically in the past and will doubtless change further in the future. What must remain consistent in the midst of these changes is the fundamental orientation of the whole Church to the fulfillment of the mission of Christ and the ordering of ministries in service of that mission.

NOTES

1. *Acta Synodalia* I/4, 142f.

2. *Vehementor Nos,* in *The Papal Encyclicals,* ed. Claudia Carlen (New York: McGrath, 1981) 3: 47–48.

3. Kenan B. Osborne, *Ministry: Lay Ministry in the Roman Catholic Church* (New York/Mahwah, N.J.: Paulist Press, 1993) 530 ff.

4. Years later, in a revised edition of his classic work, *Models of the Church,* Avery Dulles would propose this model (Church as Community of Disciples) as a "bridge model" that drew together the fundamental features of the five models of church (Herald, Servant, Institution, Sacrament, and Mystical Communion) that he had addressed in the earlier edition of his book. Cf. Avery Dulles, *Models of the Church,* expanded ed. (New York: Doubleday, 1987).

5. *Acta Synodalia* II/3, 175–178.

6. For a careful analysis of the council's treatment of charisms, see Albert Vanhoye, "The Biblical Question of 'Charisms' after Vatican II," in *Vatican II: Assessment and Perspectives,* vol. 1, ed. R. Latourelle (New York/Mahwah, N.J.: Paulist Press, 1988) 439–468.

7. John Haughey, "Charisms: An Ecclesiological Exploration," in *Retrieving Charisms for the Twenty-First Century,* ed. Doris Donnelly (Collegeville, Minn.: The Liturgical Press, 1999) 3–5.

8. Bruno Forte, *The Church: Icon of the Trinity* (Boston: St. Paul Books & Media, 1991) 54–55.

9. Cf. *Christifideles Laici,* 19, *Origins* 18/35 (February 19, 1989) 570.

10. Walter Kasper, *Theology and Church* (New York: Crossroad, 1989) 151.

11. Jerome Murphy-O'Connor, "Eucharist and Community in I Corinthians," in *Living Bread, Saving Cup,* ed. Kevin Seasoltz (Collegeville, Minn.: The Liturgical Press, 1982) 4.

12. Cf. Ludwig Hertling, *Communio: Church and Papacy in Early Christianity* (Chicago: Loyola Press, 1972); Werner Elert, *Eucharist and Church Fellowship in the First Four Centuries* (St. Louis: Concordia, 1966); Kenneth Hein, *Eucharist and Excommunication: A Study in Early Christian Doctrine and Discipline* (Frankfurt: Lang, 1975).

13. John D. Zizioulas, *Being as Communion* (Crestwood, N.Y.: St. Vladimir's Seminary Press, 1985) 140.

14. Ibid.

15. It appears a sixth time in no. 2 of the *Nota Praevia Explicativa* attached at the eleventh hour to *Lumen Gentium,* without conciliar approval, "by higher authority." Walter Kasper offers a helpful discussion of the ambiguities surrounding this phrase in *Theology and Church* (New York: Crossroad, 1989) 156–161.

16. See Jean Leclerq, "Influence and Noninfluence of Dionysius in the Western Middle Ages," in *Pseudo-Dionysius: The Complete Works* (New York/Mahwah, N.J.: Paulist Press, 1987) 31; Yves Congar, *L'Église de Saint Augustin à l'époque moderne* (Paris: Cerf, 1970) 229–230.

17. See Terence Nichols's helpful treatment of different notions of hierarchy in church tradition. Terence Nichols, *That All May Be One: Hierarchy and Participation in the Church* (Collegeville, Minn.: The Liturgical Press, 1997). This view of the Church as an ordered communion parallels in some ways Ghislain Lafont's presentation of the postconciliar church as a "structured communion." See his *Imagining the Catholic Church: Structured Communion in the Spirit* (Collegeville, Minn.: The Liturgical Press, 2000).

18. Zizioulas, *Being as Communion,* 215–216.

19. Thomas F. O'Meara, *Theology of Ministry,* rev. ed. (New York/Mahwah, N.J.: Paulist Press, 1999) 150.

20. See Wendy Wright, "The Charism of Parenting," in *Retrieving Charisms for the Twenty-First Century,* 85–101.

21. Karl Rahner, "Consecration in the Life of the Church," in *Theological Investigations,* vol. 19 (New York: Crossroad, 1983) 67. "Consecration" translates the German, *"Weihe,"* which, however, also carries the sense of "initiation," "dedication," or even "re-dedication," thus explaining Rahner's categorization of "sacraments of consecration."

22. Ibid., 64.

23. St. Augustine, *Sermon* 340.

24. James Puglisi, *The Process of Admission to Ordained Ministry: A Comparative Study* (Collegeville, Minn.: The Liturgical Press, 1996) 1: 205.

25. Ibid., 206.

26. Karl Rahner, "Pastoral Ministries and Community Leadership," in *Theological Investigations,* vol. 19 (New York: Crossroad, 1983) 75.

27. David Power, "Church Order," in *The New Dictionary of Sacramental Worship* (Collegeville, Minn.: The Liturgical Press, 1990) 214.

28. Ibid., 216. For further studies into the history and contemporary significance of the minor orders, see Winfried Haunerland, "The Heirs of the Clergy? The New Pastoral Ministries and the Reform of the Minor Orders," *Worship* 75 (July 2001) 305–320; Bruno Kleinheyer, "Ordinationen und Beauftragungen," in *Sakramentliche Feiern II, Gottesdienst der Kirche,* vol. 8, ed. Emmanuel V. Severus and Reiner Kaczynski (Regensburg: Pustet, 1984) 7–65; Walter Croce, "Die niederen Weihen und ihre hierarchische Wertung," *Zeitschrift für katholische Theologie* 70 (1948) 257–314.

29. Haunerland, "The Heirs of the Clergy?" 309.

30. See Richard R. Gaillardetz, "Shifting Meanings in the Lay-Clergy Distinction," *Irish Theological Quarterly* 64 (1999) 115–139.

31. In a similar fashion, Thomas O'Meara proposes that "perhaps one should speak of three kinds of activities by which an individual is commissioned in the church: ordination, installation, and presentation." While acknowledging the three ordinations of deacon, presbyter, and bishop, O'Meara adds that "installation is for ministers who have an extensive education and whose ministry is full-time in the parish and diocese, while presentation is for readers, acolytes, visitors of the sick, assistants to other ministries." O'Meara, *Theology of Ministry,* 224. His latter two categories correspond almost exactly to what I refer to as installed and commissioned ministries.

32. *The Rites of the Catholic Church as Revised by Decree of the Second Vatican Ecumenical Council and Published by Authority of Pope Paul VI* (New York: Pueblo Pub., 1976) 726–739.

33. Haunerland, "The Heirs of the Clergy?" 310.

34. See NCCB Subcommittee on the Lay Ministry, *Lay Ecclesial Ministry: The State of the Questions* (Washington, D.C.: USCC, 1999); Zeni Fox, *New Ecclesial Ministry: Lay Professionals Serving the Church,* rev. ed. (Kansas City: Sheed and Ward, 2002).

35. For similar proposals, see Haunerland, "The Heirs of the Clergy?" 311 and Hans Bernard Meyer, "Laien als liturgische Vorsteher: Stellen wir die richtigen Fragen?" in *Wie weit trägt des gemeinsame Priestertum? Liturgischer Leitungsdienst zwischen Ordination und Beauftragung, Quaestiones disputatae* 171, ed. Martin Klöckener and Klemens Richter (Freiburg: Herder, 1998) 11–19.

36. Haunerland, "The Heirs of the Clergy?" 313–314.

37. Ibid., 317. Haunerland speaks of a "commissioning" rather than an "installation." As will be evident in the next section, I prefer to reserve the term "commissioning" to a third category of ordered ministries in the Church.

38. O'Meara, *Theology of Ministry,* 222.

39. Marcel Metzger, "Ministères, ordinations, clergé et peuple dans les 'Constitutions Apostoliques," in *Ordination et ministères* (Rome: Edizioni Liturgiche, 1995) 209.

40. This has been demonstrated well in Kenan Osborne's essay included in this volume.

41. The question of how the diaconate relates to the apostolic office of the Church is a difficult one and cannot be addressed adequately here. The deacon's role as assistant to the bishop in the early Church suggests some connection to the exercise of the ministry of *episkope*. At the same time, there is little or no evidence of deacons themselves engaging in the pastoral oversight of a eucharistic community.

Ministry and Ministries

Thomas P. Rausch, S.J.

If there is much written about ministry in the contemporary Church, there also remains considerable controversy about the origins of ministry and its contemporary expression. Part of the difficulty stems from the fact that the New Testament data is open to different interpretations. Another complication stems from a controversy waged in the postconciliar Church over the whole question of ministry. One current seeks to expand the concept of ministry by moving beyond its exclusively clerical understanding in second-millennium Catholicism. Another, driven by feminist and anti-hierarchical concerns, has sought to reinterpret the period of Christian origins, arguing that concepts such as office, hierarchy, and priesthood are completely foreign to the egalitarian nature of primitive Christianity. A third is represented by the Roman reaction to both; it seeks to reserve again the term "ministry" for the ordained.

How can we articulate a theology of ministry that respects the distinctive ministries of ordained and lay members of the Church in the context of their shared baptism? Here we will consider, first, the development of ministerial language in the period of Christian origins. Second, we will look more closely at the above-mentioned currents concerning ministry in the contemporary Church. Finally, we will consider ordained and nonordained ministries in the context of Christian baptism.

I. MINISTERIAL LANGUAGE AND CHRISTIAN ORIGINS

The English word "ministry" has its origin in the Greek word *diakonia* (Latin, *ministerium*). It first appears in the New Testament in the letters of Paul, though it may have been in use even earlier. *Diakonia* is most often translated as "service." Paul sometimes uses *diakonia* in the more general sense of service, as in reference to his efforts to support financially the Jerusalem church (Rom 15:25, 31; 2 Cor 8:4, 19; 9:1) and for personal service (Phlm 13). But most often he uses *diakonia* and its substantive, *diakonos,* of those whose particular form of service places them in leadership roles in the community. He uses *diakonia* or *diakonos* in connection with his own apostolic ministry (Rom 1:1; 15:16; 1 Cor 4:1; 2 Cor 3:6; 6:4; 11:8; 11:23) or in reference to others claiming to be apostles (2 Cor 11:12, 15) or with recognized roles in local communities (Rom 16:1; Phil 1:1). Among the latter is a woman, Phoebe, whom he identifies as the *diakonos* of the church of Cenchreae (Rom 16:1).

Basing their arguments on H. W. Beyer's article in Kittel's *Theological Dictionary of the New Testament,* modern scholars have understood *diakonia* and its cognates as having their origin in secular life, rooted specifically in the verb *diakonein,* to serve, specifically, to serve at table. Thus the term was seen as originally secular, not religious; *diakonia* meant simply service. However, some recent scholarship has challenged this interpretation. In his book, *Diakonia: Re-interpreting the Ancient Sources,* John Collins has argued that *diakonia*/ministry comes not from profane life, but from religious or formal language, with the implications of authorization or divine representation. Ministers are "emissaries." He judges this to mean that ministry is not for all the baptized; it is based on the Word and restricted to those to whom it has been given by the community or by the Lord.[1]

The ultimate inspiration for the adoption of the word *diakonia* by the early Christians was the example of Jesus himself, who saw his own life and death as a service on behalf of others (Mark 10:45), an understanding that some scholars believe originally came to expression at the Last Supper.[2]

A Diversity of Ministries

If *diakonia* is the basic concept for ministry, the New Testament documents show a variety of names for those who exercised roles of service and leadership in the earliest Christian communities. The terminology was somewhat fluid, particularly in the earlier documents. But there was leadership from the beginning, even a certain order in the ministries.

Paul sees the community as endowed with a rich variety of gifts *(charismata)*, ministries *(diakoniai)*, and works *(energēmata)*, to be used for building up the Church as the Body of Christ (1 Cor 12:4-6). Apostles are in the first place, followed by prophets, and then teachers (1 Cor 12:28). But Paul also mentions leaders or "presiders" (*proistamenoi:* 1 Thess 5:12; Rom 12:8); the hosts or heads of house churches (1 Cor 16:19; Rom 16:5; Phlm 2); overseers and ministers or deacons (*episkopoi kai diakonoi:* Phil 1:1); and ministers (*diakonos:* Rom 16:1). Other New Testament works reflect a similar diversity of terms. Ephesians refers to apostles, prophets, evangelists, pastors, and teachers (Eph 4:11). Hebrews refers to leaders (*hēgoumenoi:* Heb 13:7, 17, 24). Prophets and teachers are still visible in later books (Acts 13:1; *Didache* 15:1). Matthew mentions prophets and scribes (or wise men: Matt 13:52; 23:34), perhaps a variant paring. Presbyters (literally "elders"), first mentioned in James 5:14, appear more frequently in the later books (Acts 11:30; 14:23; 20:17; 2 John 1; 3 John 1) as do presbyter-bishops (1 and 2 Tim, Titus, 1 Pet 5:1-4, 1 Clement) and deacons (1 Tim 3:8-13; *Didache* 15:1).

The Emergence of a Pastoral Office

It is difficult to speak of a ministerial *office* in the earliest New Testament letters, if by office is understood a position of authority, bestowed with some sign of appointment, to exercise some permanent ministry within the community. Such "institutionalized" ministries have often been opposed to "charismatic" ministries arising spontaneously through the Holy Spirit. But such facile juxtapositions are misleading, for each ministry is grounded in some charism.[3] If Paul's churches did not yet have an institutionalized office, it would be inaccurate to conclude that the only structuring principle was the diversity of charisms. The prophets and teachers named after the apostles are usually recognized as local community leaders. Schillebeeckx calls them "incipient local leaders and pioneers."[4] Wayne Meeks points to Paul's ranking of apostles, prophets, and teachers in 1 Corinthians 12:28, to a few roles common to all the lists, and to the evidence that some leaders were supported by the congregations from a very early period (Gal 6:6) as evidence "that some degree of formalization had already taken place."[5]

In the later books of the New Testament one can discern a pastoral office in the process of emerging. By then the original witnesses had passed from the scene and the churches were confronted by new challenges, among them the question of authority, succession, and leadership. This is reflected in a number of books from this period. Matthew seems concerned about a type of "nascent clericalism" which is evident in his warnings against "ostentatious religious clothing and paraphernalia... the desire for first seats at the religious meetings... and the desire to be addressed with special titles" (Matt 23:5-10).[6] A controversy over rank in the Synoptics (Mark 10:35-40; Matt 20:20-28; Luke 22:24-27) is concerned with authority and ministry in the community. A variant tradition in 1 Peter 5:1-4 instructs the presbyters to exercise their authority without "lording it over" others.[7]

Increasingly the presbyter/bishops (the two terms were not at first clearly distinguished) took over the roles exercised earlier by prophets, teachers, presider/leaders *(proistamenoi),* and probably the leaders of the house churches. While elders in the synagogue functioned as a kind of advisory council, the responsibility of the presbyter/bishops frequently included community leadership as well as preaching and teaching. The expression "pastors and teachers," introduced by a single article in Ephesians 4:11, indicates an office of pastoral leadership which included both functions. An interesting text in 1 Timothy states that "presbyters who preside well deserve double honor [or compensation], especially those who toil in preaching and teaching" (1 Tim 5:17). Timothy is also instructed not to "lay hands too readily on anyone" (1 Tim 5:22), suggesting that a sign of appointment to the presbyteral office, while not necessarily universal, is in place. Raymond Brown notes that "in churches associated with the three great apostolic figures of the NT, Paul, James, and Peter, presbyters were known and established in the last third of the century."[8] The threefold ministry of a bishop, assisted by presbyters and deacons, already evident in the letters of Ignatius of Antioch around 110 C.E., was in place throughout the Church by the end of the second century.

While the threefold ministry proved remarkably effective in providing for the pastoral care of local churches and linking them together into the universal communion of what Ignatius called "the catholic church" (Smyrn 8.2), its emergence was not without some loss. One loss was the Pauline concept of the multiplicity of charisms. In the later New Testament books, the term "charism" appears only in reference to the ministry of church leaders (1 Pet 4:10) and to those who have received the laying on of hands (1 Tim 4:14; 2 Tim 1:6). Another loss was the openness to women in ministerial roles discernible in the earliest communities. In the later New Testament books one finds a number of passages that suggest a subordinate role for women. "Household codes," or rules of domestic order subordinating wives to husbands, children to parents, and slaves to masters, were incorporated from Greco-Roman sources into New Testament letters (Col 3:18–4:1; Eph 5:22–6:9; 1 Pet 2:13–3:7; Titus 2:2-10). An injunction in 1 Timothy 2:12 against women teaching suggests that there were indeed women who were teaching in the community.

A second development in regards to the Church's pastoral office was its gradual sacralization or sacerdotalization. As early as the year 96, the author of 1 Clement compared the order of the Jewish cult, with its high priests, priests, and Levites (1 Clem 40), to the order of the Christian community, with its apostles, bishops, and deacons (1 Clem 42). As the Church became more aware of the sacrificial dimension of its Eucharist, it began using sacerdotal language for its eucharistic presiders. The *Didache* recognizes the wandering prophets as eucharistic leaders (10) and calls them "high priests" (13). The prayer of consecration for the ordination of a bishop which comes to us from Hippolytus of Rome (ca. 215) refers to the bishop as "high priest" (*Apostolic Tradition* 3.4). Tertullian (d. 225) and Cyprian (d. 258) also speak of the bishop as *sacerdos*. Cyprian extended the term to presbyters, but only in conjunction with the bishops, a usage that became traditional in the Church. It is also in Cyprian that we find the first reference to presbyters presiding at the Eucharist without the bishop (Letter 5). The gradual change of the Church's ministry of leadership into a sacral, priestly office has been well documented in recent studies. Thomas O'Meara speaks of the "metamorphoses of ministry,"[9] Edward Schillebeeckx of its "sacerdotalizing,"[10] Kenan Osborne of its "clericalization."[11]

II. MINISTERIAL CURRENTS
IN THE CONTEMPORARY CHURCH

One of the most important achievements of the Second Vatican Council was its attention to the vocation of the layperson in the Church.

The council took a number of steps to develop a theology of the laity. First, it used the biblical image of the people of God to describe the Church (*Lumen Gentium* [hereafter *LG*], ch. 2) and emphasized that the whole Church, not just priests and religious, are called to holiness (*LG,* ch. 5). Pneumatologically, it reclaimed the *charismata* or spiritual gifts, "both hierarchic and charismatic" (*LG* 4, cf. 12, 30). Most important, it stressed that both ordained ministers and all the faithful share in the priesthood of Christ, though in different ways (*LG* 10). This emphasis on the two priesthoods is foundational to the council's vision. The laity share in Christ's priestly, prophetic, and kingly functions (*LG* 31). Commissioned by the sacraments of baptism and confirmation, they share in the mission of the Church itself (*LG* 33), an affirmation that moves far beyond the pre-Vatican II language that described the "lay apostolate" as "the collaboration of the laity in the apostolic tasks proper to the hierarchy."[12]

In the years after the council, the rediscovery of the laity's participation in the mission of the Church focused particularly on the question of ministry. As we noted earlier, three currents have emerged. One is expansionist, a second deconstructive, and a third attempts again to restrict the concept. We will consider each briefly.

1. Expanding the Concept

The first approach seeks to expand the concept of ministry beyond its restriction to the ordained. In his book, *Are All Christians Ministers?* John Collins argues that this approach is a thoroughly modern one, based on a reinterpretation of Ephesians 4:12, particularly in the 1971 *Revised Standard Version* (RSV) translation.[13] By dropping a comma, so that the phrase "for the work of ministry" completes the preceding "for the equipment of the saints" rather than standing for one of the tasks of the "apostles, prophets, evangelists, pastors and teachers" mentioned earlier, the 1971 RSV suggests that all are called to the work of ministry. Though this view was contrary to that of the Reformers, it was welcomed by Protestant theologians. In a section of his commentary on Ephesians entitled "The Church without Laymen and Priests," Marcus Barth wrote that "all saints and the whole church are...clergymen of God," arguing that baptism probably included the meaning that was later attributed to ordination.[14] The 1982 World Council of Churches text, *Baptism, Eucharist and Ministry,* reflects this baptismal theology, situating its discussion of ministry in the context of the calling of the whole people of God (M 1-6).[15] Hans-Ruedi Weber sees the view that "*all* the members of the church have received grace and are therefore called to service or—to say exactly the same thing—called to ministry," as representing a "Copernican change" in theology.[16]

In the years since the council, Catholic theologians also have sought to develop theologies of ministry that go beyond that of the ordained. The first step was taken by Pope Paul VI. In *Ministeria Quaedam,* an apostolic letter which followed the 1971 Third Synod of Bishops, Pope Paul decreed that the old "minor orders" would henceforth be called "ministries" and could be committed to lay Christians.[17] This was a step forward, even if these ministries of "lector" and "acolyte" were still restricted to males and the term "ordination" was to be replaced by "installation," for what was emerging was a new language of ministries ordained or installed. The Pope also invited episcopal conferences to move on the basis of particular needs toward "the establishment of other offices from the Holy See, over and above those which are common to the whole Church."[18] It was this freedom to experiment that according to Peter Hebblethwaite led to the "ministry explosion" of the 1980s.[19]

Catholic theologians soon went even further. A considerable number have argued that all Christians are called to ministry. Thomas F. O'Meara sees baptism as the fundamental sacrament of ministry; it is "an initiation into a new eschatological life which intrinsically includes ministry."[20] Leonard Doohan speaks of "a permanent commitment to ministry that results from baptism,"[21] but his concept of ministry is so broadly conceived that any instance of help or assistance rendered another in Christ's name qualifies. Paul Bernier stresses that "ministry is a facet of baptized life, not the vocation of the few."[22] In a more nuanced treatment, Kenan Osborne uses Vatican II and subsequent church documents to argue for a specific lay vocation or status chosen by some Christians, distinct from the vocation of all the baptized. Such a vocation is a genuine ministry, "an active and specific role in the church as a servant-leader, a role which, though traditionally not involving an ordination, needs some form of credentialing or ritual of institution."[23] Recently the bishops of the United States have used the term "ecclesial lay ministers" to describe those exercising these roles.[24]

2. Deconstructing the Tradition

Another approach to a more inclusive ministry is represented by recent efforts to deconstruct what was perceived as being at the foundation of the Church's hierarchical structure and ordained ministry, the apostolic office. Some feminist scholars have challenged the idea of an apostolic office related to the Twelve. Sandra Schneiders argues that the primitive Church was an egalitarian discipleship, with "evangelical equality" as the principle of relationships within the Church.[25] According to Elisabeth Schüssler Fiorenza, the early Church emerged from the "Jesus movement," a "discipleship of equals."[26] While the early Christian communities were also "egalitarian," the equal access of men and women to roles of authority soon gave way to a more restrictive patriarchal leadership based on the male heads of households.[27] She takes the position that the Twelve did not exercise a ministry of leadership in the primitive community; their role was "eschatological-symbolical," representing the twelve tribes of Israel.[28] Thus, an ordered church should be understood as a later development, with no foundation in the work of the historical Jesus.

Others have sought to reinterpret the eucharistic role of ordained ministers. Some have proposed a charismatic "ordination of the Spirit" as opposed to traditional ordination by the bishop.[29] John Baldovin finds problematic both the "sacerdotalized vocabulary" used of ordained ministers and the idea that in presiding at the Eucharist their role is "representational," acting "*in persona Christi*."[30] Neil Darragh wants to reduce the role of the one he calls the "mono-presider" by having different leaders for the liturgy of the word, the liturgy of the Eucharist, and the liturgy of gathering and sending.[31] Gary Macy speaks of Catholics in the United States as being in the midst of a "renegotiation" of the ritual power of the Eucharist and looks forward to a new and exciting future of eucharistic celebrations without permanently ordained clergy.[32]

3. Restricting the Language of "Ministry"

A third approach, evident in more recent postconciliar documents issuing from Rome, seeks to limit the terms "minister" and "ministry" to the ordained. This approach can be seen in two recent Roman documents. In 1997 the instruction "Some Questions Regarding Collaboration of

Nonordained Faithful in Priests' Sacred Ministry" was published by eight Vatican offices,[33] while in 1999 the Vatican Congregation for the Clergy published a circular letter entitled "The Priest: Teacher of the Word, Minister of the Sacraments, Leader of the Community."[34]

The orientation of the first document is immediately clear from its title. If the Church in the years before Vatican II spoke of the "lay apostolate" as "the collaboration of the laity in the apostolic tasks proper to the hierarchy,"[35] as we saw earlier, the new language of the Curia is of the collaboration of the nonordained in the sacred ministry of priests or in their "pastoral ministry." The laity may share in the mission of the Church, but they don't yet have a proper ministry. The instruction speaks of the ministry of the clergy as "sacred" or "pastoral," while the mission of the laity is "secular" in nature.[36] Thus, the instruction betrays the familiar tendency to see the Church as the realm of the clergy and the world as that of the laity.

The "essence" of the sacred ministry is to be found in the "exercise of the *munus docendi, sanctificandi et regendi.*"[37] The role of the laity is to "assist" or "collaborate in" this ministry; they can "assume duties" or exercise forms of "pastoral activity." They can serve as "extraordinary ministers" of Holy Communion and baptism (nos. 8, 11). But they are not to assume titles such as *"pastor, chaplain, coordinator, moderator,* or other such similar titles which can confuse their role and that of the pastor, who is always a bishop or priest."[38] The bottom line is that the instruction is content to defend the status of the ordained, without any evident concern for the very real ministerial needs facing the contemporary Church.

The 1999 letter from the Congregation for the Clergy is a very traditional treatment of ordained ministry in terms of the threefold *munera.* Regrettably, it fails to show how the ordained priesthood is to serve the priesthood of all the faithful.

III. ORDERED MINISTRIES

So how can we talk about ministry in tomorrow's Church? The traditional dichotomies—clerical and lay, religious and secular, institution and charism, ordained and nonordained—are not helpful and reinforce the false church/world dichotomy. Can we speak of "ministries ordained and nonordained"? Or, even better, "ordered ministries"? A solid argument can be made that the Second Vatican Council was moving toward a more inclusive understanding of ministry.

Ministry Rooted in Baptism

In a recent article, Richard Gaillardetz writes that while the council can be read as presupposing the traditional lay-clergy distinction, on a deeper level it is moving toward a less "hierarchological" or "contrastive" perspective to one based on a "common matrix" coming from baptism.[39] Gaillardetz points to the placing of *Lumen Gentium*'s chapter on the Church as the people of God before the one on the hierarchy, the council's frequent use of the term *"Christifideles"* to refer to the baptized, its appeal to the priesthood of all believers, and its incorporation of the biblical concept of charism and thus of pneumatology alongside the more traditional christological framework.[40]

In an another important study, Elissa Rinere shows that the council applied "ministry" and "service" to both clergy and laity. The terms "minister" and "ministry" appear over two hundred times in the documents; nineteen times they are used in reference to the activity of laypeople.[41] Rinere's careful summary is worth citing at length:

Taken together, the conciliar documents considered here show a clear progression in the council's understanding of the laity as ministers. At the outset, ministry pertained to the ordained only. In *Sacrosanctum Concilium* the laity were accepted as liturgical ministers and included in the munus of sanctifying. In *Christus Dominus* they were said to share the pastoral ministry and the munus of governing of the bishop. In *Apostolicam actuositatem* and *Ad gentes,* although critical questions about the nature of lay activities carried out under official authorization from the hierarchy were not settled, laity were named as ministers both within the Church, in fulfillment of the hierarchical munera, and in the world, in fulfillment of the munera of the people of God. Source information, particularly from *Apostolicam actuositatem* and *Ad gentes,* indicates that the council consciously applied the word "ministry" to lay activities which were exercises of the common priesthood of the faithful. Finally, *Gaudium et spes* stated without qualification that everyday life in the world is ministry through which God continues to act.[42]

But, despite this progression in the conciliar understanding, in the 1983 Code of Canon Law, service and ministry belong to the ordained. The laity "may offer special services or engage in certain ministries, but only by invitation of the hierarchy."[43] Rinere attributes the more open view of the council to its emphasis on the complementarity and equal importance of the two priesthoods in *Lumen Gentium*. At the end of her essay she asks the question, "If the conciliar use of the word 'ministry' had ecclesiological significance, what are the ecclesiological consequences of the code's withdrawal of the word from the priesthood of the people?"[44]

Both articles point to baptism as the sacrament in which all ministry is rooted, explicitly in Gaillardetz's article, and more obliquely in Rinere's emphasis on the complementarity of the two priesthoods. Both authors reflect an emerging consensus in contemporary Catholic theology that recognizes baptism as the fundamental sacrament of ministry. But this is also a very traditional argument.

Vatican II's *Presbyterorum Ordinis* states that priests, marked by the special character of orders, are "configured to Christ the Priest" and so can act *in persona Christi capitis* (no. 2). But it neglects to say explicitly that all Christians are configured to Christ by the sacraments of baptism and confirmation and so share in his priesthood. According to Thomas Aquinas, the sacramental characters received by the faithful "are nothing else than certain participations of Christ's priesthood, flowing from Christ Himself."[45] All Christians "put on Christ, through being configured to Him by the character."[46]

Pope John Paul II, in giving a carefully qualified acknowledgment of lay ministry in two of his writings, calls attention to this baptismal foundation. The first, from his apostolic exhortation *Christifideles Laici,* exhorts pastors to "acknowledge and foster the ministries, the offices and roles of the lay faithful that find their foundation in the sacraments of baptism and confirmation, indeed, for a good many of them, in the sacrament of matrimony."[47] The other, an address given in 1994 at a Vatican symposium sponsored by the Congregation for the Clergy, says the following: "In some cases the extension of the term *ministry* to the *munera* belonging to the lay faithful has been permitted by the fact that the latter, to their own degree, are a participation in the one priesthood of Christ. The *officia* temporarily entrusted to them however are exclusively the result of a deputation by the church." The Pope reminds laypeople that "these tasks are existentially rooted in their baptismal ministry" and emphasizes, quoting *Christifideles Laici* (no. 23), that "the exercise of such tasks does not make pastors of the lay faithful: In fact, a person is not a minister simply in performing a task, but through sacramental ordination."[48] If this is a somewhat tentative recognition of lay ministry, it is significant that it is rooted sacramentally in baptism and the baptismal priesthood.

Perhaps we can see behind this effort to restrict "pastoral ministry" to the ordained a concern to safeguard the unique meaning of ordination. That concern is not entirely misplaced, since its importance is not infrequently overlooked in contemporary discussions of ministry. What, then, is unique to the ministry of the ordained?

The Gift of Ordained Ministry

The Catholic tradition both theologically and liturgically understands the sacrament of orders as incorporation into the Church's apostolic ministry or office. Bishops and presbyters are enabled to act in the name of the Church *(in persona ecclesiae)* and thus in the person of Christ, the head of the Church *(in persona Christi capitis),* a role they exercise in the Church's public, sacramental life. Susan Wood has used the happy term "sacrament of the ecclesial community" to describe this.[49] Like others, she argues that the "Christic" role of the priest, acting *in persona Christi,* is rooted in the ecclesial, "the Christic occurring in and through the ecclesial."[50] Deacons are ordained "not for the priesthood, but for the ministry" *(LG* 29). They assist the bishop and priests in the liturgy, the ministry of the word, and charity.

Ordained ministry cannot be understood merely as a function; it is rooted in a received identity. What is key is ordination. The Latin word for "ordain" means "to order" or "to incorporate into an order"; the ritual "orders" ministry. By ordination, the priest is incorporated into the Church's pastoral office; the Church and thus Christ act in and through the priest as their representative. A new relation now exists between the priest and the Church and, consequently, a real change has come about. The tradition expressed this by speaking of an ontological change or "character." Henceforth in exercising a sacramental ministry the priest is able to act in the name of the Church, and thus in the person of Christ.

CONCLUSIONS

1. Both the baptized and ordained ministers share in the one priesthood of Christ, though in different ways. All the faithful are "configured" to Christ through baptism, confirmation, and Eucharist and so have a participation in his priesthood. They share in the threefold functions of Christ (*LG* 31).

2. The Second Vatican Council is clearly moving toward a more inclusive concept of ministry. In *Gaudium et Spes* it praises the "ministry" of earthly service (no. 38) and the "ministry of safeguarding life entrusted to all people" (no. 51), both ministries in which the laity share.

3. Some laypeople are called to a specific lay ministry, distinct from the vocation of all the baptized. As Kenan Osborne has suggested, those exercising these ministries should be commissioned with some ritual of institution.[51]

4. The sacrament of ordination incorporates a baptized person into the Church's apostolic office and thus, for a bishop or presbyter, into its ordained priesthood. Ordination recognizes a charism for a particular service; it gives the priest a special role, not a higher status.

5. The ordained priesthood serves the common priesthood of all the faithful, particularly when the bishop or priest presides at the assembly's celebration of the Eucharist. Priests are enabled by ordination to represent the Church and to act officially in its name, and thus in the person of Christ who gathers the Church together.

6. By his communion with the bishop, the priest both symbolizes and maintains the communion that exists between the local congregation and the local church, and with the worldwide communion of the Church. The real meaning of ordination is to be found not in sacred power, a concept open to misunderstanding, but in sacramental authorization.

NOTES

1. John N. Collins, *Diakonia: Re-interpreting the Ancient Sources* (New York: Oxford University Press, 1990) 258–259.

2. Edward Schillebeeckx, *Jesus: An Experiment in Christology* (New York: Seabury, 1979) 303–305; Collins, *Diakonia,* 52–53.

3. See Thomas F. O'Meara, *Theology of Ministry: Completely Revised Edition* (New York/Mahwah, N.J.: Paulist Press, 1999) 62–63.

4. Edward Schillebeeckx, *The Church With a Human Face* (New York: Crossroad, 1985) 79.

5. Wayne A. Meeks, *The First Urban Christians: The Social World of the Apostle Paul* (New Haven: Yale University Press, 1983) 135.

6. John P. Meier, "The Antiochene Church of the Second Christian Generation," in Raymond E. Brown and John P. Meier, *Antioch and Rome: New Testament Cradles of Catholic Christianity* (New York/Mahwah, N.J.: Paulist Press, 1983) 70.

7. John Hall Elliott, "Ministry and Church Order in the NT: A Traditio-Historical Analysis (1 Pt 5,1-5 & plls)," *The Catholic Biblical Quarterly* 32 (1970) 367–391.

8. Raymond E. Brown, "*Episkope* and *Episkopos:* The New Testament Evidence," *Theological Studies* 41 (1980) 325.

9. O'Meara, *Theology of Ministry* (rev. ed.), 80–138.

10. Schillebeeckx, *The Church With a Human Face,* 144–147.

11. Kenan B. Osborne, *Priesthood: A History of the Ordained Ministry in the Roman Catholic Church* (New York/Mahwah, N.J.: Paulist Press, 1988) 145–148.

12. Pius XII, "Allocution to Italian Catholic Action," *Acta Apostolicae Sedis* 32 (1940) 362.

13. John N. Collins, *Are All Christians Ministers?* (Collegeville, Minn.: The Liturgical Press, 1992) 22–24.

14. Markus Barth, *Ephesians,* The Anchor Bible (Garden City, N.Y.: Doubleday, 1974) 481.

15. World Council of Churches, *Baptism, Eucharist and Ministry* (Geneva: World Council of Churches, 1982).

16. Hans-Ruedi Weber, *Living in the Image of Christ* (Valley Forge, Pa.: Judson Press, 1986) 71–72, italics in original.

17. Paul VI, apostolic letter *Ministeria Quaedam,* August 15, 1972, in Austin Flannery, ed., *Vatican Council II: The Conciliar and Post Conciliar Documents* (Northport, N.Y.: Costello Publishing Co., 1975) 429.

18. Ibid., 428.

19. Peter Hebblethwaite, *Paul VI: The First Modern Pope* (New York/Mahwah, N.J.: Paulist Press, 1993) 599.

20. Thomas F. O'Meara, *Theology of Ministry* (New York: Paulist Press, 1983) 139. In his revised volume (1999) he says, "Every Christian has a vocation to ministry, to serving the kingdom of God" (210).

21. Leonard Doohan, *The Lay-Centered Church: Theology and Spirituality* (Minneapolis, Minn.: Winston Press, 1984) 45.

22. Paul Bernier, *Ministry in the Church: A Historical and Pastoral Approach* (Mystic, Conn.: Twenty-Third Publications, 1992) 1–2.

23. Kenan B. Osborne, *Ministry: Lay Ministry in the Roman Catholic Church* (New York/Mahwah, N.J.: Paulist Press, 1993) 598.

24. U.S. Catholic Bishops' Committee on the Laity, *Called and Gifted for the Third Millennium* (Washington, D.C.: USCC, 1995), 17; see Zeni Fox, *New Ecclesial Ministry: Lay Professionals Serving the Church* (Kansas City, Mo.: Sheed and Ward, 1997).

25. Sandra M. Schneiders, "Evangelical Equality," *Spirituality Today* 38 (1986) 293–302.

26. Elisabeth Schüssler Fiorenza, *In Memory of Her* (New York: Crossroad, 1983) 107 ff.

27. Ibid., 286–287.

28. Elisabeth Schüssler Fiorenza, "The Twelve," in *Women Priests: A Catholic Commentary on the Vatican Declaration,* ed. Leonard Swidler and Arlene Swidler (New York: Paulist Press, 1977) 117.

29. John W. Glaser, "Anonymous Priesthood," *Commonweal* 93 (December 1970) 271–274.

30. John F. Baldovin, "The Eucharist and Ministerial Leadership," *CTSA Proceedings* 52 (1997) 74–78.

31. Neil Darragh, *When Christians Gather: Issues in the Celebration of the Eucharist* (New York/Mahwah, N.J.: Paulist Press, 1996) 16–17.

32. Gary Macy, "The Eucharist and Popular Religiosity," *CTSA Proceedings* 52 (1997) 56–58.

33. Congregation for the Clergy et al., instruction "Some Questions Regarding Collaboration of Nonordained Faithful in Priests' Sacred Ministry," *Origins* 27/24 (1997) 397–409.

34. Congregation for the Clergy, circular letter "The Priest: Teacher of the Word, Minister of the Sacraments, Leader of the Community," *Origins* 29/13 (1999) 197–211.

35. Pius XII, "Allocution," 362.

36. "Some Questions," 399.

37. Ibid., 401.

38. Ibid., 403.

39. Richard R. Gaillardetz, "Shifting Meanings in the Lay-Clergy Distinction," *Irish Theological Quarterly* 64 (1999) 119; the term "common matrix" is from Kenan Osborne, *Ministry,* 530 ff.

40. Ibid., 121–132.

41. Elissa Rinere, "Conciliar and Canonical Applications of 'Ministry' to the Laity," *The Jurist* 47 (1987) 205.

42. Ibid., 216.

43. Ibid., 226.

44. Ibid., 227.

45. *Summa Theologiae (ST),* Pt. III, Q. 63, a. 3; compare *Mediator Dei,* no. 43, which says that priests alone have been conformed to Christ the Priest.

46. *ST,* Pt. III, Q. 69, a. 9.

47. John Paul II, apostolic exhortation *Christifideles Laici* 23, *Origins* 18/35 (1989) 571.

48. "Do Laity Share in the Priest's Pastoral Ministry?" *Origins* 24/3 (1994) 42.

49. Susan Wood, "Priestly Identity: Sacrament of the Ecclesial Community," *Worship* 69/2 (1995) 109–127.

50. Ibid., 133; for a review of the debate on which representation is primary, see my article, "Priestly Identity: Priority of Representation and the Iconic Argument," *Worship* 73 (March 1999) 169–179.

51. Osborne, *Ministry,* 598.

Canon Law
and Emerging Understandings of Ministry

Elissa Rinere, C.P.

In the summer of 2001, all the participants in this extended study of the theology of lay ministry came together at St. John's for ten days of sharing and discussion. At the end of that time, we drew up a list statements concerning lay ministry on which all of us could agree, regardless of whatever else we might disagree about. This list, entitled "Points of Convergence," forms the basis of my reflections here.[1]

This presentation is divided into three major sections: traditional understandings of lay ministry as seen in canon law; emerging understandings of lay ministry; implications of these emerging understandings for canon law. The plan is to match current theological development concerning lay ministry with canon law, since the law is intended to give theology practical expression.

I. TRADITIONAL UNDERSTANDINGS OF LAY MINISTRY

Before we can look at what is emerging, it is necessary to look at what is older, fading and, one might say, submerging. It is well to keep in mind that the points we will look at have functioned in the Church for most of the second millennium. Throughout the first section we will consider six points which, when taken together, give us the context within which to see our traditional understanding of lay ministry and our progress from that point to the present. These six points are: the structure of the Church, the mission of the Church, the structure of ministry, the role of the layperson, the meaning of baptism, and the general understanding of *cura animarum*, or the care of souls.

First, we will consider these six points as they are found in the 1917 Code of Canon Law, then as they were spoken of at Vatican II, and finally, as they are developed in the 1983 Code.

Understandings Reflected in the 1917 Code of Canon Law

The Structure of the Church

The 1917 Code was built on the ecclesiology that dominated at both the Council of Trent (1545–1563) and the First Vatican Council (1869–1870), an ecclesiology that saw the Church, established by Christ, as a perfect society. Under this ecclesiology, the Church was composed of two distinct groups, clergy and laity. There was no real theology of baptism uniting the two groups.

One illustration of this is how the 1917 Code of Canon Law dealt with the laity. The third section of the second book was titled "Laity" (*de laici*), and it contained two general canons on the laity. The first stated that the laity have the right to receive the spiritual goods of the Church[2] and the second prohibited laity from dressing in clerical garb.[3] There were no canons that spoke of the Church as a unified community of the baptized.

The Mission of the Church

For several centuries preceding Vatican II, the mission of the Church was understood to be primarily internal, that is, directed to its own membership. The clergy provided for the faithful what was needed for salvation, and it was the task of the faithful to respond appropriately. There was no outward movement of the Church through ecumenism, and evangelization was reserved to religious orders dedicated to missionary activities. Because the mission of the Church was understood in this way, it followed that the mission was entrusted only to the clergy, with the laity as recipients.

The 1917 Code reflected an aspect of this ecclesiological situation when it referred to non-Catholic Christians as "heretics" and severely limited the contact that Catholics were permitted with them.[4]

The Structure of Ministry

By "structure of ministry" I mean the complex of laws, offices, and tasks through which the Church expects the mission to be accomplished. Through the early centuries of the life of the Church, the threefold hierarchy of deacon, priest, and bishop developed. Eventually the sacrament of orders developed, with the structure, as it was known, of minor and major orders.[5] Any man who received tonsure was considered a cleric, and therefore entrusted with some aspect of the mission. The minor and major orders captured, in a certain sense, all the ministerial activity of the Church. Other than by becoming a cleric, there was no way for an individual to be assigned to any of the tasks of the orders. Only clerics, of whatever level, performed ministerial tasks.[6]

The Role of the Laity

Our traditional understanding of the role of the layperson was the other side of the role of the clergy. Clergy dispensed sacraments, guidance, and grace, and the laity received. There was no sense of collaboration or cooperation, but only of reception.

The Meaning of Baptism

Traditionally, the general understanding of baptism was consistent with the general understanding of the sacrament of orders and of ministry. Baptism removed original sin and "enabled" the individual to receive salvation. The 1917 Code of Canon Law defined the juridical effects of baptism as personhood in the Church and the rights and duties of membership,[7] but there was no mention of any other effects of baptism, such as incorporation into Christ or a share in the priesthood of Christ, all of which are spoken of so freely today.

The General Understanding of the "Care of Souls"

The phrase "care of souls" or *cura animarum* is the traditional term for the work of bishops and priests. To be entrusted with the care of souls meant, briefly, to respond to the right of the baptized to the spiritual riches of the Church by making them available. Traditionally, and consistent with what has already been said, care of souls was entrusted to the clergy and was received by the laity, primarily in the parish setting.

These six points give us a good reminder of where our Church was just forty short years ago. We operated from a different ecclesiology which then gave shape to our theology, law, and practice.

Impact of Vatican II on Traditional Understandings

Even though the content of the conciliar documents is so familiar to us these days, it is important to keep in mind their relative youth and the degree of change required to move the whole institution of the Church from the traditional to the conciliar. We will take each of the six points of our study in turn.

The Structure of the Church

The council teaches in many of its documents, but especially in the Dogmatic Constitution on the Church, *Lumen Gentium (LG),* that the Church, established by Christ, is not a perfect society but is a people on pilgrimage, a people in the process of becoming.[8] Further, the council articulates so beautifully the truth that the Church is one people—the baptized. Only after the unity of the people through baptism is made clear in the second chapter of the document is the community divided into the two traditional groups of clergy and laity. However, even though there is this division, it does not mean separation.

> Though they differ essentially and not only in degree, the common priesthood of the faithful and the ministerial or hierarchical priesthood are none the less interrelated; each in its own way shares in the one priesthood of Christ. (*LG* 10)

The structure of the Church is that of a community united in baptism. There are different groups within the community, but because of the meaning of baptismal unity their differences are complementary, for the purpose of forming the unified whole.

The Mission of the Church

The mission of the Church is described differently in various conciliar documents, but in all of them, consistently and clearly, the mission is outward and it is entrusted to all the baptized. The Decree on the Church's Missionary Activity, *Ad Gentes (AG),* states it this way:

The mission of the church is carried out by means of that activity through which, in obedience to Christ's command and moved by the grace and love of the holy Spirit, the church makes itself fully present to all individuals and peoples in order to lead them to the faith, freedom and peace of Christ by the example of its life and teaching, by the sacraments and other means of grace. (*AG* 5)

While the Decree on the Church's Missionary Activity speaks of the outward movement of the Church's mission, the Decree on the Apostolate of the Laity, *Apostolicam Actuositatem (AA),* speaks of its inclusivity.

Sharing in the function of Christ, priest, prophet and king, the laity have an active part of their own in the life and activity of the church. Their activity within the church communities is so necessary that without it the apostolate of the pastors will frequently be unable to obtain its full effect. (*AA* 10)

The Structure of Ministry

Even though the council so significantly altered the concept of mission for the whole Church, it did not significantly alter the structures through which ministry would be carried out. The traditional structure of the minor and major orders was left intact, although with the restoration of the permanent diaconate.[9] However, the structure of ministry did undergo notable change in 1972, when Pope Paul VI abolished the sub-diaconate and the minor orders and then established the new installed ministries of lector and acolyte for laymen.[10] This action was a significant reordering of what had been in place for many centuries.

In addition to restructuring ministerial structures, Pope Paul also opened the door to national or regional structures for ministry in his invitation to all episcopal conferences to establish other installed lay ministries according to the needs of their territories. These national or regional lay ministries would be available to men or women. Unfortunately, up to this time, no episcopal conference has acted upon this invitation.

The Role of the Laity

We have already seen that the council placed the mission of the whole Church into the hands of all the baptized. However, there is further specification on the role of clergy and laity in carrying out the mission. In general, the council saw laypeople working to accomplish the mission of the Church "in the world," while clergy carried out their tasks in the realm of the Church, but provision was made for exceptions to this general rule. For instance,

> Finally, the hierarchy entrusts the laity with certain tasks more closely connected with the duties of pastors: in the teaching of christian doctrine, for example, in certain liturgical actions, in the care of souls. (*AA* 24)

Therefore, the council provided the laity with an active part to play in the Church, primarily "in the world." However, this model for lay activity was neither exclusive nor unyielding.

The Meaning of Baptism

We are aware of how Vatican II restored baptism as the point of unity for all Christians and the source of each one's share in the priesthood of Christ. In the words of the Constitution on the Sacred Liturgy, *Sacrosanctum Concilium (SC),*

> by Baptism men and women are implanted in the paschal mystery of Christ; they die with him, are buried with him, and rise with him. They receive the spirit of adoption as sons and daughters "in which we cry, Abba, Father." (*SC* 6)

The General Understanding of the "Care of Souls"

The council documents significantly alter the meaning of "care of souls" by extending this care to all people, believers and non-believers alike.[11] Clergy are given primary responsibility for this work, but laity are to be brought into collaboration for two reasons. First, because without their assistance, clergy cannot work with full effectiveness; and second, because laity are given gifts of service that call out for recognition and exercise.

Response of the 1983 Code

It is clear that Vatican II did much to alter traditional understandings of ministry. Now we turn to the 1983 Code of Canon Law, formulated in response to that council, and consider its articulation of these conciliar teachings.

The Structure of the Church

The 1983 Code of Canon Law maintains the structure of the Church as set out in *Lumen Gentium*. The second book of the Code, on "The People of God," begins with a presentation of the Church as the community of the baptized. Only after the Church is united in this way is it set out as an ordered community under the leadership of the hierarchy. In other words, the Code reflects the council's presentation of at least two ecclesiologies: the united community of believers and the ordered community comprised of laity and clergy.

The Mission of the Church

The conciliar principle that the mission of the Church belongs to all the baptized has found clear articulation in the 1983 Code of Canon Law.

> Canon 204, §1: The Christian faithful are those who, inasmuch as they have been incorporated into Christ through baptism, have been constituted as the people of God. For this reason, made sharers in their own way in Christ's priestly, prophetic, and royal function, they are called to exercise the mission which God has entrusted to the Church to fulfill in the world, in accord with the condition proper to each.[12]

This canon, built on *Lumen Gentium* and the Decree on the Apostolate of the Laity, *Apostolicam Actuositatem*, doesn't specifically name the mission of the Church, but clearly assigns responsibility for the mission to all the baptized. Canon 781, based on the Decree on the Church's Missionary Activity, *Ad Gentes*, indicates that the primary mission of the Church is the preaching of the Gospel.[13]

However, participation in the mission, that is, the exercise of one's share in the priestly, prophetic, and royal aspects of the priesthood of Christ, is carried out according to each one's condition or status. This principle also follows from the council, as has been seen. In the 1983 Code, forms of involvement for clergy and laity in the priestly function are spelled out in Book IV: The Sanctifying Function of the Church (cc. 834–1253). Involvement in the prophetic function is found in Book III: The Teaching Function of the Church (cc. 747–833).

A weakness of the 1983 Code is its lack of development of lay participation in the royal or governing function of the priesthood of Christ. There is no book of the Code devoted to this "Royal Function of the Church," and canons on governance apply only to clergy, with one exception.[14] This exception has led to much controversy and discussion about the nature of authoritative power, how laity are brought into cooperation with it, and what the boundaries of that cooperation are.[15]

Despite lack of clarity on this major point, the new law, in response to conciliar teaching, recognizes that the accomplishment of the mission of the Church is the responsibility of all the baptized.

The Structure of Ministry

The 1983 Code maintains the structure of ministry which comes from both the council and the actions of Pope Paul VI in 1972. This means that in the Code, clergy (bishops, priests, or deacons) have assigned tasks within the hierarchical structure, and recognition is given to the installed lay ministries for men of lector and acolyte.[16] Although laity, men and women, may be invited to undertake liturgical ministries or other functions in a parish or diocese, there are no universal structures specified beyond those for clergy and the two installed lay ministries, nor are any regional or national structures encouraged.

The Role of the Laity

This point is, of course, closely related to what has already been mentioned about the mission of the Church. The law is clear, as was the council, that laity have an active part to play in the life of the Church. However, in general the Code maintains the church/world division found in the conciliar documents. For instance, laity are called on to preach the Gospel through the witness of their lives (c. 759), but the canon that permits laity to preach in churches (c. 676) is rife with conditions and caveats that hamper implementation.

Further, although laity may serve in any number of diocesan offices, their ability to serve is not explicitly stated. Rather, the law does not explicitly bar them from assuming these positions, and therefore the opportunity is present.[17]

The Meaning of Baptism

On this point, the law is consistent with conciliar teaching that baptism is the unifying factor for the whole Church. As noted earlier, canon 204 articulates the ecclesiology of *Lumen Gentium,* which springs from the vision of the Church as first and foremost the people of God constituted and unified through baptism.

The General Understanding of the "Care of Souls"

The 1983 Code maintains the conciliar understanding of *cura animarum,* or the "care of souls," with one exception. In agreement with the council, the Code presents "care of souls" as directed to believers and non-believers alike. Also, it is parish-centered and primary responsibility for it lies with the clergy.

Unlike the council, the Code provides for laity to be brought into *cura animarum* only by exception and to supply for a lack of clergy. While this provision is in the law, the council taught that laity could be brought into "care of souls" because of gifts given them by the Spirit of God. There was no stated condition of the need to supply for a lack of clergy. It is interesting to note that, in the Code, laity are more readily accepted into diocesan-level administrative positions than they are into parish-level positions involved with pastoral care.

These few points illustrate that the 1983 Code of Canon Law responded well, almost with complete conformity, to the conciliar principles that so strongly influence our current understandings of ministry. However, since the ending of the council and the promulgation of the Code, time has continued moving forward, circumstances in the Church have continued to change, and our insights and understandings of ministry have continued to evolve.

II. EMERGING UNDERSTANDINGS OF MINISTRY

It is difficult to try and isolate all the ministerial developments that have taken place in the last twenty years. Here I will consider only two, which are based on the July 2001 symposium in which all the contributors to this volume participated: the emerging understandings of ministry coming from theology, and those coming from our own lived experience.

From Theology

First, we can identify changes in how we understand the sacrament of baptism. The council brought us back to baptism as the source of unity in the whole Church and the source of any sharing we have in the Church's mission. We now hear that baptism can be seen as the source of *all* ministerial activity, for clergy and laity alike. Generally, what is developing is a new understanding of the relationship between the sacraments of orders and baptism; and part of that evolving understanding involves awareness of a new aspect of baptism with respect to all activities taken up under its banner.

Second, we are hearing much more these days about charisms, gifts of service given by the Spirit of God, and how these charisms relate to lay ministry. Although the council taught about these gifts,[18] as well as about the rights and responsibilities that come with them, there has been little practical application of these teachings.[19] What we see today is the idea of charism moving from the theoretical realm to the practical.

A third point of theological development is seen in the difficulty of maintaining the distinctions between "sacred and secular" and "Church and world." With regard to the first distinction, once something is designated as "sacred," the other entity, by default, is understood as "other than sacred." For instance, if priestly ministry is sacred, what adjective do we use to modify lay ministry?

Likewise, there are problems with separating the Church and the world. What does such a separation imply for the nature of the two entities? Where does one start and the other stop? The council spoke of the Church being separate from the world,[20] and also of the unity of the Church with the world.[21] Various aspects of this question have been discussed for some years,[22] but new aspects of the question arise as a theology of lay ministry evolves. If laity labor primarily "in the world," what is to be understood about their efforts "in the Church"? To ask the same question in another way: How can a Christian lead a unified and integrated life if the Christian does not live in an integrated environment?

Or, if the Church is separate from the world, does that not imply that the exercise of religion is separate from everyday life?

From Our Experience of Ministry

Just as new questions are arising from theology, new questions are also arising from our actual experience of lay ministry over the last twenty-five or thirty years. First, experience has shown us that the need for effective ministry is real. That is, people are not indifferent to the sort of ministry they encounter, and many will deliberately seek out what they need in order to grow in faith. This is evidenced in the changing patterns of parish membership.

Second, experience has shown us that collaboration between clergy and laity in ministry enriches the whole Church. Parishes are able to offer more varied outreach, pastoral care, and educational opportunities because of the presence and gifts of parish lay ministers.

Third, experience is showing us that although the work of lay ministers can be very advantageous, to bring laity into significant pastoral leadership positions without providing suitable structures, stability, or even sufficient formation is harmful to minister and community alike. Some dioceses have carefully worked out job descriptions, pay scales, and diocesan-wide hiring and firing practices for lay employees. Other dioceses have not made the same progress, leaving lay ministers little job security with the coming of a new pastor or bishop.[23]

Newly Perceived Risks

Along with new developments in theology and new understandings from experience, we have encountered new concerns over the development of lay ministry. These have been articulated most clearly in official church documents.

Pope John Paul II, in a 1994 address to experts gathered in Rome to discuss collaboration between clergy and laity, mentioned the following points.[24] First, given the ever-increasing numbers of laity going into church-related ministries, he saw the possibility for confusion on the part of the faithful between the functions proper to the ordained and those proper to the laity. Related to this, the Holy Father mentioned the risk of confusion between the theological status of the priesthood of the ordained and that of the priesthood of all the baptized and a blurring of the boundaries between them, which would obscure the fact that the priesthoods differ not only in degree but in also in essence.[25] Last, he noted the risk, as more and more laity are brought into ministry, of clericalizing the laity to the detriment of the true mission of the baptized to bring the Gospel to all people.

These concerns were echoed and made more specific in the 1997 instruction issued by eight Vatican offices: "Some Questions Regarding Collaboration of Nonordained Faithful in Priests' Sacred Ministry."[26] This instruction provides very detailed limits for what lay ministers may or may not do in the course of carrying out their ministerial responsibilities. The concern of the instruction is the correct presentation and understanding of the ordained priesthood, even though, because of necessity, laity might be asked to take on actions that properly belong to the ordained.

This same concern about avoiding confusion between the priesthoods can be seen in the 1988 document issued by the Congregation for Divine Worship, *The Directory for Sunday Celebrations in the Absence of a Priest*.[27] It is interesting to note that these concerns have roots in the documents of Vatican II mentioned earlier, which admitted laity to "care of souls" but did so only after considerable debate and with some hesitancy.

III. IMPLICATIONS FOR CANON LAW

Clearly, the theological issues surrounding and supporting lay ministry have continued to develop since Vatican II and since the publication of the 1983 Code of Canon Law. This is reasonable, since the Church is a living organism, never static. However, theology and law are related disciplines. Law is not intended to reflect developing theologies. Rather, as happened after the council, law is intended to implement theological teaching that has attained a level of universal acceptance in the Church. One might say that canon law, since it applies to the entire Church, cannot explicitly address local or even national issues. This characteristic of the Code can be an asset and a liability.

Looking at the current theological developments in lay ministry we have cited here, and assuming that at some future time these developments will have to be articulated in law, let us consider what adjustments might be required in our current legal framework in order to accommodate these developments. I suggest there are at least three.

First, there will be a need for flexible universal structures that will allow nations and regions to develop stable ministerial structures of their own. Beneath this seemingly simple idea are very complex issues about the nature, role, and authority of episcopal conferences,[28] and the degree to which nations and regions can differ from one another structurally, since structural differences will denote some degree of theological difference.

Right now, as stated in *Ministeria Quaedam*, bishops of any country are free to establish installed ministries for their own territories, but the process is cumbersome and surrounded by a number of unanswered questions. The Church has issued many documents on the inculturation of liturgy. We also need some work on the inculturation of lay ministry.

Second, in consideration of current developments in lay ministry, the law will have to become better at recognizing charisms and the rights and obligations they bring with them. Vatican II gave great emphasis to charisms. Right now in the law, religious life is recognized as being based on charism, even though its charismatic nature is not explicitly stated. This recognition can be seen in the respect canon law gives to the particular law of any religious institute, since the particular law is the guardian of the charism. The recognition can also be seen in the freedom that religious institutes have to determine which individuals who seek admission are actually received, since the institute's charism is carried by the individual members.

In seminary formation and the call to ordination, the presence of charism is again implied. The formation period is the time of "discernment" and the ordination rite itself is recognition of the personal charism of service and its acceptance by the Church.

For marriage, the elements of charism are in place, but the language is seldom used. In theory, seeking the sacrament can be compared to personal recognition of the charism of marriage, and the celebration of the rite can be taken as the acceptance of the gift for the whole Church. However, without the language, the concepts are slow to develop.

In these three instances—religious life, ordination, or marriage—the charism, or call, is considered to be life-long and the vocation is "standard" throughout the whole Church. That is, the vocation is understood in basically the same way and is subject to the same legal structure throughout the Catholic world. In lay ministry developments, we see the need for recognition of charisms that might not be life-long and that need to be regional or national rather than universal. We need structures that provide a consistent and stable means of discerning and utilizing charisms of service for specific communities. This need is not utilitarian, for the sake of order, but is based on the dignity of the charisms now being given in the Church and the dignity of baptism from which they spring.

The third accommodation the law would have to make in response to current developments in lay ministry is to present a consistent commitment on the part of the institutional Church to those laity who undertake ministry. In the 1983 Code, the principle of a just wage for lay ministers is present in that the right to such a wage is recognized.[29] However, given present lay ministry developments, the need for consistent and mandated employment practices is not met by the canon. Also, the 1983 Code assigns responsibility of preparation for ministry to the lay minister,[30] while current experience has shown that this approach produces wide and unacceptable variations in ministry and in ministers. Only within the last ten years or so have dioceses been establishing formation programs for lay ministers or working with academic programs in pastoral ministry to set standards and goals. Much more is needed.

When church law adjusts to accommodate these three points, flexibility, charism, and consistent employment practices, we will know that a new stage of development for lay ministers has been achieved and that a new relationship between the sacraments of orders and baptism has been realized.

CONCLUSION

It would be beneficial, perhaps, to reiterate that law is the servant of theology, and therefore it cannot develop any more quickly than theology develops. What I have presented here is not what *should* happen for the world to be set right, but what the indicated needs are should lay ministry and its accompanying issues continue to develop as they have to date.

The canon law we now have is extraordinarily faithful to the principles of Vatican II and is a more than extraordinary step of progress from our previous code. Right now, the whole Church is in a slow and sometimes painful process of development that is taking us beyond the council. Our task today is to continue this development. We are the initiators of a new age for the Church. As we travel into this new age, we must continue to value and to balance our theology with our law, our future with our heritage, and our pastoral practice with the needs of the people of God.

NOTES

1. For a list and discussion of these points, see "Convergence Points toward a Theology of Ordered Ministries," by Susan K. Wood, S.C.L., p. 256 of this volume.

2. C. 682: "Laity have the right of receiving from the clergy, according to the norm of ecclesiastical discipline, spiritual goods and especially that aid necessary for salvation." Translation taken from *The 1917 Pio-Benedictine Code of Canon Law in English Translation,* by Edward Peters (San Francisco: Ignatius Press, 2001) 258. Hereafter cited as Peters.

3. C. 683: "It is not permitted for laity to wear a clerical habit, unless it concerns either a student in a seminary or others aspiring to orders" (Peters, 259).

4. There are many canons that illustrate this point. An example is c. 1325, §3: "Let Catholics beware lest they have debates or conferences, especially public ones, with non-Catholics without having [permission from] the Holy See or, if the case is urgent, the Local Ordinary" (Peters, 447).

5. There is an extensive history associated with the development of minor and major orders. The minor orders were porter, lector, acolyte and exorcist. The major orders were sub-deacon, deacon, and priest.

6. This structure of ministry did not change until 1972, when Pope Paul VI abolished the minor orders and the sub-diaconate and established the installed lay ministries (reserved to men only) of lector and acolyte.

7. See c. 87 of this code.

8. For instance, see *Lumen Gentium (LG)* 6.

9. See *LG* 29.

10. Paul VI, *motu proprio Ministeria Quaedam*, August 15, 1972, *Acta Apostolicae Sedis* 64 (1972) 529–534.

11. This is especially clear in the Decree on the Pastoral Office of Bishops in the Church, *Christus Dominus,* and the Decree on the Apostolate of the Laity, *Apostolicam Actuositatem (AA)*. For detailed references, see my article, "The Exercise of *Cura Animarum* through the Twentieth Century and Beyond," in press, *The Jurist* (the canon law journal published by the School of Canon Law at the Catholic University of America).

12. Translation taken from *Code of Canon Law: English-Latin Edition* (Washington, D.C.: Canon Law Society of America) 1999.

13. C. 781: "Since the whole Church is by its nature missionary and the work of evangelization must be held as a fundamental duty of the people of God, all the Christian faithful, conscious of their responsibility, are to assume their part in missionary work."

14. The exception is c. 129, §1: "Those who have received sacred orders are qualified, according to the norm of the prescripts of the law, for the power of governance, which exists in the Church by divine institution and is also called the power of jurisdiction. §2: Lay members of the Christian faithful can cooperate in the exercise of this same power according to the norm of law."

15. For comments and references on this topic, see Myriam Wijlens, "The Power of Governance (cc. 129–144)," in *New Commentary on the Code of Canon Law* (hereafter, *Commentary*), ed. John Beal et al. (New York/Mahwah, N.J.: Paulist Press, 2000) 183–194.

16. C. 230, §1: "Lay men who possess the age and qualifications established by decree of the conference of bishops can be admitted on a stable basis through the prescribed liturgical rite to the ministries of lector and acolyte. Nevertheless, the conferral of these ministries does not grant them the right to obtain support or remuneration from the Church."

17. It is well known that laity, men or women, may be chancellors of dioceses, finance officers, administrators, or tribunal officials.

18. For instance, see *AA* 3 and 30; the Decree on the Ministry and Life of Priests *(Presbyterorum Ordinis)*, 9.

19. The 1983 Code makes no explicit mention of charisms of any sort.

20. For instance, see *LG* 3, 8, 9, or 13.

21. This theme pervades the Pastoral Constitution on the Church in the Modern World, *Gaudium et Spes*, but especially nos. 40–44.

22. See, for instance, Joseph Komonchak, "Clergy, Laity and the Church's Mission in the World," in *Official Ministry in a New Age*, ed. James Provost (Washington, D.C.: Canon Law Society of America, 1981) 168–193.

23. For some comments on this issue, see Philip Murnion and David DeLambo, *Parishes and Parish Ministers: A Study of Parish Lay Ministry* (New York: National Pastoral Life Center, 1999), especially section III.

24. For the English translation of this address, see *Origins* 24 (May 11, 1994) 40–43.

25. See *LG* 10.

26. For the text of this instruction, see *Origins* 27 (November 27, 1997) 397, 399–410.

27. For the text of the directory, see *Origins* 18 (October 20, 1988) 301, 303–307. A bilingual (Spanish and English) ritual book is also available: *Sunday Celebrations in the Absence of a Priest: Leader's Edition* (New York: Catholic Book Publishing Co., 1994).

28. These topics are beyond the scope of this paper. For comments and some references, see John Johnson, "Title II: Groupings of Particular Churches," in *Commentary,* especially pp. 588–609.

29. C. 231, §2: "Without prejudice to the prescript of c. 230, §1 and with the prescripts of civil law having been observed, lay persons have a right to decent remuneration appropriate to their condition so that they are able to provide decently for their own needs and those of their family. They also have a right for their social provision, social security, and health benefits to be duly provided." (Note that c. 230, §1 stipulates that laymen installed as lectors or acolytes do not, by reason of their installation, have a right to remuneration from the Church.)

30. C. 231, §1: "Lay persons who permanently or temporarily devote themselves to special service of the Church are obliged to acquire the appropriate formation required to fulfill their function properly and to carry out this function conscientiously, eagerly, and diligently."

ORDERED MINISTRIES

Priesthood Revisited

Mission and Ministries in the Royal Priesthood

DAVID N. POWER, O.M.I.

PREFACE

Though this article was written as an unimpassioned study of sources, the topic takes on a rather sad pertinence in face of recent information about pedophilia among priests and about episcopal mismanagement in dealing with such cases. Beneath our perplexity in face of these and similar matters lies the issue: Where do we situate the ordained priesthood in the life of the Church, among the baptized with whom they share a common mission, and among ministries?

Much of what has been said in public journals is hardly borne out, especially about links between the requirement of celibacy and the problem of pedophilia among priests. There are several quite distinct issues: the common difficulties encountered in keeping faithful to celibacy, the homosexual orientation of some priests, and the sad fact that some priests have sought sex with young boys. Pedophilia, technically so defined or not, like alcoholism, is a pathology; homosexuality is not; and having problems with chastity is common to all humans. With or without obligatory celibacy, pedophilia is an issue that needs monitoring, protection for victims, as well as care for the pathological and those whom they have harmed.

In care and in protection, bishops appear to have often failed, even if we reserve all moral judgment on those responsible for this failure. One commentator has hit the mark in saying that the roots of the current problem over clerical pedophilia lie in the notion and practical realities of keeping a hierarchical order among ministries in the Church. This was intended to mean not the persons of bishops but the hierarchical vision of order and the hierarchical system of clerical training, supervision, and appointment. Actions and responsibilities of bishops, because they are seen as constituting a sacred hierarchy, are often submitted to no judgment and no oversight, except that of bishops themselves and of their appointees or representatives. In training, candidates remain within enclosed enclaves, somewhat less tightly today than before, but still bound in. In the past, unfortunately, and this is where a number of pedophiles and their victims have suffered, a certain kind of spirituality sidelined adequate sexual self-consciousness and sexual maturity. One could, therefore, within a hierarchical system, proceed to ordination without proper awareness of one's sexual tendencies. Beyond this, in mentality and law, little accountability to local communities and to the lay faithful is written into processes of ordination, appointment, reappointment, and suspension from office.

In keeping with the purposes of this seminar and symposium, the paper here presented is theological in nature. Though critique of thought was envisioned as part of the seminar's procedures, critique of practice was to be given a secondary place, except perhaps with regard to the rights and remuneration of lay ministers appointed to ecclesiastically determined tasks. The paper subjects the hierarchical theology of order to critique and in a retrieval of tradition suggests an alternate model, which is more community based and, it seems to the author, more faithful to scriptural and early ecclesial tradition, before the onset of hierarchical distinctions and orderings.

Though not spelled out in detail, there are repercussions on practical matters of candidature, clerical celibacy, ordination, appointment, removal, and suspension. There is no sacred space surrounding bishops, priests, and deacons. They belong in the *ecclesia,* as do all the baptized, and are servants of this *ecclesia*, authentic representatives of Christ only to the extent that they are obedient and humble servants. Candidates would properly have their roots in communities and not in some personal "vocation" or some personal sense of divine calling. Appointed clergy are responsible to their communities and some process of participation in appointment, accountability during tenure, and even judgment on failure within communities is juridically necessary and theologically justified. It is no simple matter to set up such procedures, but one of the implications of this paper is that they must have their place.

It is in the light of the times that these remarks are prefaced to this paper. They are not in the manuscript circulated among participants and the program organizers bear no responsibility for having generated or authorized them. However, in light of the inadequacy of the hierarchical system, unhappily supported by an inadequate theology, it seemed fitting to make some observations about the implications of theological reconsiderations and theories. If the rest of the paper seems rather technical, bear in mind that it might be far-reaching in its implications. I do not, however, think that it is good to augur change without a full and serious examination of tradition and that is what I have here tried to present. I therefore consider this kind of theological scrutiny and argumentation of vital importance to the life of the Church and the mission of Christ in which it participates, and in the long run of vital relevance to practical matters that today trouble the life of communities.

The distinction made by the Second Vatican Council's Constitution on the Church (and oft-since repeated) between the priesthood of the ordained and that of the baptized as one of kind and not only degree is in itself innocuous enough, once it fades in the light of a thousand qualifications. Inasmuch, however, as it supports a hierarchical system, in theory and in practice, it can readily give foundations to what is insupportable in the life of the Church and its internal relations. In any case, it refers to one particular notion of priesthood, which has cultic rather than evangelical moorings. It is therefore imperative, if priesthood is to be revisited and resituated, to examine carefully the evangelical and patristic images and conceptions of the priesthood of Christ and of the Church, his Body. These are ways of treating of the mission and mediation of the Son, the Word made flesh, of what he has obtained for his Body, and of the Church's participation in the grace of headship, his mission of mediation, his worship, and his ministry. They do not rely on an image of cult, though such an image is used as analogy, but on one of the combat undertaken between light and darkness, life and death. In this, the notion of priesthood applied to the Church, by way of relation to that of Christ, is about the body of the Church and about all the baptized, and only secondarily about the ordained.

THE SECOND VATICAN COUNCIL

Even before the Second Vatican Council, in discussing mission and ministry it was usual to invoke the distinction between the priesthood of the ordained and the priesthood of the baptized, even as liturgical considerations led to a greater emphasis on the participation of all in the one priesthood of Christ and of his Church. Both the emphasis on one priesthood and the distinction between the two kinds of participation were incorporated into the council's Constitution on the Church, *Lumen Gentium (LG)*. Parallel to the distinction, the document also indicated distinctive domains for the mission of the ordained and for that of the laity, assigning the sacred to the former and the secular to the latter, as in *Lumen Gentium* 31.[1]

There is, however, a long history to the idea of priesthood and distinctions within it. In fact, in reviewing the council's appeal to the notion of priesthood from a historical perspective, three observations emerge. First, the present usage of priestly terms does not exactly reflect a long tradition but has emerged over time. Second, by retrieving more traditional understandings of priesthood, one may reshape the vision of the Church's mission, even if the image itself of priesthood is given a more secondary place in light of later developments that accentuate its reference to cultic acts. Third, one sees that it is possible to use a vocabulary that is less focused on making distinctions and more oriented to an inclusive sense of mission that respects diversities within oneness.

The Question Raised by the Second Vatican Council

Before looking back to history, it is helpful to look more closely at the approach to priesthood taken at the Second Vatican Council, in order to put the inquiry in perspective. In composing their documents, the members of the council wished to account for the participation of baptized and ordained in the life and work of the Church, Christ's Body, under the movement and inspiration of the Holy Spirit. Adopting the fundamental idea of consecration for mission, based on John 10:36, the council related the Church and each and all of its members to the mission and the consecration of Christ himself. That done, differentiation within this consecration and mission was introduced through relating the members of the Church to what was distinguished as the three-fold office of Christ himself and of his Church. This followed a pattern more or less established since the sixteenth century, with John Calvin the chief but not the sole protagonist of the theoretic division.[2]

This involved distinguishing the work of Christ himself as priest from his prophetic and royal work, and associating it particularly with the offering of the sacrifice of redemption, in a way not found in early Christian writings. As far as the Church is concerned, it meant locating the Church's exercise of Christ's priesthood in the liturgy. At this point, one finds the fundamental statement that all members of the Church are given a share in Christ's priesthood, just as they are given a share in his office as king and as prophet. However, the council also declared that the share in the priesthood of Christ given through ordination differs, not only in degree but in kind, from that of the baptized (*LG* 11).

Despite this logic, the use of the word "priesthood" in the conciliar documents lacks precision. Apart from associating it with the Church's sacramental ministry and eucharistic sacrifice, the council offered no precise definition of Christ's own priesthood but seemed to take this as a given. On the priesthood of the Church, at one stage, in *Lumen Gentium* 10, the council seems to use the term "royal priesthood" as a corporate designation. Subsequently, however, this appears to refer to single members being equated with what is called the priesthood of the baptized, or the priesthood of all the faithful, or the priesthood of all believers.

In using the idea of priesthood in the way noted, the council wished to address two particular questions within a broad attribution of priesthood to the Church. One was the sacramentality of ordination to the episcopate. The other was the participation of the baptized in the priesthood of the Church and of Christ in a way that would not confuse their role with that of the ordained. Since priesthood had come to be identified during the Middle Ages with ordination to the presbyterate, so that the episcopate was often seen as a charge or an office but not a sacrament, the council was anxious to show that ordination to either role included priestly or cultic ministry along with the ministries of teaching and of government. On the subject of the laity, it was the council's intention to show that they in turn shared in the offices of Christ as priest, prophet, and king, even while holding on to a distinction between order and baptism. In stressing their part in his priesthood, the council intended especially to promote their active participation in the Church's liturgy, but in a way that would not confuse their part with the ministry of the ordained.

A further note on conciliar terminology is here appropriate. Commentators often point out that the council hesitated to use the term "ministry" in speaking of the participation of the baptized in the offices of Christ, preferring words such as "office" or "charge." In recent years, the magisterium of the church in the United States has introduced the term "ecclesial lay ministry," modified later to "lay ecclesial ministry," for those laypeople who work full-time and by appointment in exercising pastoral roles in their communities, while avoiding the word in speaking of the activity of other members of the community. While this is intended to specify roles, it adds to the distinctions affirmed within the body of the Church.

PRIESTHOOD IN TRADITION

What can be said of this conciliar teaching in the light of tradition, especially pre-medieval tradition, both East and West? What needs explanation in the first place is the sense given to priesthood when it is predicated of Christ or his work, or what it meant to say that he is priest and king, as these two terms were commonly used together. This done, it can be asked how the Church was seen corporately as a royal priesthood, and why over time some of its members came to be called priests in a distinctive way. Both these issues may be addressed by looking at scriptural and patristic foundations.

Scriptural Foundation

In the New Testament it is the Letter to the Hebrews which elaborates on the priesthood of Christ as a way of explaining his mediation of a new alliance or covenant. Elsewhere, those who adhere to Christ as redeemer are designated as a royal priesthood, particularly in 1 Peter and the Book of Revelation. The two appellations are not directly connected but have different Old Testament foundations and provide two distinct metaphors to elaborate on the mediation of Christ and on the sanctification of those who believe in him as redeemer.

Background is always of interest and one thing that is common to both the Letter to the Hebrews and the letter called First Peter is that they are each addressed to people who are suffering for their conversion to Christ. In this context, treatment of the suffering of Christ himself looms large in both works. Priesthood and sacrifice are ritual and covenantal metaphors that can make some sense of the relation of suffering to sin and to redemption.[3]

Letter to the Hebrews: The Priesthood of Christ[4]

The writer of this letter wants to show that it was through suffering that Jesus Christ fulfilled his mission to mediate a new covenant. From this it follows that those who suffer now may do so with faith in the power of his suffering and in communion with him, and so enter with him into eternal life.

The Jewish background of author and community and their familiarity with Hebraic Scriptures and ritual allow for the appropriation of the language of mediation, sonship, covenant, priesthood, and sacrifice to express the efficacy and meaning of Christ's suffering. Being God's Son and being sent by him into the world, he is one with God, but through the flesh he is also in solidarity with humankind, especially in its trials and weaknesses.

The letter's focus is on the mediation of a new covenant according to the eternal plan of God, whose intention is to save humanity and all of creation from servitude to the devil and to subject them in obedience to his own will and rule. It is through Christ, the eternal Son made flesh, that this work is accomplished (1:1-4). Through his suffering in the flesh he showed perfect obedience to the Father and became for humankind the purification for sins (10:8-13).

The comparison with God's covenant with Israel and with the Levitical priesthood and its rituals is apparently prompted by the wish to find a suitable way to convey the letter's message of salvation through Christ to its particular readership. Those addressed seem to have been nostalgic for the worship of the temple and steeped in a knowledge of the story of the covenant made with the people through Moses and sanctioned by sacrifice, as they were familiar with the rituals of Yom Kippur through which the people underwent an annual purification of their sins.

It is in demonstrating the dominance of the Son and his superiority over all creatures, his solidarity in the flesh with suffering humanity and the perfect obedience which he learned through suffering, that the author introduces the themes of covenant, mediation, priesthood, kingship, and sacrifice. There are five aspects to what is called his priesthood, developed through chapters 5 to 10. First, Christ, Son of God coming in the flesh in the fullness of time, is qualified to be a priest because he is declared so from eternity by divine oath and because he lived and suffered in perfect solidarity with those whom he is to save through his death. Second, this priesthood is perfect and unique, a priesthood according to the order of Melchizedek, not that of Aaron. Third, through the offering of his death in perfect obedience to the will of the Father, this priest entered not an earthly sanctuary but a heavenly sanctuary and there continues to exercise his priesthood on behalf of sinners. Fourth, unlike the sacrifices of the earthly sanctuary, the offering of this priest achieves once and for all the forgiveness of sins, so that no further sacrifice is needed. Fifth, the notion of kingship is conjoined with that of priesthood, because through his sacrifice Christ has gained dominion over sin and the devil and has subjected all things in obedience to the rule of God (10:13).

To these five points, a paradox is added in chapter 13. Far from shedding blood within the temple, as did the high priest on Yom Kippur, Jesus shed his blood outside the gate, outside the city, at the place of infamy where the entrails of the animals used in sacrifice were burned (13:11-13).

Looked at from another angle, it may be said that two acts constitute the exercise of this priesthood, as they are described in chapter 9. The first is the death through obedience and the shedding of blood, the piercing through the veil of the flesh into the heavenly sanctuary. The second is what results from this, the eternal priestly intercession which Christ makes for his own at the right hand of the Father.

For the writer of the letter, in his attention to the suffering of the faithful, this priesthood with its sacrifice is the foundation of the spiritual life of Christ's followers. It is to be confessed by them in faith and confidence (10:19-25). They are guaranteed the forgiveness of sin. They are given dominion over sin and the works of the flesh. They, too, through suffering, can gain their salvation because of Christ's solidarity with them and theirs with Christ. They must, however, risk going outside the camp, risk infamy in communion with him if they are to witness to the power of Jesus' suffering (13:12).

1 Peter: The Royal Priesthood of the Church[5]

The idea of the Christian community as a royal priesthood may in fact predate the elaboration of the theme of Christ's priesthood, though in hindsight it has been understood in relation to this. The most commonly invoked text is 1 Peter 2:4-10.

While this text is often called upon in support of the priesthood of all baptized, or all believers, it is to be noted that it speaks of the people as a whole or as a unity. The aim of the letter is to encourage the followers of Christ in their suffering, especially in the suffering that comes from finding themselves aliens and disregarded. They can endure these sufferings through union with the redemptive suffering of Jesus Christ. According to the author, Christ leads them on the way of suffering. He can do so because he has released them from bondage through the ransom paid by the pouring out of his own precious blood. The letter compares Christ to the Passover lamb and speaks of the death of Jesus as a sacrifice of expiation (1:18-19). The images of sacrifice and blood, rather than the image of priesthood, are here to the fore.

Though they may sense themselves a people subjected to alien powers, Christ's followers are in fact a chosen people, an elect people. They are built up as a household, or as a living temple, on the foundation who is Jesus Christ, who was himself rejected and spurned. Evoking the scene of the covenant narrated in Exodus 19, the author calls the disciples whom he addresses a "royal priesthood." The term is taken from Exodus 19:5-6, which describes a scene of election and covenant. It is because they are a chosen people, a people with whom Yahweh has made covenant, that the Israelites are a royal priesthood, that is, a nation that has dominance over its enemies through the power of God and can engage in true worship. They are indeed a people in which all may be seen as kings and priests, unlike their Gentile neighbors.

This is now applied to Christ's disciples. Chosen in Christ, redeemed by his blood, they are a royal priesthood, a people that has spiritual dominance and can announce the good news of salvation to their neighbors. They are a people in which each and all are kings and priests, all anointed by the Spirit in the building up of the one household of God. These terms apply to their whole lives, not simply to participation in acts of worship. It is the collective denomination of the terms "chosen race," "holy people," "kingly priesthood" which stands behind any application to individuals.

The text, then, as such has nothing to do with rites of worship or cult. It is about alliance and covenant, the alliance that God has now forged with the baptized as a people by reason of their ransom from sin through the shedding of the blood of Christ. The people may have confidence in the suffering of Christ and may find salvation through their own suffering in communion with his. They live as a people who give witness to the dominion over sin, a dominion that has been given to them, and who are a living testament, a "temple" erected to the glory of God.

In the letter, Christ is said to be, in virtue of the ransom paid by his blood, the foundation stone of this people, this living temple of God's Spirit. If there is any reference in the letter to Christ himself as priest, it is oblique and is contained in the idea that the people offer spiritual sacrifices which are pleasing to God "through Jesus Christ" (2:5). The idea of Christ as king is more to the fore in the letter than that of Christ as priest, for it is his rule that now leads this new people as God's rule led the Israelites of old through the desert (cf. Isa 43:20-21).

Conclusions

The examination of these two scriptural texts reveals two distinct, if comparable, adoptions of an Old Testament vocabulary of priesthood, royalty, and sacrifice. They both appropriate Old Testament images and establish the contrast that results from Christ's contention with sin and death as a new foundation for alliance and for hope.

In addition to what is here learned of the early Christian vocabulary of priesthood, it is often noted as a kind of negative constatation or salutary warning that priestly, cultic, and sacrificial terms are never applied in the New Testament to community leaders, or indeed even to the mission of the apostles, except in regard to preaching (Rom 15:16). This but underlines the fact that priesthood as cultic action is never the primary concern of the New Testament heritage when there is mention of priesthood or sacrifice. In the case of Christ, what is placed in the foreground through the use of metaphor and imagery is his mediation through suffering, the access to the Father which is opened to all for whom he gave his life. In the case of the Church, God's people, it is the dignity and salvation and hope that accrue from the expiation and redemption of Christ's suffering and death, the gift that he makes of himself in obedience to the Father of his patience or passion and which gives his disciples too the hope of being saved through suffering. This is the peculiar witness which Christ and his Body give to the world that is dominated by sin and servitude.

Far from being about cult, this scriptural foundation for the use of priestly vocabulary shows a way of expressing on the one hand the mystery of Christ's suffering and death for sinful humanity and on the other a way of speaking of the lives of those who are redeemed by the blood of Christ. They live by a new covenant and are given dominion over sin and death. In both cases, the reality of suffering undergone in obedience and faith is essential to the employment of the metaphor.

It is also clear that, as such, the language of kingship and priesthood had nothing to do with distinctions within the body of Christ, either of kind or of degree. It refers to the mediation of Christ through suffering and to the reality of the Church, of the people, of those chosen by God in Christ. It puts redemption through suffering, in the contest with sin and death, at the center of the Christian mystery.

The Patristic Era[6]

The use of the terminology of kingship and priesthood in the patristic era includes references to both Jesus Christ and his Church. There are also some more specific efforts to make a link between the two and to give this link a sacramental grounding because of what the sacraments celebrate. While the general use of the imagery corresponds on the whole to what has been seen in two scriptural texts, this is given a particular meaning as a description of the Church's worship. In such a context, a matter of specific interest is the special attribution of priesthood and regality to bishops, as ministers of worship, of Word, and of penitential discipline.

Soteriology

Though there are many aspects to the soteriology of early centuries in Eastern churches, what gives it a focus is the idea of Christ's mediation and his designation as mediator. The prevailing perception is that this is grounded in the Incarnation, that is, in the taking on of flesh of the Word or of the Son. What writers such as Origen, Athanasius, Cyril of

Jerusalem, or John Chrysostom say of Christ as priest and king fits into a broader discourse on his work of mediation and his role of mediator.

For many writers, the Incarnation in its broad reference to the works of his flesh is the act of atonement. The coming of the Logos into the world meant the taking on of human flesh, in the condition of its mortality and subjection to sin, by the Son of God. Undertaking this wondrous exchange of the divine and human natures, at his advent the Son found nothing in humanity which was worthy of God, since the original work of creation had been destroyed. Thus he incurred the task to transform it, to make it like unto his own humanity, to bring it with him to the Father, indeed to deify it, and thus to free it from sin and death. By the very fact of entering into the world to make humanity one with himself, that is to say, the Son took up the combat with sin and death.

The Fathers mentioned describe this quite dramatically and it is in the context of this description of combat that they speak of Christ as priest and king. These terms are not used as definitions from which to draw conclusions, but they are employed as a symbolic language, provided by the Scriptures, whereby to bring out the meaning and power of Christ's mediation. In fact, most of the time the writers follow the Letter to the Hebrews very closely, always with the same accent on what Christ suffered and why this suffering is redemptive.[7]

The two terms "priest" and "king" go together and do not refer to distinct functions or purposes, even if they have distinctive connotations. Priesthood can describe the passage from the original taking on of human nature to suffering and through death to the right hand of the Father. As covenant act, it connotes as well what such passage means for those whom Christ came to redeem. Kingship describes the domination over sin and over the world which Christ acquired through the combat undertaken. The Mediator is called "king" because he was victorious over sin and death and now reigns over the faithful who have been redeemed and who dominate these enemies in their own flesh, in the hope of being with Christ in eternity. Drawing especially on Hebrews, writers call him "priest" because he is said to have offered himself as sacrifice in the once and for all offering of his death, gaining entry for himself and "his sisters and brothers" into the heavenly sanctuary.

With the language of Christ's priesthood and kingship, Athanasius and Cyril use various other biblical metaphors to describe this mediation. Appeal to the image of *kenosis* found in the hymn recorded and adapted by Paul in Philippians 2 is sometimes linked with these notions. In other places, enlarging upon the language of painful but victorious conflict, they say that the Mediator paid a debt. Occasionally there is mention of paying a debt to the devil, but most of all it is said to be paid to death itself. The language of sacrifice, taken primarily from Paul in all the harshness of the victim's identification with sin, is also employed and is a way of underlining both Christ's suffering and its intent.

Commenting on Hebrews and on the Psalms, both Athanasius and Cyril contrast the priesthood of Aaron with the priesthood according to Melchizedek. They do this to show the distinctive character of the priesthood of Christ and the unique quality of his offering, through which cultic priesthood is not only replaced but surpassed. He is priest according to the order of Melchizedek because his priesthood had no origin in this world but comes from the eternity of the Word's communion with the Father. Being exercised once and for all in his transition through death to heaven, it is an eternal priesthood whose act of sacrifice need never be repeated but is forever efficacious.

Mediation, Eucharist, People, Bishop

Though Origen and the other writers had already made the connection, it was primarily John Chrysostom who linked Christ's priesthood specifically with the Eucharist. This symbolic and ritual action in which he is united with his Body is the representation of his mysteries and so of his once and for all sacrifice.[8] This includes both the act of offering through suffering and death and the priestly intercession that he took on through his access to the Father's right hand. In the bread and wine, over which the bishop prays, and through these signs, Christ's sacrifice and priesthood are represented and made present, so that all may share in them and in the access to the Father which Christ gained through his death.

It is this last point that provides the foundation for speaking of the royal priesthood of the Church. This comes into being through the Church's sacramental communion with Christ as his Body. The communion in his sacrifice and priesthood is given principally through eating and drinking of his body and blood, but this supposes that all have been initiated into this corporate union through baptism. From this sacramental communion there follows the spiritual communion whereby the Church and all of its members offer the sacrifice of a life lived according to the Gospel, including the service which they render to the poor and their songs of praise and thanksgiving. Because this spiritual communion derives from and is given expression in eucharistic communion, it is possible to speak of the eucharistic offering of the Church. There is no logical or ritual progression at issue. There is simply the fact that those who are given a sacramental participation in Christ's sacrifice, kingship, and priesthood through receiving the gift of his body and blood in these eucharistic actions express their spiritual communion with him, both in their worship and in the way they live.

Priesthood of Bishops

The assignation of the title of priest to bishops occurs within the context where the Church is called a royal priesthood, or a living sacrifice, and has a twofold foundation.

First, the transfer of names occurs within the liturgy, beginning with the *Apostolic Tradition* (and in the West in letter 63 of Cyprian of Carthage) and reaches a high point with John Chrysostom. In earlier writings, the bishop is called priest, like unto Christ, because through his prayer he sanctifies the offerings of the community and it is through this prayer that the offerings become a sacramental sacrifice. For John Chrysostom, and on this basis for later Byzantine commentators on the liturgy, the bishop also takes on a representative role in the enactment of the mysteries of Christ's flesh through the celebration of the Eucharist. Thus, the fact that he represents Christ in his liturgical office is a further reason for calling him a priest.[9]

On this score, however, it is of interest to note that what is thought to be represented in the liturgy are all the mysteries of the Word made flesh. These are summarized in the anaphora of John Chrysostom as suffering or passion, the death, the entering into the tomb, the resurrection from among the dead, the ascension into heaven, the sitting at the right hand of the Father, and the coming in judgment. Commentary on the liturgy assigns a particular representative role in all this to the bishop, a role at times given quite allegorical play, as when his ascent to the *cathedra* is likened to the Lord's ascension to his heavenly throne.

There is clearly a difference in public role here between the way in which all the baptized are joined as a royal priesthood in the priesthood and kingship of Christ and the way in which the bishop relates to Christ through the liturgical representation of his mysteries. Regardless of such a difference in public role, this special attribution of priesthood to the bishop does not take from the fundamental equality of all the baptized in priesthood and in the offering of sacrifice. As John Chrysostom puts it in a homily on 2 Corinthians:

> There are occasions when there is no difference at all between the priest and those under him: for instance, when we are to partake of the awful mysteries; for we are all alike counted worthy of the same things... before all one body is set and one cup. And in the prayers also, one may observe the people contributing much... The offering of thanksgiving is common; for neither doth [the celebrant] give thanks alone, but also all the people. For having first taken their voices, next when they assent that it is "meet and right so to do", then he begins the thanksgiving... Now I have said all this in order that each of the laity also may keep their attention awake, that we may understand that we are all one body, having such difference among ourselves as members with members, and may not throw the whole upon the priests; but ourselves also so care for the whole church, as for a body common to us.[10]

What is most basic is that all are called in the same way to share the mysteries through receiving the body and blood of Christ in the sacrament. Furthermore, while the bishop has his distinctive role in the eucharistic celebration, all are one with him in making prayers and offering the great thanksgiving prayer. The differences that exist are to be compared to the differences between members in the one body, acting together for a common purpose and in a common drama.

To see this liturgical role in full perspective, one may note a gradual attribution of priesthood to the bishop within the entire ministry through which he leads the baptized into communion with Christ. This means ascribing to him not only priesthood but kingship, for it is his whole ministry which gives the faithful access to Christ and through him to the Father. Herein is included his ministry of teaching, his leading the people on the way of penance, and his acts of binding and loosing. Inherent to this is the suffering which he endures through the exercise of his ministry, and which renders him more like Christ and so able to draw others to him. For he too, like Christ, must "eat the sins" of the people.[11]

The Contribution of the Pseudo-Dionysius

This writer is of interest because the Latin translation of his work meant an influence of Eastern thought on the Latin theology of priesthood. In the work called *The Ecclesiastical Hierarchy*,[12] the bishop is called *hierarchés* or *hierarch*. This is a pagan word, meaning one who presides at sacred rites, indeed even as high-priest. The term *hierarchia* means sacred source or principle. In its Christian usage, it is defined in chapter 3 of the *Celestial Hierarchy*[13] as a "sacred order, knowledge and activity" which assimilates one to likeness with God and from which graces may flow to others. The bishop who is at the head of the ecclesiastical hierarchy is a font or source of the wisdom that brings others into communion with God. Presbyters, next in rank, are charged with the work of illuminating or teaching the divine mysteries as expressed in rites and symbols, while deacons are charged with the work of purification of catechumens and sinners.

A Note on Ordination Procedures

In what precedes, there is an evident connection between access to ministry and a judgment on personal closeness to Christ, a capacity to embrace his suffering. What renders a person capable of leading others to Christ is his own closeness to him. This is assumed in one who is ordained a bishop. In practice, this is the reason for the need to present a bishop to the people and to have them proclaim him worthy. It is not particularly a difference in kind in the royal priesthood which is at issue in ordaining a bishop, but a large question of difference of degree in the extent of one's communion with the Mediator. The exercise of his ministry as pastor and *leitourgos* is for the bishop his way of living the royal priesthood and of sharing in the priesthood and kingship of Jesus Christ, just as others live this reality in their own respective walks of life and according to their own level of communion with Christ. The practical, visible differentiation is in the particular call and ordination to ministry, and in the degree of a person's closeness to Christ. The closeness of Christ to the Father and his readiness to suffer have to be replicated in the lives of all the faithful, but the more intimate this union, the more one may assume a ministry of service and leadership in the Church.

NEW TURNS:
DEVELOPMENTS IN THE MEDIEVAL LATIN WEST

While it could be shown that Leo the Great and Augustine are quite close to the thinking of the East, it is of more immediate interest to show how thinking about priesthood took a new turn in the Latin West from Isidore of Seville onwards. This had to do with the accentuation of the cultic priesthood of bishop and presbyter, with new parallels to the priesthood of Aaron, and then with the limitation of this language to designate eucharistic and sacramental actions. In the process, the idea of Christ's own priesthood was also affected and it became more notionally distinct from the idea of his kingship, two distinct notions taking the place of a twin metaphor.

Isidore set the tone in his treatise on ecclesiastical office by latching on to a definition almost thrown out for consideration by Augustine: *sicut rex a regendo, ita sacerdos a sanctificando.*[14] The definition still underlines the capacity to sanctify others, but is easily transferred to the power of sacramental action to sanctify things. Of this priesthood, or power to sanctify, the bishop is the prime exemplar, but presbyters share in it. It is true that in his notion of priesthood Isidore kept the pastoral office of teaching and of binding and loosing to the fore, alongside the sacramental ministry, and that for him Matthew 16:18 was the fundamental text in treating of priesthood. The etymology, however, and its application moved the primary use of the language of priesthood in the Church to its application to the ordained.

Putting the focus on sacrament and especially on eucharistic sacrifice was the work of the Carolingians, who served this interest by making stronger and stronger affinities between the Levitical priesthood and the priesthood of the ordained in the Church. In other words, it was the Aaronic and not the priesthood of Melchizedek that offered the primary metaphor for the priesthood of the ordained. Priesthood was defined in terms of the power to consecrate and the power to offer sacrifice. Not only was this a working definition for the sacrament of orders, but it was applied also to Christ, in whose work therefore priesthood and kingship are more clearly distinguished. This was also the epoch in which the exercise and power of Christ's priesthood and sacrifice came to be defined more and more in terms of making satisfaction for sin. Suffering was part of this, of course, but instead of being linked with combat it was seen to be a price paid in reparation for sin, an act of restoring the balance of divine justice.

The period of time preceding the end of the millennium was not a healthy time for the worthiness of ordained ministers, because of prolific simony and concubinage. The resultant objections of spiritual fraternities to unworthy ministers and the doubts they cast on the truth of their sacramental ministry only helped to define priesthood more narrowly as a power to consecrate and offer sacrifice, divorced from any connection with the spiritual vigor of the ordained person. Such a definition can be understood only in the context in which the eucharistic action was taken less and less as the exercise of the Church community's royal priesthood and more and more as the exercise of a power unique to the ordained.

It need not be stressed here how much this tied in with the growing practice of having priests, even those whom Agobardus of Lyons with disdain called *homiunculi,* offer Masses for the living and the dead. Had the eucharistic action been seen more as an action of the body of the Church and less as an individual action of the ordained, the spiritual brethren could have found, or been given, another answer to their problem with the undignified.[15]

Orders of the Laity

While this development occurred in the theology and practice of priesthood, the role of the diverse laity in the Church was kept through the notion of *order* within the Body of Christ and so of the diversification of members in the body.[16] Apart from its use in liturgical documents and its introduction into Christian vocabulary by Tertullian and Cyprian,[17] at least since Augustine there had existed the use of the term *ordo* to designate any particular vocational group. Augustine himself took Noah, Daniel, and Job as types of three orders in the Church, namely, leaders, contemplatives, and those busy about the affairs of temporal life. Alternating with words such as *gradus, conditio,* and *professio,* the word became commonplace in the Latin Middle Ages as a way of making such a distinction of domains of interest. There was a penchant for the number three, associated with the triad of church leadership, contemplation, and secular life, yet those mentioned varied considerably. The orders from time to time included church leaders, contemplatives, the married, virgins, peasants, kings, lords, knights, and burghers. Their variety and complementarity were compared to the organic reality of a body with many members, each contributing to the good of the Church.

Since it was hard to keep the categories firm, later writers replaced this discussion of orders in the Church with the treatise on the states of life in which one served God. It may also be that the idea of a varied active contribution to the service or mission of the Church waned. At any rate, priesthood and order become more and more elements in a strictly clerical vocabulary.

A CRITICAL CENTURY: REFORMATION AND TRENT

How Thomas Aquinas related participation in Christ's priesthood to the cult of the Church is well known, as well as how he distinguished between active and passive powers.[18] While Thomas's treatise as such was not adopted by all, the distinction between active and passive roles was commonplace. Here, this is simply presumed as background to a discussion of priesthood within the writings of the sixteenth-century Reformers.

Reformation Writers

In marked contrast with the medieval and scholastic cultic usage, the Reformers of the sixteenth century were intent on applying Christ's titles of king and priest to spiritual things and not to temporal, as they were intent to overcome the distinction between the baptized and ordained ministers associated with the doctrine of the sacramental character and priestly anointing.

Martin Luther[19]

In his writings on the role of Christ in human salvation, as well as in what he says of the baptized, Martin Luther joins the function of king with that of priest. In several of his biblical commentaries he elaborates on the sacrifice of Christ in terms that often sound similar to those found in patristic writers, but adding his own particular view of the imputation of Christ's righteousness to sinners and of justification by faith.

As Luther sees it, Christ in his incarnation took on the effects of Adam's sin, indeed took on his sin, in order to endure suffering and death on behalf of sinners and thus earn the right to have his righteousness imputed to them. It is by the death and the blood of Christ that the baptized are cleansed and sanctified.

Luther also adds a personal comparison between Christ's priesthood and that of Aaron. In his commentary on the Letter to the Hebrews, he says that by taking on the form of a servant and offering himself in the flesh, Christ is the true Aaron, or fulfills the type of the Aaronic priesthood. None can share in this priesthood, because his sacrifice is unique and once and for all and does away with all sacrifices. On the other hand, Christ's anointing as priest according to the order of Melchizedek is associated more readily with his present role in heaven and his present relation to the Church. By his anointing, Christ, like Melchizedek, is both king and priest and he enters into these offices through the sacrifice of his death. Along with this, Luther emphasizes the role of Christ as testator, the one who left the testament of the forgiveness of sins to those who would believe in him and in his word, and whose testament was sealed by the Father's oath. For sinners and believers, this means that they receive this testament when they hear it proclaimed and respond in faith. Of this gift, a seal is given in the sacrament of the Lord's Supper. Receiving the testament in faith, they receive the freedom of believers, which is a spiritual reality that keeps them free from the domain of sin and from subjection to the Law.

All faithful Christians have a share in Christ's kingship and priesthood because of the freedom they have been given through Christ and their faith in him. In virtue of a spiritual power, the Christian is king and lord of all things spiritual and cannot be harmed by evil, even though of course one is still subject to suffering and the onslaught of the devil. As priests, Christians are able to appear before God and pray for others, as well as to teach one another spiritual things.

In the *Babylonian Captivity*, Luther elaborates on the many spiritual offerings that the baptized can make because of their life in Christ. These include prayer and almsgiving and the self-offering in which they cast themselves upon Christ. In this, as in other polemical works, Luther is scathing about calling ministers priests and the Eucharist their sacrifice. In later years Luther evolved his teaching on ministry in a positive and pastoral way. While he recognized the need and gospel mandate for ordained ministers of Word and sacrament, he did not acknowledge any participation in Christ's kingship and priesthood other than that of baptism. For ministers to preach the Word and duly administer the sacraments, as they are called to do, is their way of exercising their baptismal priesthood. As far as Luther is concerned, it is not a ground for distinctions within this priesthood.

John Calvin

While the division of the three offices of Christ had already been developed to some extent by Erasmus, Osiander, and Bucer, in the sixteenth century it received its fullest and most lasting treatment from John Calvin in the *Institutes of the Christian Religion*.[20] For all three offices, Christ was anointed by the Father when he was sent into the world. The prophetic office was and is exercised through the proclamation of true doctrine. The royal office is the rule that he has over believers through his resurrection from the dead and his sitting at the right hand of God. To explain the priestly office,[21] Calvin predicates it of his role as mediator and looks both to the sacrifice of his death and his heavenly intercession.

For Calvin, there is a sense in which the baptized participate in both roles of Christ's priesthood, that of offering and that of prayer. "We are," he writes, "defiled in ourselves, yet we are priests in him, offer ourselves and our all to God, and freely enter the heavenly sanctuary that the sacrifices of prayer and praise that we bring may be acceptable and sweet-smelling before God."[22] On the other hand, he rejects the special priesthood of the ordained and nowhere uses the word "priest" when writing of ministers. In fact, to speak of another priesthood, as to speak of the Mass as an immolating of Christ, is "detestable."[23]

Council of Trent[24]

For its part, the Council of Trent defended the particular priesthood of the ordained as the power to act as Christ's ministers in offering the Mass and in ministering the sacraments. In the decree on the sacrifice of the Mass, the council allowed that the faithful may be said to partake of Christ's sacrifice through spiritual offerings, but it made no room for their active liturgical share in Christ's priesthood in the sacraments or in the Eucharist. The council also persisted in defining priesthood and sacrifice, whether that of Christ or that of the memorial action of the Church, as an act of making satisfaction for sin. In effect, because of the council's apologetic and polemical approach, it was unable to go beyond received ideas about priesthood and its particular application to the ordained. Luther and Calvin had retrieved elements of an earlier patristic tradition, but Trent seemed unable to incorporate these into its own perspectives on order and ministry, given its desire to keep the distinction between laity and ordained firmly intact.

CATHOLIC THEOLOGY LEADING UP TO VATICAN II

To get the Second Vatican Council's own use of terms in focus, a number of things are worth recording about what led up to the council, however briefly this has to be done.

While post-Tridentine theology developed an ecclesiology centered on hierarchy and focused on the cultic aspects of ordained ministry, the French school associated with Saint Sulpice[25] gave evidence of a broader perspective, which in fact had a large influence on priestly spirituality.

The French School's notion of the priesthood of Christ and of the ordained was quite broad and was based on the symmetry between activity and holiness of life. Christ himself acted, and acts, as a priestly mediator because he was chosen by God, because of a communion in Spirit with the Father, and because he engaged in the activities of teaching and healing, making sacrifice, and making intercession. His compassion with sinners is central to this priestly reality. The one who is priest by ordination needs to model his life completely on this. Holiness of life in communion with Christ and all his ministerial activities is included in the notion of being a priest. The French School also retained the notion of the priesthood of all the baptized because of the union with Christ the Priest to which they are called. However, the writings of this school made no room for an active and public part in the service of the Church to be exercised by the baptized.

Starting with the nineteenth century and the liturgical movement, and taking a fresh point of departure in 1903 with the thought and pastoral activity of Lambert Beaudoin, writers were more and more intent on accounting for an active part of all the baptized in the life, liturgy, and mission of the Church. Two avenues of research and inquiry were

pursued. First, due to the impact of the liturgical movement, more attention was given to the share of the baptized in the one priesthood of
Jesus Christ. Second, terms were sought whereby to allow for the participation of all the faithful in the mission and apostolate of the Church,
a participation seen to result from their baptism and membership in the
Body of Christ.[26]

Nonetheless, by and large, writers seemed, as it were, stuck with the
application of priestly terminology to liturgy and extended the term beyond this at best to include spiritual sacrifices. Thus it was that at the
Second Vatican Council the distinction between the three offices of
Christ and the threefold mission of the Church was adopted as a way of
including all three kinds of ministry in the sacrament of orders, and of
giving a part to all the baptized on all the fronts of the Church's mission.

REFLECTION: THE CHURCH'S MISSION IN FOCUS

At the beginning of this essay, the primary texts and orientations of
the Second Vatican Council were noted. Behind and beneath the terminology of the three offices of Christ and his Church, what is foundational is the Church's participation in Christ's mission and consecration.
Each and every member of the Church shares in this, but it is the body
as a whole which presents Christ to the world.

Commentaries point out that in the aftermath of the council, the
pastoral constitution *Gaudium et Spes* provided a necessary comple-
ment to *Lumen Gentium,* as it gave substance to the emerging view of
the Church's mission in the contemporary world. This should not be
forgotten in discussions of ecclesial mission and ministry. In each age,
according to the conditions of the time, the mission of the Church takes
on a particular expression and works with specific purposes in mind. As
the Church takes its presence today in a largely secularized society, and
in face of the evils and injustices of a global community, a retrieval of
what was intended originally by using the vocabulary of priesthood and
kingship may help us to formulate the sense and direction of its mission. This would also have consequences for developments in the theology and reality of ministry.

From what has been surveyed, it appears that as far as the origins of
the vocabulary of priesthood are concerned, what was lost at the council

was the direct association between Christ's priesthood and kingship, and attention to the suffering endured in the combat with sin and death, undertaken in the service of humankind's deification. Priesthood and kingship are terms that qualify each other as they are applied to the one mediation and mission of Christ and the Church's share in it. In this context, the suffering of Christ is not portrayed as a satisfaction for sin rendered to God, but as testimony to God's love and truth in face of evil and death. Whether we refer to the failures of the modern world, to the disasters of the postmodern, to the circles of hell in which millions abide, or to what the magisterium has called the culture of death, as a Church we look to Christ as the fount of life. In so doing, we recognize that the Church's mission is to witness to life and to enlist in the efforts of a self-giving love to overcome sin, death, and their consequences. It is to this that the Church today is called more than ever, and it is this which needs to be the focus and direction of developments in mission and ministry. The location of all forms of ministry is within the communion of the Church with Christ in the action whereby life, love, and reconciliation, even through suffering, prevail over hatred, divisions, and death. If the cultic aspects of what the New Testament calls priesthood (and kingship) are overemphasized and separated from other activities, much of what this terminology was meant to say is lost.

There is, however, a problem with the terminology itself on account of its medieval history and even on account of the way it was used at the Second Vatican Council. The terms "priesthood" and "kingship" no longer serve quite so well to express the sense of Christ's own mission and the union of the Church with him in this mission as they did in early centuries. In order not to lose the substance of what royal priesthood originally meant, it may be necessary to find a new vocabulary.

As was seen, at the council the distinction between ordained and baptized was spelled out on the basis of a difference in kind in their respective share in Christ's priesthood. The difficulty with this is threefold. First, it rests on too sharp a distinction between the priesthood and the kingship of Christ. Second, it gives priority to the nature of the Church as institution, with its different offices, while these are simply meant to support the life of the community as a body. Third, it seems to support a distinction between spiritual sacrifice and priesthood and sacramental sacrifice and priesthood. By way of contrast, a different vision of the Church emerges when one concentrates on the fundamental participation of the Church as body and mystery, or as royal priesthood, in the royal priesthood of Christ by which he gained victory over sin and death and brought humanity into a communion of reconciliation with the Father.[27]

The Communion of the Church in Christ and His Spirit

To distinguish and order roles within the Church, we might well borrow from the relational ecclesiology of some Orthodox theologians such as John Zizioulas, now metropolitan of Pergamon.[28] The Church is revealed in its being and reality as a participation in the mystery of the Trinity, itself known to us through the relationality of the persons of Father, Son, and Spirit in the economy of salvation. The gift of the Spirit which is given to the Church is the Spirit which reposes on the well-beloved of the Father and brings the Church into the communion of the paschal mystery. In this, the Church in its relation to the Trinity is essentially an eschatological being; it exists and acts in virtue of its expectation of fullness. This nature of the Church is manifested and realized primarily at the eucharistic table, where, as a corporate personality, all receive the gift of the body and blood of Christ and with it the gift of the Spirit, "for the forgiveness of sins and for immortality." It is inherent to the reality of Christ himself as mediator to be one with his Church, to realize his own sonship, his own priesthood, his own kingship, in and through the Church.

Institutions and roles are necessary, and by no means a contradiction of this basic corporate oneness of the royal priesthood. They are better understood as relations and responsibilities within the one body than in terms of power and office, and need to be placed within the context of the eucharistic and eschatological community. They are secondary to the union expressed and realized at the eucharistic table, where all receive the gift of the body and blood of Christ, and through it a participation in his mission of love and his presence to humanity, or what in the patristic era was called his sacrifice and his royal priesthood.

The liturgy itself manifests this oneness and ordering. The bishop who presides at the liturgy is one with all the baptized in being convoked by the Word, in being invited to the table, in being in communion with Christ in his priestly prayer, in eating and drinking of the body and blood of Christ. It is only on this basis that in certain moments of the celebration he can speak in the name of the body, that he can proclaim the prayer of Christ, that he can manifest the relationship of Christ to his Church and of the Church to Christ. Especially in the eucharistic prayer and in some of the visual rituals, he symbolizes the presence and relationship of Christ to the Church, so that it may know itself in and through this relationship. But this distinction of the bishop from the Church recedes into the background in the oneness of the eucharistic table and in the eschatological expectation of fullness in Christ and in his Spirit.

Every service, ministry, and office must find its place within this eucharistic and eschatological communion. In what sense does a ministry contribute to that communion which is oneness with Christ in the reception of the Spirit and the witness to the call to be children of God the Father, receiving with the Son the gift of love? To what extent does it recede and fade before the eucharistic communion of the whole and the anticipation of eschatological plenitude? Practical questions of appointment, ordering, and remuneration are necessary, but they need to be pondered with the horizon of eucharistic and eschatological communion in the mystery of the Trinity.

Ordering Ministries

The question of how to differentiate between ministries can be considered within this perspective. As noted above, even though the Second Vatican Council proclaimed the participation of all in the priesthood and kingship of Christ, it used these terms to measure the differences within the one body, with the result that the biblical and historical meaning and signification of the terms was obscured. Rather than relying overmuch on reference to priesthood and kingship to differentiate roles, functions, or ministries, the notion of order and ordering within the one body and communion, in pursuit of the one mission, seems more profitable. This, moreover, avoids the distinction of domains in which ordained and baptized are respectively engaged, as when the secular is apportioned to the laity and the sacred to the clergy. The body as such is in the world, and for the world, and is internally ordered into groups, each adopting a way in which this mission is enacted, so that the witness of the body is rich and variegated in its testimony to Christ's redeeming love and its testimony against death.

For whatever reason, the terms of order and ordination are today used most regularly of those who receive the laying-on of hands, even though historically they had a broader usage. Every distinct group in the Church in early centuries was called an order within the body, as this is still recalled in the bidding prayers of the Good Friday liturgy of the Roman rite. Thus the Church recognized the orders of bishop, presbyter, deacon, acolyte, lector, catechumen, penitent, virgin, and widow within the one body. All of these, in their distinctive ways, expressed the multi-faceted reality of the Church and all in one way or another contributed to its building-up in communion with Christ and to its evangelical testimony. As already seen, in the Middle Ages an attempt was made to employ the word "order" even more widely so as to account for the different ways in which laity, as well as clergy and monks, contributed to the life, the good ordering, and the mission of the Church. In *Ministeria Quaedam* in 1972, Paul VI made some modest, if not immediately fruitful, attempts to restore a sense of ordering in and to the ministry of the Church among all the baptized and in this he was in line with early Church tradition. For a variety of reasons, however, this attempt was not much pursued in further developments of law and order.

The notion of order and ordering also embodies the possibility of change. The ordering of groups within the Church and of its ministries is not the same in every age, whatever the lines of continuity. Learning from what has been seen about early teachings on priesthood, today we can join the sense of ordering the body of the Church with the sense of its mission as service of the world, through witness and even suffering with Christ, in fostering the victory of a God-given life over sin, evil, and death. In such a context, some new ordering may well emerge, since the issue has to do with those groups or orders that best serve, in the power of the Spirit, the service of a mission so conceived.

Already in many local churches the order of catechumens has re-emerged with new vigor as a vital and life-giving component of a Church whose "new evangelization" is the witness for life and protection against the evils of contemporary trends. Some of the lay movements that mark the life of churches today are sometimes grouped under new forms of consecrated and evangelical life, but some might find a better placement within a larger conception of ordering toward mission. The sending of baptized persons on mission to countries in need of aid and human development is already practiced, but is not this a fresh

order, deserving perhaps of its particular canonical recognition and ritual, at least at local levels?

The service of peace and justice in the world is a special sort of
mission, and one that requires a keen communion with Christ in his witness through suffering and self-giving love to the Father. It is exercised
with much variety of roles and offices, and therefore with an inner differentiation. How developments in its composition and mission affect
the very image of the Church may be illustrated through one example. It
has been pointed out that immigration, including that of refugees, af-
fects the life and mission of Church communities.[29] Are immigrants
within the Church not themselves a particular "order," testifying to the
very reality of the Church as the communion of the reconciled and the
home of the socially alienated? And is it not a service of their need to be
located within a contemporary focus on mission that derives from communion with Christ's life-giving *kenosis?* And, consequently, how are
we to locate and conceive the ministries ordered to this mission?

Certainly within any emerging of ordering related to mission, there
would remain differences of kind because of what the ordering signifies
about the Church. This, however, seems better related to the Church as
the visible and sacramental body of Christ than directly to Christ and
his priesthood in a way that sets him off from the Church as the one exercising power over it (while in fact he exercises his power within it
through the Spirit). Within the differences in ordering, needless to say,
the role of what has been called the "apostolic office" will always stand
out, because of what it signifies about the Church in relation to its apostolic foundation and its universal communion between churches. It is
not without bearing on our time, however, that the early Church, even
with its consciousness of its apostolic origins and mission, chose secular terms to designate its leaders. Nor does the continuity mean that the
apostolic office itself may not need to take new forms in order to be effective in giving form to the Church's mission.

In the church in the United States, most of the effort at ordering the
contribution of those not ordained but actively engaged has to do with
services within existing communities. There is a double concern here.
One is to properly designate their relation to bishops, the other is the desire to assure proper compensation for the commitment of time and effort. The name of ecclesial lay ministry, or lay ecclesial ministry, has
been put to use in these regards. Perhaps, however, this fails to respect

the diversity of ministries and what is new among some of those who commit themselves strongly to service within the one royal priesthood, without always involving issues of delegation of power, allotment of times, and compensation.

In looking at the matter on a basis of order and ordering within the service of a common mission, one can see that some groupings are emerging that could be seen as church orders within themselves. Examples are pastoral associates, catechists, church musicians, marriage counselors, and directors of ministries caring for justice in the name of Christ. Appropriate names can be hard to come by, but that new kinds of ministry constitute new groups of people in the Church is quite clear. In the face of such a reality, theology has to be humble and canon law creative and fluid, lest the Spirit be quenched.

CONCLUSION: RETROSPECTIVE AND PROSPECTIVE

If there is one distinctive characteristic in the kinds of service that emerge in the Church today, and in the spirituality that motivates them, it may well be the sense of sharing in the *kenosis* of Christ, in the self-emptying that love demands when in Christ members of the Church give themselves to the service of the Church and its mission in a broken world. This, however, is the essential nature of participation in Christ's royal priesthood and it is shared by all the baptized who are called in the Spirit to give of themselves in mission and ministry.

On the question of appropriate terms and theorems to account for ministry, we know that words, images, and metaphors have a history. They need to be interpreted in their proper context, both literary and historical. In different contexts, their point of reference, their signification, and their meaning may change. With this in mind, the present overview of tradition has brought to light three ways of using the image or the idea of priesthood. It has also resulted in a conclusion about our way of conceiving the Church's mission and the manner of differentiating roles and ministries within the Church in the service of the one mission.

The first usage of the language of priesthood has its origin in Scripture and patristic writings. Christ is called the priest or king of the new covenant; his death is called the sacrifice by which sin and death are blotted out and through which humanity is given access to God. This priesthood is from eternity because it springs from the Father's love and fidelity. It endures into eternity where Christ sits in his risen flesh at God's right hand. Priesthood, kingship, and sacrifice are terms used by the Scriptures and by ecclesiastical writers to express the identification of the Son of God with weak humanity and the strength of the suffering through which he took on the powers that would undo humankind.

Transformed in their own flesh by reason of the taking flesh of God's Son and their sacramental communion with him, those who are given access to God through Christ, the Church as his body and his people, are a royal priesthood. In this, there is no difference of kind among his members and the only difference of degree is in the depth of communion with him, in the splendor of holiness that manifests and transmits God's love, in the testimony of a service rendered in total self-surrender. It is this which readies for ministry and ordination to the service of others.

A second attribution of priesthood follows from this, with a new referent, namely the Church's sacramental celebration, especially but not exclusively its Eucharist. The communion of Christ and his members in the one Body is sacramentally celebrated through rituals of initiation and in the eating and drinking of his life-giving flesh and blood. Sacramental communion is the basic act of the royal priesthood and the offering of spiritual sacrifices flows from the sacramental gift. Within this context of sacramental representation, the role of the bishop takes on its own representative character. His actions in the sacramental mystery represent the presence and the action of Christ and his teaching and pastoral ministry lead the faithful to this mystery. Hence there emerges a special attribution of priesthood, as well as of kingly power, to bishops, and in consequence to presbyters. In other words, within this general sacramental usage the bishop as primary celebrant sometimes becomes the particular referent of the imagery of representation and action. However, this usage remains firmly grounded in the priority of the sacramental representation of Christ's life-giving sacrifice in the gift of his body and blood and so in the prior attribution of royal priesthood to the whole Church.

A third attribution of priesthood emerges later, particularly in the Latin West, and it emerges when the vocabulary refers in particular to the ordained, in virtue of their role and power to act as instruments of Christ in the sacraments and especially in the Eucharist. This attribution manifests a change of concern, language, and thought-structure wherein categories of being, power, order, and office prevail. The concept of Christ's own priesthood is affected, for it is closely related to his action in the sacraments and in the offering of the Eucharist. The combat with sin, suffering, and death, which is foremost in the Letter to the Hebrews, recedes in favor of the language of cult and satisfaction for sin. Instead of being used as metaphors to express the meaning of this combat and its efficacy, priesthood, sacrifice, and kingship are used as definable concepts in their own right, with bishops and presbyters as their principal referents.

In terms of the exercise of instrumental power, participation in Christ's priesthood was distinguished into passive and active, into being recipient and being instrument. Enough was retained of the scriptural and patristic imagery of priesthood, as in the French School of Spirituality, to see that being an ordained minister must mean close identification with Christ in his suffering and his service of others. However, the concepts of office and power continued to dominate. To be a bishop or a priest is a call to communion with Christ, priest and victim, but it is fundamentally a communication of power.

Contemporary documents and theological writing, rather than attributing a passive power to the priesthood of the baptized, speak of them as having an active part in liturgy and in offering spiritual sacrifices in virtue of their baptism. The underlying concepts in the distinction of offices, however, remain those of power and hierarchy. Hence it is that in regard to the third attribution of priesthood the doctrine of the Second Vatican Council speaks of a difference not only in degree but in kind (*LG* 10). The meaning is clear and a distinction of offices and roles in the Church is necessary for the sake of the ordering of community and of communion. The language of power is indeed tempered by the language of service and it is often repeated that the mission of the ordained priesthood is to serve the priesthood of all the baptized. However, to speak of differentiation in priesthood through kind obscures the fundamental sacramental mystery of the royal priesthood of the Church as a sacramental and spiritual body, one that lives a deep communion with Christ in his work of mediation.

It was suggested that in the light of the history of terms, a preferable use of language to speak of the service of the Church and of its mission may be to note the complementarity of orders and ministries in mission and service. This would be more respectful of the first, fundamental, and most original use of the language of priesthood. This has to do with the power of Christ's suffering for sinful humanity and with the royal priesthood of his people, whereby those who have been saved through this mystery give witness to its efficacy and share in the redemptive mission which Christ, through the Spirit, now enacts in his body. There is no need to be very rigid in the use of terms and attributions. We are in a period comparable to New Testament times, when charisms were given by the Spirit, some listings of charisms and services made, but no definitive count taken. Counting may be one of the ways of quenching the Spirit.

NOTES

1. The distinction given at the beginning of the chapter on the laity precedes all discussion of their prophetic, kingly, and priestly roles in the Church.

2. For a survey of historical and current use of these distinctions, see Geoffrey Wainwright, *For Our Salvation: Two Approaches to the Work of Christ* (Grand Rapids, Mich.: Wm. B. Eerdmans, 1997).

3. What is found in these two letters could then be compared with the ready use of the imagery of sacrifice in the letter to the Romans, also in connection with the price of suffering.

4. See the article, G. Mathon, "Sacerdoce," *Catholicisme* (Paris: Letouzey & Ane, 1948–2001) 12: 245–260, with bibliography.

5. Ibid.

6. More detail is given in the forthcoming article "Priesthood" in the revised edition of the *New Catholic Encyclopedia* and the bibliography there cited. For reference purposes, the collection of texts offered in Paul Dabin, *Le sacerdoce royal des fidèles dans la traditionne ancienne et moderne* (Paris: Desclée, De Brouwer & Cie, 1950), is useful.

7. What could be further studied is the use of this vocabulary in commentaries on the psalms, especially Psalm 2 and Psalm 109.

8. See, in particular, Albert Houssiau and Jean-Pierre Mondet, *Le sacerdoce du Christ et de ses serviteurs selon les pères de l'église* (Louvain-La-Neuve: Centre d'Histoire des Religions, 1990).

9. See Hugh Wybrew, *The Orthodox Liturgy: The Development of the Eucharistic Liturgy in the Byzantine Rite* (New York: St. Vladimir's Seminary Press, 1990).

10. Homily XVIII in 2 Cor., Par, 3. *Library of the Fathers of the Holy Catholic Church*, vol. 27 (Oxford, 1848) 216–217.

11. The expression is taken from Origen, Homily V on Leviticus, and Homily XI on Numbers. See *Homélies sur les Nombres*, introduction et traduction de André Méhat. SC 29 (Paris: Ed. du Cerf, 1951).

12. See English translation, *Pseudo-Dionysius: The Complete Works*, trans. Colm Luibheid (New York/Mahwah, N.J.: Paulist Press, 1987) 193–259.

13. Ibid., 143–192.

14. Treating of the *ordo sacerdotalis* in the *Etymologiarum*, Liber VII.12 (*Patrologia Latina* 82, 291–292) and the *De Ecclesiasticis Officiis*, Liber II.5-7 (*Patrologia Latina* 83, 780–788) Isidore includes bishops and presbyters in this priesthood. The definition of *sacerdos* is "to give the sacred or holy (*sacrum dare*)." The word comes, he says, from *sanctificando*, just as *rex* comes from *regendo*.

15. During this same period, there was some attempt to relate the power of princes and emperors to the kingship of Christ, especially during the struggles between *sacerdotium* and *imperium*. This, however, was not ultimately successful, for Gregory VII and Innocent III were subtle enough to tie in Christ's kingship with more spiritual matters and to give the *sacerdotium* of the Church, especially of the pope, some say in temporal matters without claiming that he had a direct role in rule in this domain. It was simply the subordination of the temporal to the spiritual in the divine order of things that allowed him to intervene when temporal rulers seemed to reverse the order. The kingship of Christ was to be defined in terms of his power over sin and his power to bring all things to subjection to God through the preeminence of the spiritual in God's own kingdom. This theory was given classical status in the treatise of Thomas Aquinas, *De regimine principum*.

16. See David Power, "Church Order," *The New Dictionary of Sacramental Worship*, ed. Peter Fink (Collegeville, Minn.: The Liturgical Press, 1990) 212–233.

17. Reference will be made in the text that follows to the early meaning of distinguishing orders in the Church.

18. Thomas Aquinas, *Summa Theologiae* III, q. 63.

19. See the study by Karin Bornkamm, *Christus—König und Priester. Das Amt Christ bei Luther im Verhältnis zur Vor- und Nachgeschichte* (Tübingen: Mohr Siebeck, 1998).

20. *Institutes*, Book II, 15.

21. Ibid.

22. Ibid., II, 15.6.

23. Ibid.

24. The decrees on the Eucharistic Sacrifice and on the Sacrament of Order are the pertinent conciliar texts. Denzinger-Schönmetzer, 1636–1658, 1764–1778.

25. See, in particular, *Traité des saints ordres, publié par M. Tronson selon les écrits et l'esprit de Jean-Jacques Olier* (Paris: Ed. du Vieux Colombier, 1953), together with the critical perspective of G. Chaillot, "Formation liturgique au séminaire et tradition sulpicienne," *Bulletin de Saint-Sulpice* 23 (1997) 190–239, where more account is taken of the original ideas of Olier himself.

26. One might here mention the contributions of Emil J. Scheller, *Das Priestertum Christi im Anschluss an den hl. Thomas von Aquin. Vom Mysterium des Mittlers in seinem Opfer und unserer Anteilnahme* (Paderborn: Verlag Ferdinand Schöningh, 1934), and Paul Dabin, *Le sacerdoce royal des fidèles dans la traditionne ancienne et moderne* (Paris: Desclée, De Brouwer & Cie, 1950).

27. There is some insinuation of this in the concilar Decree on the Ministry and Life of Priests, no. 2, where it is affirmed that it is only on the basis of their baptismal reality that one can speak of the ministry of the ordained.

28. The writings of Zizioulas are most readily available in English in the volume of essays, *Being as Communion* (Crestwood, N.Y.: St. Vladimir's Seminary Press, 1985).

29. See "Les étrangers en situation illégale en Europe. Conclusions d'un colloque organisé par le Conseil pontifical pour la pastorale des migrants," *Documentation catholique* XCI (1994) 1074–1077.

Laity, Ministry, and Secular Character

Zeni Fox

In the last fifty years, we have seen the emergence of a new group
of ministers, neither clergy nor vowed religious, who are serving the
life, communion, and mission of the church community. Many roles
once filled and functions once exercised almost exclusively by priests,
sisters, and brothers are now held by laypeople.[1] These laypeople usually have had considerable preparation for their ministry and often serve
with the intention of life-long commitment to work within the Church.
Bishops in the United States first officially recognized this development
in 1980 when they observed:

> Growing numbers of lay women and men are also preparing
> themselves professionally to work in the Church... Ecclesial
> ministers, i.e., laypersons who have prepared for professional
> ministry in the Church, represent a new development. We wel-
> come this as a gift to the Church.[2]

More recently, after six years of studying these new ministers, the U.S.
Bishops' Subcommittee on Lay Ministry issued a report. Two of their
conclusions are particularly relevant:

> Some, whom we are naming lay ecclesial ministers, are called
> to a ministry within the Church as a further specification and
> application of what all laity are called and equipped to do...
>   Lay ecclesial ministry is experienced by many to be a call to
> ministry, a vocation. It is the role and responsibility of the entire
> Church (including the bishop and the local parish community)

to foster, nurture, encourage, and help discern all vocations to ministry.[3]

The bishops had listened to laypeople involved in church ministry and had heard them speak of their call. Based on the survey reports of pastors and church members, the bishops judged this ministry to be a gift to the community and determined that the official Church needed to respond. *Lay Ecclesial Ministry: The State of the Questions* summarized their deliberations and called for ongoing work by the U.S. Bishops' Conference relative to various issues they had outlined.

However, some voices have expressed concern about the increasing numbers of lay ecclesial ministers, noting that laity are defined by a secular character, and that their primary ministry is in the world.[4] An early articulation of this concern, in 1978, was presented by a group of laypeople and clergy in the "Chicago Declaration of Christian Concern." They charged that the role of laity in the world was being overshadowed by an emphasis on institutional church-related activities.[5] Most recently, when the Subcommittee on Lay Ministry presented its report at the annual meeting of the Bishops' Conference in November 1999, similar points were raised. Both in small group discussions and during the floor discussion, the secular character of laity and their role in the world were named as cautionary notes in any affirmation of lay ecclesial ministers. Present at the bishops' meeting as an invited observer was a layman who has worked for the Church for over twenty years. After listening to the floor discussion he said, "I wanted to put my head down and cry. After all this time, they still cannot accept and affirm our ministry in the Church." Many lay ecclesial ministers shared his sentiment.

Laity. Ministry. Secular character. These are key words in the discussion. The bishops who prepared the report, *State of the Questions,* those bishops who raised objections or concerns about it, the lay observer at the meeting (and many of the thirty-thousand-plus lay ecclesial ministers in our parishes) all have different perspectives on these key words. In what follows we will explore the relationship of these terms, tracing their evolution from the early work of Yves Congar, through debates at the Second Vatican Council, relevant council documents, and the later work of Congar with a view to shedding light on the present situation. We will conclude by looking at how the concepts of laity, ministry, and secular character may be creatively focused to positively evaluate the church development named lay ecclesial ministry.

BEFORE THE COUNCIL

Before the last half of the twentieth century, the Church had no authoritatively defined or formally posited theology of the laity. The theology of the laity that has emerged in our times must be seen in the context of the dominant ecclesiology that developed after Trent, largely as a response to the sixteenth-century Reformers. Luther held that "since the church is the congregation of those who have faith and since faith is invisible, the true church is invisible."[6] Robert Bellarmine, a leader of the Catholic Reformation, stressed that the Church is a perfect society, one that is fully visible. Each criterion of membership he proposed has a visible element: the profession of faith (not simply belief), the reception of the sacraments, and submission to legitimate pastors. This understanding of the Church as a visible society highlighted the structure of government as the formal element in the society and defined the Church primarily in terms of its visible structures, especially the rights and powers of its officers. The powers and functions of the Church were understood as teaching, sanctifying, and governing.

> The division of powers leads to further distinctions between the Church teaching and the Church taught, the Church sanctifying and the Church sanctified, the Church governing and the Church governed. In each case the Church as institution is on the giving end ... identifying the Church itself with the governing body or hierarchy.[7]

The laity, therefore, were seen as passive subjects in the Church. Intensifying this perspective was the fact that the Reformers emphasized the priesthood of all believers, leading the Catholic reformers to emphasize the role of the clergy as primary.

The life of the Church in the period after Trent was also influenced by many cultural changes as Western society moved from the understandings and social patterns of medieval society into our so-called modern times. Kenan Osborne notes the importance of the French and

American revolutions and traces the patterns of thought that influenced both those revolutions and views in the Church about the laity. A central tenet of the revolutions in France and America, the inalienable rights of the individual, gave rise to such ideas as "religious tolerance, the rights and privileges of 'citizens' and their relationship to internal church matters, and the lack of a preferential position for the 'one true church' within a kind of pluralistic society."[8] However, "although the role of the lay person, both in the church and in western culture generally, was undergoing a radical change, Roman Catholic Church leadership failed to understand some of the basic issues behind these changes."[9] Nonetheless, within the Church, laypeople were becoming increasingly active, in part because of their heightened sense of themselves as subjects. Other contributing factors were the ideas and example of Protestant churches and the increased level of education and wealth in society, which empowered laity in new ways.[10]

In the context of nineteenth- and twentieth-century cultural changes and ecclesiology, various lay movements arose. Some of these movements became international in membership and purpose; often they were independent of hierarchical dominance. In the late nineteenth century, in the United States, two lay congresses were held, as well as five Catholic congresses of African-Americans. Despite these efforts of well-educated and well-trained laity, there was a slow but sure negative response from the higher clergy. Pius X (1903–1914) declared that lay Catholic Action must be sanctioned by hierarchical approval to be acceptable.[11]

Pius XI issued the call to laity "to participate in the apostolate of the hierarchy." However, that effort was hierarchically inspired, defined, and controlled; it had two goals, the formation of its members spiritually, morally, theologically, and the spreading of Christ's kingdom throughout the world. Inherent in the goals of Catholic Action was the understanding that the Church's mission extends outward to the world and its salvation. Especially since the hierarchy had limited impact on society (as opposed to the time when the Church exercised great influence), the role of the laity was important.[12]

In the United States, some lay organizations were characterized by their reliance on the hierarchy. The National Councils of Catholic Men and Women and the Confraternity of Christian Doctrine were mandated by diocesan bishops. Groups such as the Sodality of the Blessed Virgin and the Catholic Interracial Councils existed with hierarchical approval.

At the same time, other groups, such as the Grail, Young Christian Students, Young Christian Workers, and the Christian Family Movement, were more autonomous.[13]

YVES CONGAR: 1953

In order to understand the development in the theology of the laity that is expressed in the council documents, it is necessary to place it in the context of the writings of Yves Congar. His work also is instructive in regard to our task of understanding lay ecclesial ministry. Congar's *Lay People in the Church,* published in France in 1953, is the first developed theology of the laity. He sets his vision against the background of the liturgical movement, which recognized that the laity are a consecrated people with an active part in public worship, and of the pastoral work of Catholic Action, which emphasized the dignity and demands of the Christian obligation. He affirms that a total ecclesiology is needed, of which a theology of the laity would be a part, but does not undertake that task in this volume. His concern is the mission of the Church to the world:

> Many people do not realize sufficiently that a big space is left empty between, on the one hand, a rigid canonical attitude in sacred things, wherein all the emphasis is on the receptive position of the faithful and their subordination to the clergy, and, on the other hand, the field of social and international secular activity. Nowadays lay people are becoming conscious that it is their business too to fill that empty space, through a properly spiritual activity, an active role *in the Church.*[14]

Before making this affirmation, he comments on the "old medieval comparison of the two parts of the body Christian, sacerdotal and lay, corresponding respectively to the spiritual and the temporal" and says that the laity ought not be "confined solely to the purely secular tasks of temporal activity."[15]

As he describes his plan for the book, Congar makes an interesting comment about method. He indicates that although he tried to summarize all the action of the laity under the traditional rubrics of the priestly, kingly, and prophetic functions, he was not able to do so without doing violence to the lived experience. The reason is that the categories did not adequately encompass the actual reality of the Church's life. Catholic Action, so influential in shaping Congar's thought, he judged to involve all three, and to require additional formulations about the Church as community and its apostolic mission. We see, therefore, that pastoral realities helped to shape his theological construct.

Congar's first question is: "What is a layman?"[16] He develops his answer by tracing the emergence of laity, clergy, and monks in the early history of the Church. He says this eventually becomes a division into men of religion and men of the world, defining laity by a secular way of life. Furthermore, their engagement in the things of the world is seen as a concession to human weakness. Congar states that in canon law the layman can be defined only by distinction from the cleric, a definition dependent on the layman's not having the faculty or authority for office. Congar expresses his reservation with this approach, stating that it omits both the laity's place in the building up of the Church and the specifically Christian work, within human history, of transforming the world. He resists both the tendency to see the lay state as existing by favor of a concession and the view of the laity simply in negative terms of what they are not and cannot do. He concludes that

> there is no need to suppose that the distinction between laymen and clerics (canonical view), coincides with a distinction between people who have only a secular field of action and people who have a sacred or holy field of action. Lay people too exercise sacred activities. Not for a moment may we entertain any idea of them that is inconsistent with their membership in the people of God to which the very etymology of their name bears witness.[17]

The purpose of his book is to study the sacred state of the Christian laity.

Central to his conception is the idea that "lay people are Christians in the world, there to do God's work *in so far as it must be done in and through the work of the world.* [This work can be done] only through a full, real participation in the world's travail."[18] Furthermore, it must be done without undue regulation by religious authority, and must grant full respect to earthly human things. This is not to exclude the transcendent, the supernatural. Rather, it means that "the relative [is] not to be absorbed by the absolute to the point of evaporation...Reference to the First Cause should not do away with the reality of second causes and the internal truth of all that fashions the world and the history of men."[19] Congar concludes,

> A lay person is one for whom things exist, for whom their truth is not as it were swallowed up and destroyed by a higher reference. For to him or her, Christianly speaking, that which is to be referred to the Absolute is the very reality of the elements of this world whose outward form passes away.[20]

Methodologically, Congar's work at times unfolds like a meditation on two texts, that of the tradition of the Church and that of the lived experience of the contemporary community. He affirms that the Church is a people, a community of faithful. It requires a priesthood and a public worship, which includes a people and an apostleship, a shepherding of the Church's whole life. He concludes that these aspects of church life have always existed, and now exist in good measure in a lived ecclesial life.

The themes set in these early pages of his work are unfolded in chapter 3 and in the remainder of the volume. Congar draws on Scripture, patristic theology, Thomas Aquinas, and contemporary theologians to develop the role of the laity. So, for example, the biblical image of the temple is meditatively explored.

> God wills to make the world the temple of his power and his glory; he wills to make mankind his temple built of living stones, his body made of free persons, in a word, the temple of his fellowship. This is whither it all tends: that God wills to dwell and to be praised in mankind as in a single temple.[21]

A second biblical image, the kingdom, is developed at length. Congar views the kingdom as both having come and yet to be realized in its fullness. The not-yetness of the kingdom is the time of the Church, a time of cooperating with Jesus, the priest-king, a time in which it is recognized that in both Church and world Christ reigns. Christ's kingship

within history takes two different directions. It is both a spiritual authority in the Church and a temporal authority in whatever concerns the
order of this world. Congar does not, however, take a dualist view.
Christ's power is universal and cosmic; the work of salvation is for the
whole world, restoring meaning to creation and bringing to completion
that germ and vocation he has, as Word and Wisdom of God, already
given to it. Church and world have the same ultimate end, serving the
coming of the kingdom. The Church participates directly and properly
with Christ, making the whole world his temple and all persons his fellowship temple. The world strives to attain wholeness and reconciliation. It desires to overcome the tensions that cause suffering. For
Congar, the world is seeking the kingdom cosmically, if not spiritually
and religiously. Nevertheless, the full realization of the kingdom will be
God's gratuitous gift.[22]

Two points important for understanding the nature of the laity are
clarified in this chapter. One is Congar's understanding of "world." He
indicates that two meanings are given in Scripture: the cosmos as the
order of nature and the world as the realm of Satan. Concerning himself
only with the former, he says that Christ chooses not to exercise his
power now, not until the fullness of the kingdom. Furthermore, he
makes a division between world and Church; the latter is made up of
those who by faith choose to submit to Christ. Congar finds in the
teachings of Jesus a sharp distinction between the Church, which is a
spiritual kingdom of faith, and the natural world of men and history, the
realms of God and of Caesar. Second, Congar sees this way of looking
at things as important because it establishes the independence and the
stability of the temporal order, separate from the authority of the
Church. And yet, through the relation of persons with the world, it will
be transformed and renewed, it will pass into the kingdom. Therefore,
the regenerating power that will finally operate is already at work,
though now its presence is transient, precarious, fragmentary, and generally unperceived.[23]

Finally, Congar describes the roles of the hierarchy and of the lay
faithful. The hierarchy are given a ministry for the benefit of all the others, having powers for promoting the life of the body, the functions of
priest, prophet, and king. Through the laity Christ's saving powers are
revealed within history and the world, so as to bring all the richness of

creation back to God.[24] Therefore they too exercise the three functions of priest, prophet, and king. Part two of Congar's work is an explication of these themes.

In summary, the context of Congar's thought is, first, the prevailing understanding of laity as having no role in the Church, (only "the purely secular tasks of temporal activity"), of being defined in terms of what they are not, and of their being passive subjects in relation to the clergy. Second, the context includes the lived experience of the Church, in which many laity are very active through Catholic Action and other lay engagements. It is also the experience of the history of the Church, with the tendency of the hierarchy to claim authority over all aspects of life, without due regard for "secular" knowledge beyond their competence. Congar's theological starting point is that laity first and foremost are baptized Christians, members of the people of God. Therefore, of necessity, they exercise sacred activities. These activities are performed particularly in the world, but this is a world that is ruled by Christ—even as the Church is ruled by Christ. Both Church and world are radically oriented to the coming fullness of Christ's reign, the kingdom. Therefore, laity participate in the priestly, kingly, and prophetic functions of Christ, and contribute to the communal life and apostolic task of the Church. However, their exercise of these functions is different from that of the clergy.

AT THE COUNCIL

In reading commentaries on the council, including various speeches during the sessions, it becomes clear that there was a significant difference between those who emphasized the understandings of Church and laity dating from the Catholic Reformation, and those who, while not denying classical definitions, held ideas put forth by contemporary theologians, such as Congar. Although the discussions on the laity were a somewhat minor theme, these must be read against the larger debate of the council. Initially, the debate was between those who had drafted the preparatory schemas and those who found the repetition of traditional ideas inadequate for addressing the concerns of Christians at that point in time. Beginning with the first day of the conclave, when the bishops rejected the proposed slate for members of the conciliar commissions, this struggle was evident. During the first session, the fathers subsequently re-formulated the decree on the liturgy, rejected (though not without the intervention of the Pope) the draft on revelation, and began the debate on the schema on the Church. Writing after the council on the significance of these actions, Cardinal Ratzinger said:

> We would like to make clear once more just what all this meant. The Council had asserted its own teaching authority. And now, against the curial congregations which serve the Holy See and its unifying function, the Council had caused to be heard the voice of the episcopate—no, the voice of the universal Church. For, with and in the bishops, the respective countries, the faithful and their needs and their concerns were represented... [This was not] an expression of a particular theological school... [but] rather... the school of their very office, the school of communion with their faithful and with the world in which they lived.[25]

Between the first and second sessions of the council, a new schema on the Church was prepared. It was based on the critique that had been offered. One of the criticisms regarding the original chapter 6, "The Laity," was that "much more should be made of the layman's worth, his witness to the faith, the doctrine of the charismata, lay spirituality, marriage as a principle of the church's growth, the competence and autonomy of the layman in the world, where he does have something else to do besides carrying out the instructions of the hierarchy."[26]

In the working out of the council's teachings about the laity, various voices of reform were strong. Cardinal Suenens, emphasizing the charismatic dimension of the Church, stressed the importance of prophets and teachers, as well as of the apostles and their successors. He also says:

> Do we not all know laymen and laywomen in each of our own dioceses who we might say are in a way called by the Lord and endowed with various charisms of the Spirit? Whether in catechetical work, in spreading the Gospel, in every area of Catholic activity in social and charitable works?... It is the duty of

pastors...through a kind of spiritual instinct to discover the charisms of the Spirit in the Church, to foster them and to help them grow.[27]

The dignity and role of the layperson were addressed by Bishop de Smedt: "Jesus Christ actually lives here and now in the layman by baptism and makes him share actively in his roles of priest, prophet and king." Furthermore, de Smedt emphasized this active role, saying that though one "begins by hearing Catholic teaching from the Apostles and their successors...[the layperson] has an active part" whereby he or she understands and applies it to daily life. And, "through the layman [Christ] wants gradually to extend his peaceful rule to the *whole world order*."[28]

Bishop Primeau spoke to the concerns of laity regarding their role in the apostolate, the problem of being treated as "passive member[s] submitting blindly to the authority of the Church" and the desire "to be heard when issues come up in which they have some special competence which the clergy frequently lacks." He spoke against too much emphasis on "obedience, reverence and submission" and not enough on "individual responsibility" and "freedom of initiative."[29]

This theme of responsibility was continued under the rubric of subsidiarity by Bishop Höffner, who said that "those things which the layman can accomplish on his own initiative and responsibility should not be taken over by the clergy." He stressed that the lay apostolate is not a matter of fulfilling tasks assigned by the hierarchy, but "the example of a truly Christian life and the acceptance of responsibility to renew the temporal order in accordance with the principles of justice and love."[30]

Cardinal Léger spoke to the theme of holiness in the Church. He noted that "holiness extends to large sectors of life...married and conjugal life...[and] all the activities of human life—daily work, political affairs, cultural activities, leisure and recreation—through which and in which holiness is to be developed." He also stressed that not only those who take vows, but all Christians "are called to perfection, to holiness and to the imitation of Christ by their very baptismal consecration."[31]

However, the voices of these more progressive bishops do not give the full range of opinions which shaped the discussion. For example, Cardinal Ruffini said that the laity do not have a mission directly from

Christ, but only through the hierarchy. "They do not share in the mission conferred by Christ on the Apostles." Other prelates attacked statements about the priesthood of the faithful, thinking this whittled away the distinction between a hierarchical priesthood and the rest of the faithful. Some charged that granting more freedom to the laity would endanger the hierarchy's freedom of action or authority; others said the text should emphasize the need for obedience more clearly.[32]

In the United States, many laypeople were discussing and writing about the place of the laity in the Church. Bishop Wright of Pittsburgh captured some of their concerns, as he stressed the historical and theological importance of the document:

> The faithful have been waiting for four hundred years for a positive conciliar statement on the place, dignity and vocation of the layman." [Bishop Wright] said that the laity knew that their priesthood differed from the ministerial priesthood of the clergy, but that they wanted the hierarchy... to put an end to the false notion that the Church was only "clerical." The traditional negative attitude toward the layman—he was *not* a cleric, *not* a religious—must be replaced by a more positive approach.[33]

The secular character of the layperson was apparently not debated by the council bishops. Klostermann posits that the council considered the secular nature or position of the laity of special importance because it denotes the particular share in Christ's offices which falls to them and their special exercise of the mission of the Church.

> The secular character specifies the modus of the layman's share in the offices of Christ and the part he has in the mission of the People of God. And therefore we may safely assume that it affects the mission of the layman not only "in the world" but to a considerable extent in the Church as well. Then it is observed that "a secular quality is proper and special to laymen" [though] ...not used in an exclusive sense...
>
> Laymen are declared to have [their] proper vocation...in and through temporal activity...Here it is that God chooses and calls them...The task of the secular layman is...summed up as the transfiguration and ordering of all temporal things.[34]

As Klostermann continues his commentary on article 32, he consistently uses the phrase "the secular layman." The importance of this will be explored below.

As one reviews the progress of the discussion on *Lumen Gentium,* the Dogmatic Constitution on the Church, it must be said again that the role of the laity was a minor theme in the total debate. The clearest evidence of this is that the great crisis of the second session, resolved through the taking of five crucial votes relative to the schema on the Church,[35] did not include any point concerning a theology of the laity. It was not until 1964 that *Lumen Gentium* was finally approved. The final vote was 2,130 yes and 10 no, days before the closing of the third session.[36]

Apostolicam Actuositatem, the Decree on the Apostolate of the Laity, is certainly a significant document (Rynne says: "It was the first time, incredibly, that official attention has been given by the Church to the corporate function of the laity as forming an integral part of the People of God"[37]), and yet in may ways it is simply an explication of the dogmatic themes already presented in chapter 4 of *Lumen Gentium.* One must read it in the context of that earlier document, particularly the treatment of "The People of God" in chapter 2 of the schema, so that a fuller sense of the layperson does emerge. This "ensures that the place of ecclesiastic and layman in the Church is seen in due perspective, [and] also brings home to us the inner bond and cohesion between individual members of the New Testament People of God and their office-bearers, and the fundamental equality of both as regards vocation, dignity, and commitment."[38]

The original version of *Apostolicam Actuositatem,* already the object of much revision, was presented at the third session, but was not accepted for a vote.

> The bishops evidence a certain disappointment: the schema lacks depth; it appears too clerical; it seems in fact to have been conceived in original sin—the sin of clericalism. Nonetheless it has certain advantages in that it speaks not only of the lay apostolate in the narrow sense, but also of lay witness in family and public life and of vocation.[39]

Much of the debate centered on the nature of Catholic Action.[40] The focus on the apostolate emphasizes the idea that in relation to the laity, "it is easier to describe what they do than what they are."[41]

The decree was voted on for the first time in September, 1965; the second and final vote was in November, 1965. Only two votes were "no."[42] For the purposes of this essay, much of what has been said already about the debate in the council is adequate for defining the issues before us. A few additional points, however, are relevant to our task. First, it is instructive to recognize that the title of the decree was a cause of much discussion. The decision to use the phrase "the apostolate of lay people" roots it in "that mission which proceeded from the Father, who sent his Son into the world... The mission concerns every member of the Church" and is not simply identified "with the apostolic office of the New Testament writings."[43] Second, reiterating concepts from *Lumen Gentium,* it again emphasizes the secular activity of laity, but avoids a dichotomizing of clergy and laity in terms of tasks, respectively, in the Church or in the world, which the vision of *Gaudium et Spes,* the Pastoral Constitution on the Church in the Modern World, further develops.[44] The emphasis is on the consecration of the world to God, through the coming of Jesus. "Thus, the whole world, by virtue of the sacred and the divine, is no longer something 'sacral' outside the world; it can exist in the midst of the profane world."[45] Finally, in article 22 of the decree there is acknowledgment of a new reality: laity who are especially devoted to the service of the Church. Klostermann says:

> Entirely new categories of ecclesiastical vocation have arisen in the last decades in which the laity, married or single, can place "themselves and their professional skill" at the service of the Church... This refers primarily to laymen who work in a full-time official capacity in the Church's service... A completely new "state" of Christians in the Church is developing... Strictly speaking, we are no longer concerned here with Christians in the world, but with a new category of Christians.[46]

For Klostermann, these are not "secular laymen"; for Congar, also, they would not fit this category. Klostermann stresses the growing importance of these laity, and says that it "becomes more and more urgent" that the problems of just remuneration be solved. It is interesting to note that the questions of laity in special service to the Church and of the laity in foreign missions were "already to be found among the wishes of the bishops for topics to be dealt with at the Council."[47]

PERSPECTIVES FROM VATICAN II:
MINISTRY IN THE CHURCH

Commentary on laity and ministry is very limited in the documents of Vatican II, and what we now call lay ecclesial ministry is barely envisioned. The first decree passed, on the liturgy, refers to those serving as servers, readers, commentators, and members of the choir as exercising "a genuine liturgical ministry" and states that they ought to "carry out their functions with the sincere piety and decorum which is appropriate to so exalted a ministry."[48] This document, the dominant theme of which was full, conscious, and active participation by all the faithful, affirms that within the community of the faithful some members have designated roles, particular functions, a ministry to fulfill. The liturgy is both the summit toward which the activity of the Church is directed and the fount from which her power flows. The identification of diverse roles in the worshiping community can be seen as an expression as well of the ongoing life of the people of God as a ministering community. Although this decree is neither a commentary on the varied ministries of the community, nor even an invitation to their emergence, the full, conscious, and active participation of laity at the Eucharist, with some having particular roles and functions, can be seen as an early sign of what has unfolded in the Church today.

Ad Gentes, the Decree on the Church's Missionary Activity, reflects on those who undertake missionary work, stating that whether they are priests, religious, or laypeople, they have "a special vocation...Having been sent by legitimate authority they go forth in faith and obedience to those who are far from Christ, as ministers of the gospel, set aside for the work to which they have been called."[49] *Apostolicam Actuositatem* also explicitly acknowledges the participation of laity in the work of the Church, though the language is not that of vocation and ministry.

Deserving of special respect and praise in the church are the laity, single or married, who, permanently or for a time, put their person and their professional competence at the service of institutions and their activities. It is a great joy to the church to see the continuing increase in the number of lay people who are offering their personal service to associations and works of the apostolate, whether in their own country, or abroad, or, above all, in the catholic communities of the missions and of the young churches.[50]

The sentences immediately following this text speak of the requirements of justice and "resources necessary for the maintenance of themselves and their families," making it clear that the laity identified make their living through this work.[51] The same decree also affirms that laity, "sharing in the priestly, prophetical and kingly office of Christ, play their part in the mission of the whole people of God in the church and in the world."[52]

PERSPECTIVES FROM VATICAN II: SECULAR CHARACTER

Lumen Gentium treats of the laity in chapter 4, first emphasizing that by baptism they are "incorporated into Christ, are constituted the people of God, who have been made sharers in their own way in the priestly, prophetic and kingly office of Christ and play their part in carrying out the mission of the whole christian people in the church and in the world." Then the fathers treat of the secular character, noting that "to be secular is the special characteristic of the laity." Those in Holy Orders may pursue a secular profession, but nonetheless they "are principally and expressly ordained to the sacred ministry."[53]

It is the special vocation of the laity to seek the kingdom of God by engaging in temporal affairs and directing them according to God's will. They live in the world, in each and every one of the world's occupations and callings and in the ordinary circumstances of social and family life which, as it were, form the context of their existence. There they are called by God to contribute to the sanctification of the world from within, like leaven, in the spirit of the Gospel, by fulfilling their own particular duties.[54]

Apostolicam Actuositatem continues an emphasis on the role of the laity in the world.

> The mission of the church, consequently, is not only to bring people the message and grace of Christ but also to permeate and improve the whole range of temporal things. The laity, carrying out this mission of the church, exercise their apostolate therefore in the world as well as in the church, in the temporal order as well as in the spiritual.[55]

The concept of secular character is related to the baptismal mission of the faithful; it is part of their priestly, prophetic, kingly identity. In *Gaudium et Spes,* the ideas first outlined in the two documents quoted here are brought to a fuller articulation. The "world" is the world already hallowed by the Incarnation, already redeemed by Christ's Pasch, awaiting the fullness of its transformation at the Second Coming. The pairings, sacred and secular, Church and world, do not represent points of antithesis, dichotomies in a strict sense, but rather categories of thought that describe mutually interpenetrating realities. The exercise of the secular character is a holy work, the sanctification of the world—which is the work of the whole Church.

AFTER THE COUNCIL:
PERSPECTIVES ON LAY ECCLESIAL MINISTERS

In 1972, Pope Paul VI reflected on changes occurring in the Church, commenting that "at one time many functions which went with them [minor orders] were in fact exercised by the laity, as is now happening once again."[56] Therefore, to better meet the needs of the present time, and in faithfulness to the call of the council for renewal of the liturgy, the Pope declared that the offices of lector and acolyte would be conferred by installation, would be called ministries, and could be committed to laypeople. However, these ministries were limited to men, a constraint which some see as the reason why installation of lay ministers is seldom used. The Pope also indicated that episcopal conferences could request the establishment of other offices, according to what would be necessary or very helpful.[57] At their November meeting in

1973, the United States Bishops' Conference "agreed by a large majority to seek Vatican permission to establish two new lay ministries open to both men and women," ministries of religious education and music.[58] The permission has not been granted. Nonetheless, the church in the United States continued to foster the active role of the laity in the mission of the Church through ministry in the Church and in the world.

The bishops' 1980 document, *Called and Gifted,* reflected on the laity's "call to ministry," which was further designated as "Christian service: ministry in the world" and "ministry in the Church."[59] A study published by the bishops in 1986 indicated that 123 dioceses had ministry training programs of at least two years' duration. These included degree (40 percent) and non-degree (60 percent) programs.[60] Significant numbers of laypeople took part in these programs; many became what today we call lay ecclesial ministers. Studies of these ministers indicate that the single factor most influencing their initial involvement as lay ministers was a priest. Studies also show that lay ecclesial ministers increase the numbers of other laity involved in ministry in their communities.[61] As this brief commentary indicates, bishops, laity, and priests have all been part of the development of lay ecclesial ministry in the United States.

Most recently, Cardinal Mahony and the priests of his archdiocese issued a pastoral letter on ministry, which states:

> It has taken the shortage of priestly and religious vocations to awaken in us an appreciation of a broadly based shared ministry and a realization that it is in the nature of the Church as the Body of Christ to be endowed with many gifts, ministries and offices. What some refer to as a "vocations crisis" is, rather, one of the many fruits of the Second Vatican Council, a sign of God's deep love for the Church, and an invitation to a more creative and effective ordering of gifts and energy in the Body of Christ.[62]

It is necessary to note that while documents from the American bishops have been quite affirming of lay ecclesial ministry, documents from Rome have been more cautious. For example, in *Christifideles Laici* we read:

> The various ministries, offices and roles that the lay faithful can legitimately fulfill in the liturgy, in the transmission of the faith

and in the pastoral structure of the church ought to be exercised in conformity to their specific lay vocation, which is different from that of the sacred ministry... "Their own field of evangelizing activity is the vast and complicated world of politics, society and economics as well as the world of culture, of the sciences and the arts, of international life, of the mass media."[63]

In 1997 eight Vatican offices issued an instruction expressing concern about the collaboration of laity and clergy. The document states that "the sacred ministry of the clergy" is a restricted area.

In this ministry the lay faithful, men or women and nonordained members of institutes of consecrated life and societies of apostolic life, are called to assist... Since these tasks are most closely linked to the duties of pastors (which office requires reception of the sacrament of orders), it is necessary that all who are in any way involved in this collaboration exercise particular care to safeguard the nature and mission of sacred ministry and the vocation and secular character of the lay faithful.[64]

One German bishop, Cardinal Karl Lehmann of Mainz, who criticized the document, said that it indicated a "climate of mistrust for the laity."[65] Many lay ecclesial ministers in this country interpreted it that way, despite the fact that Bishop Hubbard said the instruction "was prompted by European concerns and hence was not meant to apply to the American situation."[66] What is notable is that in both these recent documents "sacred ministry" and "secular character" are presented in some way as opposites, as antithetical. While the same concepts are articulated in the documents of Vatican II, there the emphasis is more on a sharing in mission, as in *Lumen Gentium:*

The sacred pastors, indeed, know well how much the laity contribute to the well-being of the whole church. For they know that they were not established by Christ to undertake by themselves the entire mission of the church to the world. They appreciate, rather, that it is their exalted task to shepherd the faithful and at the same time acknowledge their ministries and charisms so that all in their separate ways, but of one mind, may cooperate in the common task.[67]

YVES CONGAR: 1964, 1972

When Congar's *Lay People in the Church* was re-published in 1964, he added notes to the text. And in 1972 he wrote an article expanding his thinking. Some of his revisions are helpful for our topic.

In the introduction to the new edition, Congar says that he arranged his initial study within a rather rigid framework. He adds that "by continually considering lay faithful in relation to the ministerial priesthood, we have run the risk of in some degree opposing laypeople to clerics, of hardening the distinction between them (and this in spite of a final attempt at restoring the synthesis)."[68] He sees a flaw in his own method, too focused on the functions as structure rather than on their actual working in practice. He wonders whether it would have been more helpful to use the categories of witness, service, fellowship, praise, and worship, and asks:

> Would it perhaps have been better thus to avoid defining the things by which the faithful live by reference to those which are the concern of the priestly hierarchy? Have we clung too much to the recognized categories of classical ecclesiology?[69]

In 1972 Congar again reflects on his original formulations. In regard to naming "two titles of participation or two fashions of participating in the priesthood, kingship and prophetic office of Christ" he says, "I now wonder whether this is a happy mode of procedure." While affirming that his thought followed Catholic doctrine, Eastern as well as Western, he says, "The inappropriate element in my procedure of 1953 was perhaps to distinguish too nicely."[70]

The theological clarification that Congar offers is profound and has many implications. Rather than following a linear scheme, which says that Christ makes the hierarchy and the hierarchy makes the Church as the community of the faithful, he chooses a perspective drawn more from "pastoral reality as well as the New Testament. It is God, it is Christ who by his Holy Spirit does not cease building up his

Church...the Savior actively and incessantly intervening."[71] A result of this formulation is that it focuses on the total community, priests and faithful together, formed by Christ and his Spirit, before considering the roles of clergy and laity. This echoes the work of the council which first considered "The People of God" and then the distinct groups within the community.

Further, Congar reflects on the idea of ministries, stressing that the plural form is essential. He affirms both presbyteral ministry and "a multitude of diverse modes of service, more or less stable or occasional, more or less spontaneous or recognized and when the occasion arises consecrated, while falling short of sacramental ordination."[72] Again, Congar looks to the lived life of the Church and notes many examples of such ministries, such as mothers at home catechizing the children of the neighborhood, those who initiate help to the unemployed, people engaged in services that relate to the upbuilding of the Church itself or to its *diakonia*. These ministries proceed from gifts of nature or grace, from charisms, since they are given for the common good.

> They do actually exist but up to now were not called by their true name, ministries, nor were their place and status in ecclesiology recognized. To move on to this double recognition is extremely important for any just vision of things, for any satisfactory theology of the laity. As to terminology, it is worth noticing that the decisive coupling is not "priesthood/laity" as I used it in *Jalons* [the abbreviated French title for *Lay People in the Church*], but rather "ministries/modes of community service."[73]

Congar places hierarchical priesthood within the community, and so avoids viewing the people in a state of minority, impotent and passive, but also stresses that God has willed a structured community, within which he chose the Twelve. "From the start and throughout his ministry, at the foot of the Cross and in the Upper Room at Pentecost there were disciples with the Twelve."[74] The structured community instituted by Christ is entirely holy, priestly, prophetic, missionary (cf. *Ad Gentes*), apostolic.

> It has ministries at the heart of its life, some freely raised up by the Spirit, others linked by the imposition of hands to the

institution and mission of the Twelve. It would then be necessary
to substitute for the linear scheme a scheme where the community appears as the enveloping reality *within which* the ministries,
even the instituted sacramental ministries, are placed as *modes of
service* of what the community is called to be and do.[75]

SUMMARY

The conceptualizations of laity, ministry, and secular character developed by the council fathers emerged from a historical context which
helps us understand both the strengths and limitations of the ways in
which the concepts were articulated. The council wanted to provide a
positive theology of the laity, to emphasize the place of laypeople as
members of the people of God, to assign them a part in the mission of
the Church, and to provide for a valuing, and therefore a certain independence from clerical authority, of "the things of the world." The
council fathers desired to move beyond the rigid division of the Church
into two parts, clergy and laity, with a very high valuation of the former
—and almost none of the latter—group. The preeminent thinker influencing their work was Congar, who had addressed these questions in his
Lay People in the Church. The council articulated the laity's role in the
Church and in the world, particularly in *Sacrosanctum Concilium, Ad
Gentes, Lumen Gentium,* and *Apostolicam Actuositatem.* A place for
laity in the ministry of the Church was affirmed, though quietly, at
times implicitly. Much greater emphasis was given to their role in the
world, especially through the idea of the secular character proper to the
laity.

In Congar's writing in 1953, there is a great effort to present the
roles of clergy and laity as part of a whole, as united in a communion,
not as dichotomized. For the most part, the council formulations do not
dichotomize the roles of clergy and laity, but since the council there has
been some tendency to do this. Rather than identifying a problem in
today's Church, the problem of not sufficiently embodying the vision of
the laity's work toward the transformation of the social order, the issue
is addressed in a dichotomizing way: "There is too much emphasis on
church ministry; the laity are being clericalized." It is true that there is
too little reflection on and implementation of the vision of *Gaudium et*

Spes, of the Church *in* the world. At the same time, we are faced with a pastoral development, lay ecclesial ministry, which requires a theological and episcopal response that will serve to properly incorporate these ministers into our relational, organizational, and conceptual frameworks in a way that serves communion.

Congar's later work (1964, 1972) provides a helpful theological construct that could move us beyond the dichotomizing dynamic too easily arising when one begins with the ordained priesthood and moves from that to a theology of the laity. Rooted in the realization of Christ's ongoing activity in the life of the Church through the Holy Spirit, this view affirms multiple and diverse ministries, which is the situation we find in the Church today. (Cardinal Mahony's pastoral letter articulates this vision.) Such an understanding of ministry is helpful, too, in more realistically assessing the role of vowed religious throughout history in the ministry of the Church, as described by John O'Malley.[76]

In ascribing a secular character to the laity, the council did not mean to exclude them from activity within the community of the Church, building up the Body and sharing in her service and mission. The documents are clear on this. For example, in *Apostolicam Actuositatem* we read: "The laity, carrying out this mission of the Church, exercise their apostolate therefore in the world as well as in the Church, in the temporal order as well as in the spiritual" (no. 5). Furthermore, the council names the reality of persons who put their professional competence at the service of the Church, and of laity involved in missionary work, and assesses these developments positively. Indeed, this was a topic the bishops wished to have dealt with at the council. In the thinking of Congar, and in the commentary by Klostermann on the text, these are not the "secular laymen" who are defined primarily by their mission to the secular order.

It is instructive to realize how deeply rooted the distinctions between sacred and secular and Church and world really are. Even where the council tried to move beyond a negative dichotomizing, we find today a reading of the texts that reinstates the dichotomies. It is in this context that we need to ponder the concrete reality of a large number of laypeople involved in a stable manner in ministry in the Church. How are we to understand them?

The emergence of these lay ecclesial ministers may be seen as an expression of desires implicit and explicit in the council documents.

These laity affirm that they feel called to what they do in the Church, and that they are empowered by their baptism. They are living out a dimension of the council's vision for the laity, with consciousness and commitment. Furthermore, they have extensive preparation for their roles, and many indicate that they intend a life-long commitment. They are laity whose involvement in ministry is similar in preparation and stability of commitment to that of a priest. In their persons they represent a place between the destructive dichotomies of clergy and laity, and they invite an emphasis on the communion of the people of God. Symbolizing the shared call to mission, in their lives as people who are married or single, living "in the world," not "set apart" in a monastery or rectory, yet ministering in the Church, they are one embodiment of the Church *in* the world, in a particular dialogue with the joys and hopes, sorrows and aspirations of the world. By their ministry they invite us to move beyond constructs that invite passivity among the laity, and undue control by the clergy, and to embrace a vision of the Church as a community of disciples. Perhaps just as vowed religious symbolize in a special way the call to holiness of all the faithful, lay ecclesial ministers symbolize the call to mission of all the faithful.

With Congar, we recognize that throughout the ministry of Jesus there were disciples with the Twelve, and all were called into mission. We see that today many laypeople are involved with clergy in diverse ways in ministry in the Church, and that lay ecclesial ministers are part of this much larger group. We realize that we need to move toward official recognition of these lay ecclesial ministers.[77] As Congar says, these ministries "do actually exist, but up to now were not called by their true name, ministries, nor were their place and status in ecclesiology recognized. To move on to this double recognition is extremely important for any just vision of things."[78]

NOTES

1. Statistical studies of laity in parish ministry in the Untied States have been done in 1985, 1992, and 1997. The first was part of my unpublished dissertation ("A Post-Vatican II Phenomenon: Lay Ministries: A Critical Three-Dimensional Study," Fordham University, 1986); the more recent studies are those by Philip Murnion, *New Parish Ministers: Laity and Religious on Parish Staffs* and, with David DeLambo, *Parishes and Parish Ministers: A Study of Parish Lay Ministry*

(both published in New York: National Pastoral Life Center, 1992 and 1999, respectively). Similar in-depth studies of laity involved in such other ministries as diocesan leadership, campus and prison ministry, and chaplaincy work are not available. A summary of some of the data available is offered in my book, *New Ecclesial Ministry: Lay Professionals Serving the Church,* rev. ed. (Kansas City: Sheed and Ward, 2002), especially chapters 1–4. An area needing further study is that of laity involved as leaders in Catholic institutional ministries: education, health care, and social services.

2. National Conference of Catholic Bishops, *Called and Gifted: The American Catholic Laity*—Reflections of the American Bishops Commemorating the Fifteenth Anniversary of the Issuance of the *Decree on the Apostolate of the Laity* (Washington, D.C.: United States Catholic Conference, 1980) 4.

3. A Report of the Subcommittee on Lay Ministry, *Lay Ecclesial Ministry: The State of the Questions* (Washington, D.C.: United States Catholic Conference, 1999) 16, 20. There are various objections to the term "lay ecclesial ministry," including both the idea of making such a distinction and theological problems associated with the language used. This essay will not explore that question, but will simply use the language adopted by the United States bishops, using it as a description of a phenomenon in the Church of our day.

4. Another concern is that the increasing numbers of lay ministers may be contributing to the decline in the numbers of sisters, priests, and brothers. That concern does not bear directly on the topic of this essay, but is a significant factor, spoken or not, in discussions.

5. "Chicago Declaration of Christian Concern and Responses," *Commonweal* 105 (1978) 108–116.

6. T. Howland Sanks, *Salt, Leaven and Light: The Community Called Church* (New York: Crossroad, 1997) 80.

7. Avery Dulles, *Models of the Church* (Garden City, N.Y.: Doubleday and Company, Inc., 1974) 34.

8. Kenan Osborne, *Ministry: Lay Ministry in the Roman Catholic Church, Its History and Theology* (New York/Mahwah, N.J: Paulist Press, 1993) 467.

9. Ibid., 508.

10. Ibid., 474.

11. Ibid., 493, 501, 504–505. See also John Tracy Ellis, "The Catholic Laity: A View from History," *American Benedictine Review* 37 (September 1986).

12. Robert L. Kinast, *Caring for Society: A Theological Interpretation of Lay Ministry* (Chicago: The Thomas More Press, 1985) 8–10.

13. Michael E. Engh, "Catholic Action," in *The HarperCollins Encyclopedia of Catholicism,* ed. Richard P. McBrien (San Francisco: HarperCollins, 1995) 241. A fuller treatment of developments in the United States is offered by Patrick Carey, "Lay Catholic Leadership in the United States," *U.S. Catholic Historian* 9/3 (Summer, 1990) 223–247. Carey provides historical detail regarding movements and individuals against the backdrop of key themes in American culture. Particularly helpful in differentiating the hierarchically dependent and collaborative models of clergy lay leadership is the essay by Debra Campbell, "The Struggle to Serve: From the Lay Apostolate to the Ministry Explosion," in *Transforming Parish Ministry,* ed. Jay P. Dolan et al. (New York: Crossroad, 1989) 203–280; see especially pp. 214–221.

14. Yves Congar, *Lay People in the Church* (Westminster, Md.: The Newman Press, 1967), xv.

15. Ibid.

16. Congar indicates that the term is not a biblical one (p. 3). A contemporary assessment of this point is offered by Osborne, in *Ministry,* 10–31; the implications he draws from his textual and historical analysis are given on pp. 31–37.

17. Congar, *Lay People in the Church,* 18.

18. Ibid., 19.

19. Ibid., 23.

20. Ibid., 24.

21. Ibid., 59.

22. Ibid., ch. 3.

23. Ibid., 79–80, 83, 91–92.

24. Ibid., 108–118.

25. Joseph Ratzinger, *Theological Highlights of Vatican II* (New York: Paulist Press, 1966) 28. See also Xavier Rynne, *Vatican Council II* (New York: Farrar, Straus and Giroux, 1968): "The Council and particularly the first session seemed to indicate that a major turn-over in Catholic thinking had occurred. Beginning with the discussion on the liturgy, slowly but with deliberate intent, a majority of the bishops, by a process resembling that of parliamentary debate, had begun gradually to strip the Roman Church of the juridical accumulations of centuries" (p. 128).

26. Ferdinand Klostermann, "Dogmatic Constitution on the Church: Chapter IV," in *Commentary on the Documents of Vatican II,* vol. 1, ed. Herbert Vorgrimler (New York: Herder and Herder, 1967) 231. See also Jorge Medina Estavez, "The Constitution on the Church: Lumen Gentium," in *Vatican II: An Interfaith Appraisal,* ed. John H. Miller (Notre Dame: University of Notre Dame Press, 1966) 101–122.

27. Leon Joseph Suenens, "The Charismatic Dimension of the Church," in *Council Speeches of Vatican II*, ed. Yves Congar, Hans Küng, and Daniel O'Hanlon (London: Sheed and Ward, 1964) 19–20.

28. Emile Joseph de Smedt, "The Priesthood of All Believers," in *Council Speeches*, 25–27. Also notable was de Smedt's speech in which he criticized the tone of the first schema on the Church for its triumphalism, clericalism, and juridical emphasis. Rynne, *Vatican Council II*, 112.

29. Ernest Primeau, "Responsible Freedom for the Layman," in *Council Speeches*, 54–55.

30. Joseph Höffner, "The Lay Apostolate and the Principle of Subsidiarity," in *Council Speeches*, 57.

31. Paul-Émile Léger, "Holiness of All in the Church," in *Council Speeches*, 58–59.

32. Rynne, *Vatican Council II*, 192–194. Robert McAfee Brown, an official Protestant observer at the council, said: "Cardinal Ruffini...was...dead set against giving the laity more power in the church...His presentation was...hopelessly out of date. He acknowledged that the laity exist, but he did not acknowledge that they have any such 'mission' as the schema implies." *Observer in Rome* (Garden City, N.Y.: Doubleday & Co., Inc., 1964) 76. Klostermann summarizes the position of those opposed to the schemas as one that regards the layman as a purely passive element in the Church, and the relationship between hierarchy and laity as one of authority and obedience ("Dogmatic Constitution on the Church," 233). The final vote on chapter 4, "The Laity," at the third session, took only one ballot, whereas two chapters took five ballots, and chapter three forty-two (Estavez, "The Constitution on the Church," 119).

33. Rynne, *Vatican Council II*, 193. At this time in the Untied States, articles by lay Catholics were calling for an acknowledgment of the role of laity. See, for example, *Looking Toward the Council*, ed. Joseph E. Cunneen (New York: Herder and Herder, 1962), especially the article by John F. Bannan, "The Council and the American Catholic Experience," originally published in *Cross Currents* 12 (Spring, 1962) 57–60. McAfee Brown noted that Wright also said that the Church cannot leave to the churches of the Reformation the task of developing a genuine theology of the laity (*Observer in Rome*, 78).

34. Klostermann, "Dogmatic Constitution on the Church," 237–238.

35. Rynne, *Vatican Council II*, 206–215. Ratzinger's comments are instructive: "It cannot be denied that the debate on the laity remained somewhat colorless and tedious...It was especially striking that despite all efforts no one was able to provide a positive definition of the layman" (*Theological Highlights of Vatican II*, 56). Klostermann states: "The whole approach indicates that no essential, theological definition is to be offered but simply a description *ad hoc*" ("Dogmatic Constitution on the Church," 236). And Estavez, commenting on the first session, says: "The

criticisms concerning the doctrine on the laity were not too numerous, but there were some" ("The Constitution on the Church," 107).

36. Mario von Galli, *The Council and the Future* (New York: McGraw-Hill, 1966) 53.

37. Rynne, *Vatican Council II,* 322.

38. Klostermann, "Dogmatic Constitution on the Church," 234.

39. von Galli, *The Council and the Future*, 53. "The sin of clericalism" was the judgment of Bishop Carter, from Canada (Rynne, *Vatican Council II,* 324).

40. Rynne, *Vatican Council II,* 322–328.

41. Derek J. H. Worlock, "'Toil in the Lord': The Laity in Vatican II," in *Vatican II Revisited: By Those Who Were There,* ed. Alberic Stacpoole (Minneapolis, Minn.: Winston Press, 1986) 242.

42. von Galli, *The Council and the Future,* 59. For detailed information on the voting, see Ferdinand Klostermann, "Decree on the Apostolate of the Laity," in *Commentary on the Documents of Vatican II,* vol. 3, ed. Herbert Vorgrimler (New York: Herder and Herder, 1969) 298–302.

43. Klostermann, "Decree on the Apostolate of the Laity," 304, 305.

44. Ibid., 308–310, 312. "The Commission was again and again in danger of being forced into extreme positions...one wished to limit [the apostolate] to the Christian orientation of the temporal order, and the other to the direct support of the hierarchical apostolate...[On the one hand] there was danger of a new 'ecclesialization' of the world while the other side wished to have the difference between the two so strongly marked that the two orders, would appear to stand, unconnected, side by side, by which the apostolic character of the secular activity of the laity would appear to be obscured" (p. 309). Not unrelated to the status of laymen especially devoted to the service of the Church is a comment by Congar regarding laypeople in congregations of vowed religious without priests. "Theologically and canonically, such religious are lay people, but they are not altogether so from the point of view of a theology of laity even...in the case of 'secular institutes.' Their life is not the life proper to laity...[but] rather a 'fourth kind of Christians' not of the really lay condition that serves us here" (*Lay People in the Church,* 268–269).

45. Klostermann, "Decree on the Apostolate of the Laity," 367.

46. Ibid.

47. Ibid., 368.

48. *Sacrosanctum Concilium* 29. It is interesting to note Congar's observation: "It is in the liturgical movement that we first find a renewed consciousness of the

mystery of the Church and of the ecclesial character of laity" (*Lay People in the Church,* xii).

49. *Ad Gentes* 23.

50. *Apostolicam Actuositatem (AA)* 22. Beginning with the second session of the council, lay representatives of international Catholic organizations were admitted as auditors. Their names were not published; they were referred to as "professional laymen" (von Galli, *The Council and the Future,* 208).

51. *AA* 22.

52. *AA* 2.

53. *Lumen Gentium (LG)* 31.

54. Ibid. This formulation is dependent on the division of the Church into two classes, clergy and laity. A helpful critique of this basic schema, long traditional in the Church, is offered by John W. O'Malley, "Priesthood, Ministry and Religious Life: Some Historical and Historiographical Considerations," *Theological Studies* 49/2 (June, 1988) 223–257. He argues that the history of the religious orders, especially the Franciscans, Dominicans, and Jesuits, is a history of ministry. "In the vast majority of orders and congregations founded since the 13th century, ministry has been at the center of their self-understanding" (p. 255). Further indicating a plurality of ministries is Klostermann's comment: "If . . . we take seriously what is said about the variety of services and callings in the one mission of the Church, and if we see these callings as divine callings for the proper fulfillment of which God sends his specific gifts, the charisms, then it is simply not true that within Christendom there are only two special vocations, one of priestly office and one of the religious state; there are many more different states without which the Church could never fulfill its mission" ("Decree on the Apostolate of the Laity," 313).

55. *AA* 5. See also no. 7, f.

56. Paul VI, *Ministeria Quaedam,* in *Vatican Council II: The Conciliar and Post Conciliar Documents,* ed. Austin Flannery, O.P. (Northport, N.Y.: Costello Publishing Co. 1984) 427.

57. Ibid., 428–429.

58. Alan F. Blakley, "Decree on Apostolate of Lay People," in *Vatican II and Its Documents: An American Reappraisal,* ed. Timothy E. O'Connell (Wilmington, Del.: Michael Glazier, 1986) 155.

59. *Called and Gifted,* 3.

60. Elsesser, Suzanne, *Preparing Laity for Ministry: A Directory of Programs in Catholic Dioceses throughout the United States,* Bishops' Committee on the Laity and Office of Research (Washington, D.C.: United States Catholic Conference, 1986).

61. Philip J. Murnion, *New Parish Ministers*, 37, and Zenobia Fox, "A Post-Vatican II Phenomenon," 216–217. See also the more recent study, *Parishes and Parish Ministers*, by Philip J. Murnion and David DeLambo. "The data regarding the new ministers presented in chapter 4 suggest that they are instrumental in developing a more ministerial Church. They invite people into various roles, and the people say yes. They also form committees, planning teams and advisory boards, giving a broader group of laity a part in shaping and implementing the mission of the local community" (Fox, *New Ecclesial Ministry*).

62. *As I Have Done for You* (Chicago: Liturgy Training Publications, 2000) 18.

63. John Paul II, apostolic exhortation *Christifideles Laici* 23, *Origins* 18/35 (1989) 572.

64. Congregation for the Clergy et al., instruction "Some Questions Regarding Collaboration of Nonordained Faithful in Priests' Sacred Ministry," *Origins* 27/24 (1997) 399.

65. "Sweet Vindication: German branded disloyal gets red hat," *The Catholic Virginian*, February 19, 2001, p.1.

66. "Bishop says norms not intended for U.S.," *National Catholic Reporter*, April 24, 1998, p. 4.

67. *LG* 30.

68. Congar, *Lay People in the Church*, xxi.

69. Ibid.

70. Yves Congar, "My Path-Findings in the Theology of Laity and Ministries," *The Jurist* 32 (1972) 174.

71. Ibid., 175. See also Congar's "The Laity" in *Vatican II: An Interfaith Appraisal*, 197–207. So also Klostermann, arguing for an emphasis on the many callings and ministries in the Church so as to eliminate clericalism and even laicism: "In addition, one would not be subjected to the painful spectacle of attempts to try to find something 'positive' in the lay state. For what is concretely positive is not to be found by contrasting it with the clergy, but in its own specific charisms" ("Decree on the Apostolate of the Laity," 314).

72. Congar, "My Path-Findings," 176.

73. Ibid.

74. Ibid., 177.

75. Ibid., 176–178. An echo of this is heard in Klostermann: "Just as it would not have much meaning to divide the citizens of a state arbitrarily into officials and non-officials . . . it does not appear to be particularly practical to divide the New Tes-

tament people of God into clerics and non-clerics (laymen). Merely as a group contrasted with the clerics (even if one included the religious as well) there is still no proper *status* or *ordo laicorum* but only very different kinds of 'lay' ministries, or perhaps one should rather say ministries which could be practiced by laymen as well, since what is typical for them is not their lay character." He states that the secular character cannot be characteristic of all laity: "With perfect right 'laymen' who have given their whole life and work for decades in the service of the Church and who, by their calling, stand in the direct ministry of the Church in the world, explain that they feel themselves in no way to be laymen in the world, though they have never considered entering an order or even a secular institute" ("Decree on the Apostolate of the Laity," 314–315). A more recent theological exposition placing ministries within the community is given by Thomas F. O'Meara, *Theology of Ministry* (New York/Mahwah, N.J.: Paulist Press, 1999), especially chapters 4 and 5.

76. See O'Malley, "Priesthood, Ministry and Religious Life."

77. Elsewhere I have proposed that the most helpful way to officially recognize these new ministers is by utilization of installation to a lay ministry, according to the norms presented by Pope Paul VI in *Ministeria Quaedam*. Such an action would be a first step toward relationally, organizationally, and conceptually integrating these new ministers into the structures of church life (Fox, *New Ecclesial Ministry,* chapter 17).

78. Congar, "My Path-Findings," 176.

The Secular Character
of the Vocation and Mission of the Laity

Toward a Theology of Ecclesial Lay Ministry

AURELIE A. HAGSTROM

The most recent magisterial document from Rome concerning the topic of ecclesial lay ministry was the instruction "Some Questions Regarding Collaboration of Nonordained Faithful in Priests' Sacred Ministry," published in 1997.[1] In the foreword to the document, there is a call for a "full recovery of the awareness of the secular nature of the mission of the laity."[2] The pertinent footnote refers the reader to *Lumen Gentium* 31 and *Christifideles Laici* 15, both of which treat the so-called secular character of the vocation and mission of the laity.

The purpose of this essay is to explore the concept of the secular character of the lay vocation and mission, especially in its implications for ecclesial lay ministry. The basic questions that arise are: How can a theology of ecclesial lay ministry integrate an appreciation of the secular character of the vocation and mission of the laity? Is it necessarily the case that the conciliar call for the laity to transform the secular order with gospel values negates the possibility of an intra-ecclesial lay ministry? Or, perhaps, is there a way in which this secular character actually enhances and enriches ecclesial lay ministry, making it distinctive in the life of the Church? Could the secular character be understood as a gift that ecclesial lay ministers bring to their ministry, rather than a hindrance?

Presently, there seem to be three common interpretations of the notion of secular character that can be discerned in recent magisterial documents. The first two interpretations can be supported by the documents

of the Second Vatican Council, and the third interpretation was introduced by Pope John Paul II in his 1988 apostolic exhortation, *Christifideles Laici*. What are these three interpretations?

The first basic way to interpret the characteristic secularity of the
lay vocation and mission is by means of a typological or phenomenological description. In this sense, the lay vocation and mission are seen
from more of a sociological viewpoint. Secular character, according to
this view, refers to the life situation of the laity rather than a theological
or ontological condition. This interpretation of secular character would
seem to be supported by the conciliar statement in *Lumen Gentium* 31.
In the *Relatio* for this section of the document, it is stated that *Lumen
Gentium* 31 intended to give a typological or phenomenological description of the lay state, as opposed to an ontological definition.

The second basic interpretation of secular character is theological
or ontological. This view states that the understanding of the vocation
and mission of the laity is not to be derived from sociological considerations, but rather from a theology of creation and redemption. This second position would argue that the council did in fact make an
ontological statement about the lay state in *Lumen Gentium*. According
to this interpretation, the laity's secularity does not stem from the fact
that a majority of laity live in the world, but from their vocation in
Christ. Secularity is not something external and sociological; it is vocational. Through baptism, the laity are called to full participation in the
mission of the Church, and their participation is characterized by secularity. This interpretation gives secularity a theological and ecclesiological value. The secular character is rooted in the Incarnation and based
on the nature of the Church, which is sent into the world to continue the
salvific mission of Christ.

The 1988 apostolic exhortation *Christifideles Laici* seems to view
the secular character as both a sociological fact and a theological condition: "Thus for the lay faithful, to be present and active in the world is
not only an anthropological and sociological reality, but in a specific
way, a theological and ecclesiological reality as well."[3] However, while
emphasizing secular character as both a sociological fact and a theological condition, the Pope seems to be pointing toward yet another way of
understanding the secular character of the laity.

This third understanding of secularity is to be found in the perspective of the theological view of mission. The whole Church has a secular

dimension and every member is called to the mission of transforming the world. Secular character does not place the laity "outside the Church," but rather is a dimension that finds expression in a particular way through the laity within the mission of the Church. The laity have a particular secular character within the wider secular dimension of the whole Church. The secular condition of the laity, which is distinctive, is not intended to create a separation from—much less an opposition to— the other members of the Church.

In order to appreciate these three interpretations of secular character and to evaluate them theologically, it will be necessary to review conciliar teaching and survey the 1983 Code of Canon Law and recent official documents that treat the secular character of the vocation and mission of the laity. A review of these texts should provide a solid foundation for a fruitful understanding of secular character in relation to the question of ministry.

VATICAN COUNCIL II

The ecclesiology of the Second Vatican Council was unprecedented in its reflection on and articulation of the identity, role, and spirituality of the laity in the Church and in the world. This renewal of ecclesial thought and practice was due to an emphasis on the biblical theme of the Church as the people of God, the dignity and equality—rooted in baptism—of the members of the Church, and the common sharing in the threefold mission of Christ as priest, prophet, and king. Vatican II was the first council to treat the laity from a theological, rather than an exclusively canonical, point of view.

Lumen Gentium

In its consideration of the vocation and mission of the laity, the council described the vocation of the laity in terms of what belongs properly and exclusively to them, namely, their secular character (*Lumen Gentium* 31, 33). The laity seek for the kingdom of God in temporal affairs and thus have a specific relationship with the secularity of the world. This secular characteristic is presented as a distinctive qualification of the laity. The council admits that clergy and religious engage in secular activities, but their competence is not specifically related to the world, as is the laity's.

Lumen Gentium contains two interpretations of the secular character of the laity. One interpretation is typological or phenomenological, in the sense that the life situation of the laity in the world is highlighted. But *Lumen Gentium* also stresses the theological interpretation by explaining the secular character in light of the laity's baptismal vocation in Christ.

Lumen Gentium 31

In the final drafting stages of the text of *Lumen Gentium* 31, a change was made to affirm that the proper vocation of the laity is to be found in their search for the kingdom of God by caring for and, according to God's will, setting in order temporal matters.[4] The change involved inserting the phrase *search for the kingdom of God (regnum Dei quaerere)*. What was the reason for this change? Some of the council fathers feared that, without this insertion, the secular character of the laity would not be understood in its ecclesial sense. The new phrase pointed to the specifically *Christian* character of this task, as opposed to a purely ethical approach to setting in order the things of this world.[5] The laity are not merely *secular* people, but members of the Church in the temporal world.[6]

It was not the council's intent to provide a theological definition of the laity in *Lumen Gentium* 31. As noted earlier, according to the *Relatio*, what was provided was a typological description as opposed to an ontological definition. The council addressed not only what the laity have in common with all the other members of the faithful but also what makes them different, that is, what belongs properly and exclusively to them, namely, secular character.

Lumen Gentium 33

Lumen Gentium 33 explains what gives the lay apostolate its unique character within the salvific mission of the Church. The laity's relationship to the world gives the lay apostolate a special character. The emphasis here is on identity, not on function. While the council did not define the apostolate of the laity formally, in ecclesiological terms, it did spend a great deal of time addressing the question of the secular quality of the laity's mission (much the same as it did not provide an ontological definition of the lay state, but rather provided a typological description based on the laity's positive relationship to the world). There are certain circumstances and places where the Church can be the salt of the earth only through the laity. The laity, because of their secular character, make the Church present and operative in the world in a way distinct from that of clerics or religious.

This conciliar insight stresses that the Church is not present to the world merely through the hierarchy, since the laity are not merely the "representatives" of the Church in the world, but rather, they *are* the Church in the world.[7] The laity are uniquely responsible for the function of the Church as a sign in the midst of the world. The Church must find its visible manifestation through the laity who are witnesses and living instruments of the mission of the Church. Concretely, this means the lay apostolate will be *typically* carried out in and through engagement in temporal affairs. The council is here affirming the redemptive value of the daily activities of the laity in the family, workplace, school, and society.

These sections of *Lumen Gentium* provide an understanding of the dogmatic basis for the identity and function of the laity, an identity and function derived from the sacramental structure of the Church. That is, the vocation and mission of the laity are based on their sacramental configuration to Christ. Another important contribution made by *Lumen Gentium* 31 and 33 is the explanation of the secular character of the laity. Because of their Christian relationship to the secularity of the world, the laity have a unique vocation and mission. This secular character must be an essential part of any theology of the laity, since it provides the specific element of any description of the laity's identity and function.

Apostolicam Actuositatem

The Decree on the Apostolate of the Laity, *Apostolicam Actuositatem,* is founded upon the ecclesiology and theology of the laity set forth in *Lumen Gentium.*[8] The council wanted to write a document concerning the nature, character, and forms of the apostolate of the laity.

Apostolicam Actuositatem 2

One element of *Apostolicam Actuositatem* 2 is the affirmation that the lay apostolate is characterized by the secular character, that is, the fact that the laity accomplish the mission of the Church by engaging in temporal activity. This is consistent with *Lumen Gentium* 31, which outlines the concept of the secular character of the laity. Since it is proper to the laity's state to live in the midst of the world and engage in secular transactions, they are called by God to burn with the spirit of Christ and to exercise their apostolate in the world as a kind of leaven.

The typical mark or special characteristic of the laity's participation in the mission of the Church is an apostolate exercised in and through direct concern with secular affairs. In other words, the Christian penetration of the temporal order of things implies apostolic activity.

> Accordingly, the whole life of a Christian, his worldly life included, also has part in the mission of the Church as the life of one who is baptized, and in that it is taken up in faith it always has at the same time an ecclesial and therefore apostolic character.[9]

The secular character of the laity is not merely concerned with physical presence in the world—since every member of the Church is in the world in this sense—but with a living presence that involves commitment to and immersion in the temporal order. This understanding of the lay apostolate emphasizes that the life of the laity should be considered *in itself* as an instrument of the apostolate. The world is not only "where" but also "how" the laity exercise their mission. If the life of the laity in the world is *in itself* an instrument of the Church's mission, then the everyday activities of the laity can take on a redemptive value. Thus, temporal activities are not simply a *means* but also an *end* in themselves to exercising the apostolate of the laity.

This brief analysis has demonstrated how *Apostolicam Actuositatem* 2 expands and deepens the teaching of *Lumen Gentium* 31 by explaining the nature and the scope of the lay apostolate in the Church and in the world. The council gave the laity a renewed sense of co-responsibility in the life of the Church by stressing their active participation in its saving mission. Like *Lumen Gentium*, this document also seems to emphasize the theological interpretation of the secular character.

Gaudium et Spes

The Pastoral Constitution on the Church in the Modern World grappled with the complex question of the relationship between the Church and the world. In this document, the council expressed a far more positive attitude toward the modern world than ever before. In *Gaudium et Spes* 36 the council acknowledged a legitimate and proper secularization of the world and used the word "autonomy" to refer to earthly affairs. According to *Gaudium et Spes* 4, the Church must be aware of and understand the aspirations, the yearnings, and the often dramatic features of the world. There are basically three realities that are highlighted in *Gaudium et Spes* in order to explain the Church's positive relationship with the world: the dignity of the human person; the reality of the human community; and the meaning of human activity in the world.

Unlike *Lumen Gentium*, *Gaudium et Spes* 40 emphasizes the secular mission of the *entire* Church, and not just the members of the laity. The whole people of God has a secular mission to serve as a leaven in the world, in such a way that, without compromising the autonomy of the secular, it cooperates with the Spirit to bring about a transformation of the world according to God's will. The approach of *Gaudium et Spes* seems to flow from a theology of creation and redemption. The whole Church has a secular dimension, and, within this, the laity have a particular secular character. Within the overall secular mission of the Church, the laity are highlighted. *Gaudium et Spes* 43 indicates that the secular character of the lay apostolate is the means by which the mission of the Church is actualized in the world.[10]

According to the three conciliar documents discussed above, it is not simply the fact of the laity being situated in the world, but rather the laity's Christian relationship to secular affairs or temporal realities that gives their vocation its uniqueness. In terms of the mission of the laity, the secular character is not simply a form of the apostolate, but is instead something that qualifies the whole life of the laity, in the Church and in the world.

His Christian relationship with the secular world... is something that specifies the whole life of the layman—as a qualifi-

cation of membership in the church and therefore also of his active contribution as a non-office bearer to the primary, religious
mission of the church... What should be made clear is that the
layman's Christian relationship with the world colors his whole
active being as a Christian.[11]

The secular character of the laity is a gift which they bring to the
life of the Church. It is a source of theological insight and practical action which can best be enunciated and implemented by the laity. The
laity's Christian relationship with secularity is a special grace and a special authority for action in the temporal sphere. They are called in a preeminent way to incarnate the Church in the world. The laity are to bring
the Church into the heart of the world while bringing the world into the
heart of the Church. The experience of the laity in the world, which is
brought into the heart of the Church, is a legitimate source of theology
and ministry. This can be realized only if their secular character is affirmed and valued as a gift to the Church.

The Council sought to establish the Christian and ecclesial significance of the everyday life of the lay person as in itself a real
share in Christ's and the Church's mission and to establish also
that the Church itself, in its primary task of self-realization, needs
from the laity precisely those insights, perceptions, orientations,
which only life in the world makes likely or even possible.[12]

The secular character of the laity influences and colors the laity's
activities not only in the world, but also in the Church. The activities of
the laity in intra-ecclesial affairs, such as ecclesial lay ministry, flow
from the secular character which the laity bring to these services and
ministries. The identity or being of the laity, which includes the secular
dimension, influences and determines even the intra-ecclesial functions
or activities carried out by the laity. Their secular character actually enhances and enriches ecclesial lay ministry, making it distinctive in the
life of the Church. It is a gift, not a hindrance, to full participation in the
life of the Church *ad intra*.

Thus the function to be fulfilled *in the Church* by the Christian as one who is baptized, confirmed and strengthened by

the eucharistic sacrifice, will also always be determined by the layman's characteristic position in the world.[13]

1983 CODE OF CANON LAW

During the revision of the Code of Canon Law after Vatican II, one important element in the description of the apostolate of the laity was the distinctive character of this apostolate. As seen above, the distinctive element in the vocation of the laity is their secular character, that is, the fact that the laity are called to live the Christian life in the world. This element in the vocation of the laity has an effect on how the laity specifically exercise the mission of the Church. The specific character of the lay apostolate is the fact that the laity give testimony to Christ and seek the kingdom of God in temporal affairs.[14]

Canon 225

Canon 225 is located in Book II, on "The People of God." The lay apostolate is seen within the wider understanding of the mission of the whole people of God. It is the general obligation of all the *Christifideles* to carry out the mission of the Church, and canon 225 specifies the role that the laity have in that work.

No longer are the laity seen as merely participating in the apostolate of the hierarchy. Rather, as canon 225 affirms, the laity have the general right to participate in the mission of the Church. This is not only a right, but also a duty or obligation which, by virtue of their sacramental identity, the laity share with every other member of the Church.

A key element of canon 225 is the call of the laity to transform the temporal order. Because of the secular condition of the laity, they are bound by a special duty to bring the values of the Gospel to secular activities in the temporal order. They give witness to Christ precisely when they are engaged in these secular duties. The duty to permeate and perfect the temporal order is not something that is "over and above" their daily lives or natural existence. It is exactly in and through their temporal affairs that the laity give witness to Christ. This special duty or task is proper to the laity because of the unique secular character of their vocation.

The nucleus of canon 225 is the duty that the laity have, by virtue of their vocation, to animate and perfect the temporal order. Every member of the Church is called to engage in the mission of the Church (c. 211), but the laity in particular have a unique role to play in this work. Canon 225 outlines that which makes the laity's participation in the mission of the Church unique—their call to transform the temporal order with the spirit of the Gospel. In other words, secularity is the fundamental component of the specific mission of the laity in the Church's mission.

Among all the members of the Church, it is the laity in particular who have the obligation to bring the values of the Gospel to the cultural, political, economic, social, and domestic spheres. The major contribution or "breakthrough" of this canon is that it gives an ecclesial character to the daily secular activities of the laity. It is precisely when the laity engage in temporal affairs that they are engaging in the mission of the Church. This is prior to any ecclesiastical mandate or authorization, since the laity are deputed to this task through baptism and confirmation. The approach of the 1983 Code to secular character reflects the theological or ontological approach of the conciliar documents mentioned above.

CHRISTIFIDELES LAICI

The next magisterial document that attempted to grapple with the question of the vocation and mission of the laity was Pope John Paul II's 1988 post-synodal apostolic exhortation *Christifideles Laici,* On the Vocation and the Mission of the Lay Faithful in the Church and in the World. It is one of the fruits of the work of the 1987 Synod of Bishops, whose topic was the vocation and mission of the laity in the Church and in the world twenty years after Vatican II. It is in this document that a third possible interpretation of secular character emerges. Three key texts, *Christifideles Laici* 9, 15, and 23 are concerned with the secular character of the laity.

Christifideles Laici 9

Christifideles Laici 9 reiterates the typological description of the laity from *Lumen Gentium* 31. As seen above, this description highlights

the dignity of baptism and the secular character of the laity. The Pope
says that the council

> opened itself to a decidedly positive vision and displayed a
> basic intention of asserting *the full belonging of the lay faithful
> to the Church and to its mystery. At the same time it insisted on
> the unique character of their vocation*, which is in a special
> way to "seek the Kingdom of God by engaging in temporal af-
> fairs and ordering them according to the plan of God."[15]

Christifideles Laici 15

In *Christifideles Laici* 15, the Pope begins by grounding the equality of all the members of the Church in the mystery of baptism. Baptism
gives to all the members of the Church not only a dignity but also a responsibility for the mission of the Church. The way in which the laity
fulfill the mission of the Church is different from the way in which
clergy and religious fulfill this mission. The reason for this, according
to the Pope, is that the laity are defined on the basis of the Christian
newness that results from baptism and they are characterized by their
secular character.

The Pope then attempts to provide a deeper theological understanding of this secular nature in light of God's plan of salvation and in the
context of the mystery of the Church. The basis for understanding the
secular character of the laity is the fact that the whole Church itself has
an authentic secular dimension. The Church is in the world, but not of
the world. Therefore, *all* the members of the Church share in this secular dimension, but in different ways. The laity have a unique sharing in
the secular dimension of the Church, according to the Pope. The secularity of the laity is not mere *physical* presence in the world, but rather a
living presence involving commitment to and immersion in the temporal order.

The world is where the laity receive their call from God. Therefore, the world becomes the place and the means for the laity to fulfill
their vocation. The world is not only an external and environmental
framework; it also has a definite place in God's plan of salvation. "The
world itself is destined to glorify God the Father in Christ."[16] The secular character of the laity is the *locus* where the laity are called to live as

baptized people and it is a reality that finds the fullness of its meaning only in Christ. Therefore, the vocational character of secularity also constitutes its theological content.

The laity have been given a vocation by God to contribute to the sanctification of the world. How does this sanctification come about? The Pope quotes *Lumen Gentium* 31 and affirms that:

> In fact, in their situation in the world God manifests his plan and communicates to them their particular vocation of "seeking the Kingdom of God by engaging in temporal affairs and by ordering them according to the plan of God."[17]

The secular character of the laity, then, is not only an accidental or circumstantial feature of the laity, but also a positive and genuinely theological characteristic. The secular nature of the laity has to be understood in the light of God the creator and redeemer who has handed the world over to men and women so that they might participate in the work of creation. The task of the laity is to free creation from the influence of sin and to sanctify themselves in their daily lives, in marriage or the celibate life, in a family, in a profession, and in the various activities of society.[18] Baptism does not take the laity *out* of the world. Rather, baptism calls the laity to live a Christian vocation *for* the world.

Is there any development in the notion of secular character in *Christifideles Laici* 15? That is, does the Pope simply re-state the description of secular character found in *Lumen Gentium* and *Apostolicam Actuositatem*? Or is there a further elaboration or a new definition of secular character here? The reason why this is important is because of the differing interpretations of secular character that can all be supported by the conciliar documents. The two basic interpretations, as seen above, are that the secular character of the laity can be understood in either a phenomenological or a theological way.

The question, then, is which interpretation is supported by *Christifideles Laici* 15? During the discussions of the 1987 Synod, both views were expressed by various bishops. But it was left up to the Pope to offer a definitive understanding of the secularity of the laity. In *Christifideles Laici* 15, the Pope seems to have struck a compromise position. This section of the apostolic exhortation contains both views of the lay secular character. *Christifideles Laici* 15 seems to say that the secular character is both a sociological fact and a theological condition. "Thus for the lay faithful, to be present and active in the world is not only an anthropological and sociological reality, but in a specific way, a theological and ecclesiological reality as well."[19] So, while definitely affirming a secular dimension to the lay vocation, the Pope does not seem to explicitly choose one interpretation of that dimension over another.

Instead, in *Christifideles Laici* 15, the Pope seems to be pointing toward yet a third way of understanding the secular character of the laity. He does state that in order to "understand properly the lay faithful's position in the Church in a complete, adequate and specific manner it is necessary to come to a deeper theological understanding of their secular character."[20] This is obviously a theological approach. But he also states that "the 'world' thus becomes the place and the means for the lay faithful to fulfill their Christian vocation,"[21] which seems to support a sociological or phenomenological approach to understanding the secular character.

The Pope here provides a third understanding of secularity in the perspective of the theological view of mission. Secularity does not mean "outside the Church"; rather, it is a dimension that finds expression in a particular way through the laity within the mission of the Church. The mission of the laity will bear fruit in proportion to the respect given to their secular nature in the fulfillment of this mission. The secular condition of the laity is not intended to create a separation from or an opposition to the other members of the Church. Rather, it serves to qualify the laity in relationship to all the other members of the Church.

At the end of *Christifideles Laici* 15 the Pope gives a description of the place of the laity in the Church.

> The lay faithful's *position in the Church,* then, comes to be fundamentally defined by their *newness in Christian life* and distinguished by their *secular character.*[22]

The two elements in the Pope's description of the vocation of the laity in *Christifideles Laici* 15 are baptism and secular character. The laity are fundamentally defined by their baptismal identity and are distinguished from the rest of the baptized by their secular character. And secularity here is more of a theological mission than a purely ontological condition.

Christifideles Laici 23

What does the Pope mean when he says that the laity are to fulfill the salvific mission of the Church according to their own specific vocation? He is once again referring to the secular character of the laity. In *Christifideles Laici* 23 he quotes Pope Paul VI's *Evangelii Nuntiandi* describing the mission of the laity according to their secular condition.

> Their own field of evangelizing activity is the vast and complicated world of politics, society and economics, as well as the world of culture, of the sciences and the arts, of international life, of the mass media. It also includes other realities which are open to evangelization, such as human love, the family, the education of children and adolescents, professional work, and suffering.[23]

The Pope seems to place the question of the secularity of the laity in the overall context of the laity's call to mission. While it is true that all the members of the Church live in the world and have a responsibility for the Church's mission in the world, the laity have a particular competency within this common mission. The common dignity and responsibility of the laity in the mission of the Church are characterized by the special place chosen for them by God in which they might respond to the call of evangelization. This third interpretation of secular character recognizes that the whole Church has a secular dimension, but, within the Church's mission, the laity have a distinctive secular character.

1997 INSTRUCTION
"SOME QUESTIONS REGARDING COLLABORATION OF NONORDAINED FAITHFUL IN PRIESTS' SACRED MINISTRY"

The next magisterial document that will be highlighted in an attempt to trace the secular character of the laity is the 1997 Vatican instruction on ministry in the Church.[24] It was issued by eight Vatican dicasteries and released *in forma specifica*, thereby carrying the weight of papal authority. In the foreword to the document, there is a call for a "full recovery of the awareness of the secular nature of the mission of the laity." The instruction states, however, that its purpose is not to develop the theology of the laity, since it has already been treated in *Christifideles Laici*.

> This is not the place to develop the theological and pastoral richness of the role of the lay faithful in the church, which has already been amply treated in the apostolic exhortation *Christifideles Laici*.[25]

Instead, the document answers various questions concerning the pastoral activity of the Church. The document begins with a theological review of principles by which its thirteen articles are to be understood and implemented. The four theological principles are: the essential difference between the common priesthood of the faithful and the ministerial priesthood; the unity and diversity of ministerial functions; the indispensability of the ordained ministry; and the collaboration of the nonordained faithful in pastoral ministry.

Since the focus of the document is the theology of the ministerial priesthood, there is no full-blown treatment of the theology of the vocation and mission of the laity. There is a call for a recovery of the awareness of the secular character of the laity, as noted earlier, but there is no theological explanation of this character. In fact, the secular character of the laity is mentioned only in the foreword to the instruction and is presented in the context of the Church's mission:

> In this great field of complementary activity, whether considering the specifically spiritual and religious or the *consecratio mundi*, there exists a more restricted area, namely, the sacred ministry of the clergy. In this ministry the lay faithful ... are called to assist.[26]

It is made clear that the laity can only *assist* and not substitute for the sacred ministry of the clergy. Within the collaboration of assistance between the clergy and the laity in ministry, particular attention must be given to preserving the distinction of the vocations of each.

> It is necessary that all who are in any way involved in this collaboration exercise particular care to safeguard the nature and

mission of sacred ministry and the vocation and secular character of the lay faithful. It must be remembered that *collaboration
with* does not, in fact, mean *substitution for*.[27]

What is the understanding of the secular character of the laity in
this document? The instruction seems to rely on the theology of *Christifideles Laici*. As seen above, *Christifideles Laici*, while employing both
the phenomenological/sociological and the theological/ontological understanding of secular character, definitely seems to offer a third interpretation within the perspective of the theological view of mission. So,
which one does this instruction emphasize? It seems that the instruction
relies on the theological interpretation of the secular character of the
laity. The whole thrust of the document seems to be toward a hard and
fast separation and distinction between the clergy and the laity.[28] Therefore, the secular character of the laity is described ontologically, and not
simply typologically.

Although the conciliar documents and *Christifideles Laici* recognized that all the members of the Church share in secularity (*Lumen
Gentium* 31; *Gaudium et Spes* 40, 43; *Christifideles Laici* 15), as seen
above, the 1997 instruction apparently goes back to the pre-conciliar understanding of "two realms"—sacred and secular. That is, the instruction
seems to promote the view that there are two distinct spheres of action,
with the temporal sphere belonging to the laity and the sacred to the
clergy. This is evidenced in the emphasis on the ontological interpretation of the secular character of the laity in the document. Also, the word
"sacred" is applied only to the clergy and the ministry of the ordained.
This distinction is the basis for exclusion of the laity from service within
the Church. The focus of the mission of the laity, according to the instruction, should be the consecration of the world, as opposed to intra-
ecclesial ministry, which is the responsibility and mission of the clergy.

> The laity, by virtue of the holiness of their baptism, have an ur-
> gent duty toward the material and spiritual world, but what is
> purely lay—that is, the consecration of the world—is different
> from what is concerned by ministeriality.[29]

While this approach to the laity can certainly be based on the conciliar documents and even *Christifideles Laici*, it does not seem to do

justice to the fullness of the treatment of the laity in these texts. As seen above, the notion of secularity or the secular dimension of the Church was never restricted solely to the laity in the conciliar documents or in the Pope's apostolic exhortation. In fact, the "two realm" approach was criticized by theologians before and after the council.[30]

Yves Congar admitted the inadequacy of the "two realm" approach to the laity in his famous *retractatio*. He suggested that a new model be employed, that of community/ministry, rather than that of laity/clergy. In this ecclesiology, the focus would be on the global view of the whole people of God rather than on just what is specific or distinctive about the laity.[31] Since then, other theologians have taken Congar's lead. The result has been a new theology of ministry which emphasizes the missionary nature of the whole Church and the universal ministeriality of all the baptized members of the people of God. In this diversification of ministries, many roles in the Church that had previously been restricted to the clergy are now open to the laity.[32] In this new theology of ministry, secularity is described as a dimension of the entire Church, which is "ministerial" in its entirety. The laity/clergy divide is overcome in favor of an ecclesiology of communion and the unity of the people of God.[33]

The 1997 Vatican instruction was written precisely to draw the line between the laity and the clergy more clearly, and therefore it adopted the "two realm" approach to ministry. In response to what the instruction describes as a misunderstanding of true ecclesial communion, the secular character of the laity is "hardened into a normative definition...whereby the Church becomes the realm of the ordained and the world the realm of the laity even though Vatican II...makes no such hard and fast distinction"[34]

The 1997 instruction *does* seem to differ from *Christifideles Laici* in its treatment of the secular character of the laity. As seen above, the Pope had placed the question of secularity in the context of the divine vocation to mission addressed to the laity. While the Church's mission in the world is the responsibility of *all* its members, it is also the place where the laity discover their particular place and competency.[35]

All the members of the Church share in its secular dimension and all are called to continue the salvific mission of Christ, which includes the renewal of the temporal order. In *Christifideles Laici*, the Pope placed secularity in the ecclesiological context of the Church's mission.

Christifideles Laici did not pose the secular character of the lay vocation in opposition to lay participation in the life of the Church. The unity of the Church's mission demonstrates that there should be no dichotomy between the laity's mission in the Church and mission in the world. The mission of the laity includes both intra-ecclesial activities and evangelization of the world.

But this does not seem to be the approach of the 1997 instruction, which emphasizes the ontological definition of the secular character and the "two realm" approach to mission. The instruction makes a dichotomy between the spiritual order of the Church's mission, which is to be typically restricted to the clergy, and the temporal realm of the Church's mission, which is to be the responsibility of the laity. Therefore, the instruction does seem to be a departure from the teaching of *Christifideles Laici* in its interpretation of the secular character of the laity.

CONCLUSION

This essay has attempted to explore the notion of the secular character of the lay vocation and mission by surveying several magisterial documents. Its particular focus has been on how the secular character of the laity might be considered in the context of ecclesial lay ministry. Is it necessarily the case that the conciliar call for the laity to transform the secular order with gospel values negates the possibility of an intra-ecclesial lay ministry? Or, perhaps, is there a way in which this secular character actually enhances and enriches ecclesial lay ministry, making it distinctive in the life of the Church?

In the brief survey of each of the documents mentioned above, three basic interpretations of the secular character of the laity have emerged. First, secular character can be viewed as a sociological or phenomenological datum about the laity in the Church. That is, the fact that the world is the place and the means by which the laity live out their vocation is a sociological fact. The laity engage in secular affairs in the experiences of family life, politics, society, economics, culture, science, and the arts.

The second interpretation of secular character is that it is a theological or ontological datum about the laity. This approach makes secular character a necessary theological element in any description of who the laity are and what they are called to do. The fact that the laity live in the world and seek the kingdom of God in temporal affairs is what gives a uniqueness to their vocation and mission. In this interpretation, the laity's Christian relationship to secularity is a *locus theologicus,* a source or starting point for a theology of the laity.

The third interpretation emphasizes the understanding of secularity in the perspective of the theological view of mission. Secularity, in this approach, is a dimension of the whole Church, a dimension that finds expression in a particular way through the laity within the mission of the Church.

The first two interpretations of secular character have their own strengths and weaknesses. One of the strengths of the first, or phenomenological, approach is that the world is viewed in a much more positive light. The term "secular" is also seen in its positive sense and is not confused with secularism or secularization, that is, worldly values and value systems that are contrary to those of the Gospel. It is understood, rather, in light of the act of God, the creator and redeemer who has handed over the world to men and women so that they may participate in the work of creation, free creation from the influence of sin, and sanctify themselves in marriage or the celibate life, in a family, in a profession, and in the various activities of society. One weakness of this interpretation, however, is that it is not only the laity who live in the world; rather, all the members of the Church share in this phenomenon. Clergy and religious also engage in secular activities and sometimes even practice secular professions. The whole Church has a secular dimension. So, it is difficult to see how this sociological interpretation would apply exclusively to the laity.

One strength of the second, or theological, interpretation of secular character is that, by stressing secular character, the Church's teaching on the laity affirms the redemptive value of the daily activities of the laity in the family, workplace, school, and society. The laity give witness to Christ precisely when they are engaged in these secular activities, which have an ecclesial character because of the secular nature of the lay vocation. One weakness of this interpretation, however, is that it can easily develop into a "two realm" theory of the mission of the Church. A theological or ontological approach to secular character can restrict the mission of the laity simply to activity in the world, without a corresponding mission *ad intra*, or within the inner life of the Church. A "two realm" approach can restrict the mission of the laity to only "worldly obligations" and prevent them from taking on important intra-ecclesial roles.

It seems that in the Pope's 1988 post-synodal exhortation *Christifideles Laici* there might be the outline of yet a third possible interpretation of secular character. This third interpretation would recognize that the entire Church has a secular dimension. Even clergy and religious live in the world and engage in temporal affairs. Nevertheless, the laity have a particular secular character within this secular dimension. Their unique relationship with secularity is one characteristic of their vocation and mission. This third interpretation would not emphasize exclusively either a sociological/phenomenological approach or a theological/ontological approach to secular character. Instead, it would place the secular character of the laity in the context of the divine vocation to mission. While the Church's mission in the world is the responsibility of all its members, the laity have a particular relationship with secularity, which characterizes their participation in this mission. The secularity of the laity is not a mere physical presence in the world, but rather a living presence involving commitment to and immersion in the temporal order.

This third approach would make no dichotomy between the laity's mission in the Church and the laity's mission in the world, as if the former were primarily "spiritual" and the second restricted to the "worldly" realm. Because the Church's mission is both spiritual and temporal, the laity are called to the building of ecclesial communion *(ad intra)* as well as to the transformation of the world with gospel values *(ad extra)*. In this third approach, the secular character of the laity is not posed in opposition to their participation in the inner life of the Church. The laity have the right and responsibility to engage in intra-ecclesial ministries and promote the life of the Church. This third approach would view the secular character as a gift which ecclesial lay ministers bring to ministry, rather than a hindrance.

Perhaps in the ongoing attempt to formulate a theology of ecclesial lay ministry it is possible to remain grounded in the magisterial texts on the theology of the laity while also moving forward in interpreting secular character in light of the postconciliar phenomenon of lay ministry. The activity of the Holy Spirit in the dramatic increase in lay ministries could also prompt the Church to reconsider secular character in the context of the inner life and communion of the Church. In this way, ecclesial lay ministry would not be seen as an abandonment of the proper identity of the laity. On the contrary, it would be viewed as a manifestation of the dignity and responsibility of the laity who are called to be full sharers in the life and mission of the Church.

NOTES

1. Congregation for the Clergy et al., instruction "Some Questions Regarding Collaboration of Nonordained Faithful in Priests' Sacred Ministry," August 15, 1997. English translation in *Origins* 27/24 (November 27, 1997) 397–410. Cited hereafter as "Some Questions."

2. Ibid., 399.

3. John Paul II, apostolic exhortation *Christifideles Laici (CFL)* 15, *Acta Apostolicae Sedis* 81 (1989) 393–521. English trans. Libreria Editrice Vaticana (Vatican City, 1988).

4. *Acta Synodalia*, Vol. III, Pars VIII, p. 811.

5. Edward Schillebeeckx, *The Mission of the Church*, trans. N. D. Smith (New York: Seabury Press, 1973) 100.

6. See part of the Commentary on the first pre-Conciliar schema—*Acta Synodalia*, Vol. II, Pars I, *Notae* 17, p. 266.

7. Pius XII in an allocution on February 20, 1946, *Acta Apostolicae Sedis* 38 (1946) 149.

8. See *Relatio* in *Acta Synodalia*, Vol. III, Pars III, p. 385; Vol. IV, Pars II, pp. 308–309.

9. Ferdinand Klostermann, "Decree on the Apostolate of the Laity—History of the Text," in *Commentary on the Documents of Vatican II*, vol. 3, ed. Herbert Vorgrimler (New York: Herder & Herder, 1969) 309.

10. Michael Place, "In The Manner of a Leaven—The Lay Mission to the Secular World," *The Jurist* 47 (1987) 86–102.

11. Schillebeeckx, *The Mission of the Church*, 114–115.

12. Joseph Komonchak, "Clergy, Laity and the Church's Mission in the World," in *Official Ministry in a New Age*, ed. James Provost (Washington: Canon Law Society of America, 1981) 174.

13. Edward Schillebeeckx, *The Layman in the Church and Other Essays* (New York: Alba House, 1963) 50.

14. From the deliberations of the Study Group on the Laity in 1966 during the revision of the Code. *Communicationes* 17 (1985) 172.

15. *CFL* 9.

16. *CFL* 15.

17. Ibid.

18. Ibid.

19. Ibid.

20. Ibid.

21. Ibid.

22. Ibid.

23. Paul VI, apostolic exhortation *Evangelii Nuntiandi* 70, *Acta Apostolicae Sedis* 68 (1976) 60; quoted in *CFL* 23.

24. "Some Questions," 397–410.

25. Ibid., 400.

26. Ibid., 399.

27. Ibid.

28. See Richard R. Gaillardetz, "Shifting Meanings in the Lay-Clergy Distinction," *Irish Theological Quarterly* 64 (1999) 115–139.

29. "The Instruction: An Explanatory Note," *Origins* 27/24 (November 27, 1997) 409.

30. Karl Rahner, "Notes on the Lay Apostolate," *Theological Investigations*, vol. 2 (London: Darton, Longmann, & Todd, 1963) 3; Schillebeeckx, *The Mission of the Church*, 125. See also *The Layman in the Church and Other Essays*.

31. Yves Congar, "My Pathfindings in the Theology of the Laity and Ministries," *The Jurist* 2 (1972) 169–188.

32. See Thomas O'Meara, *Theology of Ministry* (New York/Mahwah, N.J.: Paulist Press, 1983); David Power, *Gifts that Differ: Lay Ministries Established and Unestablished* (New York: Pueblo Publishing Co., 1985); Remi Parent, *A Church of the Baptized* (New York/Mahwah, N.J.: Paulist Press, 1987); Richard McBrien, *Ministry* (San Francisco: Harper & Row, 1987); Kenan Osborne, *Ministry: Lay Ministry in the Roman Catholic Church* (New York/Mahwah, N.J.: Paulist Press, 1993).

33. See Bruno Forte, *The Church: Icon of the Trinity—A Brief Study* (Boston: St. Paul Books and Media, 1991).

34. Jon Nilson, "The Laity," in *The Gift of the Church*, ed. Peter Phan (Collegeville, Minn.: The Liturgical Press, 2000) 408.

35. *CFL* 36.

Presbyteral Identity within Parish Identity

Susan K. Wood, S.C.L.

Presbyteral identity has generally been addressed in terms of priestly identity.[1] Such an approach tends to emphasize only the priestly dimension of the threefold office of priest, prophet, and king. This leaves unaddressed a number of issues, such as the need to distinguish presbyteral identity from episcopal identity, since both presbyters and bishops are priests,[2] and the need to connect the priestly office with the other two presbyteral offices of pastoral leadership and prophetic witness and teaching.

Lumen Gentium distinguishes these three roles when it states that presbyters are consecrated in order "to preach the Gospel and shepherd the faithful as well as to celebrate divine worship as true priests of the New Testament."[3] Within the threefold office, the pastoral role of the ordained is not simply folded into the priestly role. Although not separate, these roles are distinct. A pastoral charge implies a flock, a community, and a church with which the ordained is in relationship.

In this essay I will suggest that an analysis of ordained ministry in relationship to ecclesial structures and pastoral leadership may provide a way forward to an enriched understanding of presbyteral identity.[4] Even though not all actualizations of the Church occur in parish structures, not all priests are parish pastors, and other models of the priesthood are operative within religious communities,[5] the diocesan parochial model is normative for the theology of ordained ministry articulated in the documents of Vatican II and necessary for understanding the interrelationship of bishops and presbyters. Since ordained ministry is in service to the Church, it makes sense to examine such ministry in terms of the church structures it serves, for presbyteral identity does not

175

exist for itself or in a vacuum, but in relationship to Christ, other presbyters, the bishop, and the Church. In this essay I will attend to this last
relationship, the presbyter's relationship to the Church as actualized in
the parish. In doing so, I have no intention of slighting the importance
of the other relationships. They simply are not the subject of this particular essay.

This essay is not intended either to refute or to replace the work
done on priestly identity, much of which has revolved around the
priest's ability to act *in persona Christi* or *in persona ecclesiae*.[6] The
theology of the priesthood underlying this work emphasizes the priest's
role in the sacramental life of the Church and finds support in the rite of
ordination, where the promises of the ordinand and prayer of ordination
stress the presbyter's sacramental responsibilities. The theological discussions around this role have greatly contributed to a theology of the
priesthood, but they are not sufficient in and of themselves for articulating a theology of priestly identity.

These disclaimers seem necessary in the often polemical climate of
contemporary discussions of the priesthood. Priests reading books and
articles on the priesthood want to see themselves reflected there. Consequently, members of religious communities sometimes resist descriptions of priestly identity tied too closely to parochical structures.
Others look for descriptions centered on sacramental capabilities and
their role of representing Christ. In the past we have attempted to ar-
rive at an articulation of priestly identity that would suffice for all instances of the priesthood. The *in persona Christi / in persona ecclesiae*
analysis did that, since all priests preside at the Eucharist. However,
precisely because this understanding is grounded in a priest's sacramental ministry, it tends to be a-historical, universal, and essentialist
insofar as sacraments are signs and symbols that represent sacred realities. An understanding of priestly identity and ministry requires a
complementary referent that is historical, particular, pluralistic, and
contingent, dependent upon the particular circumstances of ministry.
Our failure to attend sufficiently to the contextualized character of the
presbyterate may be one of the reasons why priestly identity has been
so elusive.

This essay is an attempt to correct this by looking at one specific
context of priestly identity, the parish, as a lens through which to view

presbyteral identity. The point is that presbyteral identity is broader than priestly identity, even though the two terms are often used interchangeably. Priestly identity is concerned with the ability to offer sacrifice, to represent Christ and the Church. The emphasis is on a role within the worship of the Church. Presbyteral identity, on the other hand, requires attention to the kingly/shepherding and prophetic offices which are regularly exercised within the parochial life of the Church, even if exceptions and exemptions exist.

A theology of presbyteral identity requires both an understanding of a priest's relationship to his bishop and an adequate theology of the parish, both fairly new contexts for a theology of the priesthood. Vatican II taught that the bishop possesses the fullness of the sacrament of orders. This necessarily had the effect of shifting the theology of priestly identity at the same time as it opened reflection on the relationship between the priesthood of the bishop and his role in governing a particular church. The theology of the threefold office of priest, prophet, and king made it clear that governance was not simply an exercise of jurisdiction added to priestly ordination, but was itself an exercise of the sacrament of orders.

Similarly, a presbyter's identity is intrinsically linked to his pastoral charge. In the case of pastors, this charge is identified by the ecclesial structure it serves, the parish. Our current difficulties in defining priestly identity may be due to inattention to the offices of prophet and shepherd conferred by ordination as well as an insufficient theology of the parish.

Today we need to place the sacramental action of the presbyter and his corresponding priestly identity within a broader ecclesiological framework. Three principles guide this effort. First, the Church precedes any ministerial service to the Church. Ministry arises from the Church for the Church. Second, the sacrament of orders reflects the order of the Church. The order of the Church is that it is a communion of communions. The universal Church is a communion of particular churches, defined as altar communities under the sacred ministry of the bishop.[7] Particular churches are themselves usually regional groupings of parishes and specialized ministries within a diocese. Parishes are themselves small communions, and they and their pastors must be in communion with the larger particular church and its ordained minister, the bishop.

Third, ministry serves the unity and communion of the Church. A correlation of various levels of communion with various ordained ministries shows that there is an ordained ministry that specifically serves each level of communion. The bishop of Rome exercises the Petrine ministry for the unity and communion of the universal Church in communion with the college of bishops. Residential bishops serve the communion of their particular churches and represent those churches in the communion of churches through their membership in the episcopal college. As successors to the apostles, bishops also serve the communion of the Church throughout time with the apostolic tradition. Presbyters serve the internal communion of parishes and their communion with the particular church.

This view of the relationship between ordained ministry and the Church assumes the diocesan priesthood and residential bishops as normative for understanding ministerial and ecclesial identity. This was the operative presupposition of the theology of bishops and priests in *Lumen Gentium*, and this theology of the local church is also reflected in various provisions of the 1990 ordination rites. For example, since a priest is ordained for the sake of the entire local church, the clergy and other faithful are to be invited to his ordination. Likewise, it is fitting that the diocesan bishop be the minister of the ordination of a deacon to the presbyterate. After the gospel reading, the local church asks the bishop to ordain the candidates. Finally, the relationship to the local church is underscored by the promise of obedience that ordinands, including those from religious communities, make to the diocesan bishop.

Actual ecclesiastical practice is, however, more complicated. Titular bishops do not function as pastors of actual particular churches. Not all priests serve as pastors of parishes, since many serve special ministries within dioceses. Not all priests are incardinated into a diocese. Many are members of religious communities and are subject to being assigned to ministry in any of a number of dioceses or may do limited pastoral work. Consequently, a theology of priestly identity based on a theology of the parish within the particular church does not address the identity of all priests. However, it does begin to fill out what was missing in Vatican II, that is, a theology of ordained ministry that corresponds to a level of ecclesiality. It also begins a theology of priesthood that is historical and contextualized.

MINISTRY CORRELATED TO LEVELS OF ECCLESIALITY

A contextualized view of ministry sees ministry as arising from the Church in service to the Church. Roman Catholic theology has tended to define the basic unit of the Church in terms of the minister (an altar community under the sacred ministry of the bishop),[8] rather than defining the minister in terms of the church (a bishop is the pastoral leader of a particular church and a presbyter is a pastoral leader of a parish).[9] Nevertheless, the Church has tended to organize itself along geographical divisions rather than around ministers. As Karl Rahner notes, "the normal pattern is not of personal episcopal jurisdiction or personal parishes, but local sees and local parishes."[10] A minister is never identified apart from the church he serves. A bishop, even a titular bishop, is always designated as a bishop of a place. The same is true of presbyters insofar as there can be no absolute ordinations and presbyters are incardinated into a diocese or are members of religious communities.

Although the particular church, the basic unit of the Church in Roman Catholicism, is defined as an altar community under the sacred ministry of the bishop, most Roman Catholics never experience the diocese as a eucharistic community. Their most concrete experience of Church occurs in the parish. Within the local community of the parish the faith is professed, the community receives the baptized, and the Eucharist celebrates and proclaims the sacramental presence of Christ within the community. Consequently, the theology of the particular church articulated by Vatican II is at some variance with the most common Roman Catholic experience of Church. Vatican II's theology of the particular church needs to be complemented and completed by a theology of the parish. Just as a theology of the episcopacy and the particular church go hand in hand, so must a theology of the presbyterate and the parish mutually inform each other.

Vatican II focused on ministry rather than on levels of ecclesiality. Thus chapter 3 of *Lumen Gentium* focuses on various offices within the hierarchical church, emphasizing bishops, with only a section each devoted to priests and deacons. The pope is aptly identified as head of the college of bishops.[11] In his Petrine ministry he is "a lasting and visible source and foundation of the unity both of faith and of communion."[12] However, the text does not specify whether this refers to the unity of the bishops or the unity of the churches. The emphasis is on the bishops as successors to the apostles. The communion of particular churches is more implicit than explicit in the text, particularly in number 23, which describes the mutual relations of individual bishops with particular churches and with the universal Church. Each bishop represents his own church, presumably within the communion of churches, "whereas all of them together with the pope represent the whole church."

Sacrosanctum Concilium, the Constitution on the Sacred Liturgy, identifies the principal manifestation of the Church as "the full, active participation of all God's holy people in the same liturgical celebrations, especially in the same Eucharist, in one prayer, at one altar, at which the bishop presides, surrounded by his college of priests and by his ministers."[13] Here the Church is defined ministerially through the presence of the bishop and eucharistically as most manifest in the Eucharist. However, even though the Eucharist over which the bishop may preside is normative, it is not the most common experience for most Catholics, who experience the Eucharist most frequently within their local parish.

Vatican II describes priests in terms of their relationship to their bishop, to each other with the presbyterium, and to the eucharistic assembly where they exercise their sacred functions in a supreme degree.[14] One sentence refers them to a local community: "Having gladly become examples for their flock (see 1 Pet 5:3), they should preside over and serve their local community in such a way that it may deserve to be called by the name which is given to the one people of God in its entirety, that is to say, the church of God (see 1 Cor 1:2; 2 Cor 1:1; and *passim*)."[15] Although this passage strikingly identifies the local community as the Church of God, there is really no theology of the parish within the documents of Vatican II and no indication of how parishes are related theologically to the larger particular church, usually the diocese. Priests serve a local community, but their identity derives from their service of the Eucharist. A contextualized theology of presbyters and deacons requires an account of the relationship between the particular church with its bishop and the parish with its presbyter in his prophetic and pastoral functions as well as in his priestly ones.

THE PRESBYTER AND THE BISHOP

Vatican II's teaching on the episcopacy influenced subsequent perceptions of priestly identity. A theology of the episcopacy and the particular church, a task that had been left unfinished due to the abrupt
close of the First Vatican Council, was one of the great accomplish-
ments of the Second Vatican Council, which taught that the bishop has
the fullness of the sacrament of orders. Prior to Vatican II, this had been
a disputed theological question in the Church. Those who held that the
presbyter had the fullness of orders connected that fullness with the
ability to consecrate the Eucharist. A bishop was someone to whom
something—namely jurisdiction—had been added. If, however, according to the teaching of Vatican II, the bishop now had the fullness of the
priesthood, a priest had something less than that fullness, even though
he had full powers to consecrate the Eucharist and offer it in the name
of the Church. This had the effect of shifting the perceived relationship
between bishop and presbyter. Rather than a bishop being something
more than a priest, now the priest was perceived as being something
less than a bishop. This shift must be taken into account in the search
for a definition of priestly identity today.

The sacramental roles of bishop and presbyter no longer adequately
distinguish their respective identities. Presbyter and bishop essentially
fulfill the same role when presiding at the Eucharist. A presbyter can
now administer sacraments once reserved for the bishop, such as confirmation. In the early Church, the bishop was also the minister of baptism
and penance. Even though presbyters cannot ordain, this has not been
universally true in the history of the Roman Catholic Church.[16]

However, what does distinguish bishops and presbyters is their relationship to the communion of churches. A bishop represents his particular church in the communion of churches within the universal Church,
and a presbyter does not. A bishop presides over a grouping of the faithful that is identified as fully Church, and a presbyter does not. The presbyter's priesthood shares in the priesthood and mission of the bishop.[17]
Depending upon the bishop in the exercise of his own proper power, the
presbyter takes the place of the bishop in presiding over groupings of
the faithful, since it is impossible for the bishop always and everywhere
to preside over the whole flock in his church.[18] Even though, as we have

seen, a comparison of episcopal identity with priestly identity reveals limited differences in terms of sacramental powers, from an ecclesiological point of view, one finds a much greater difference.

This rather negative description of the priesthood of a presbyter as a partial realization of the priesthood of the bishop can be corrected by a positive description of that segment of the local church he serves, the parish.

A THEOLOGY OF THE PARISH

Years before the Second Vatican Council, Karl Rahner attempted to articulate a theology of the parish.[19] He points out that the parish and the pastor are *jure divino* in the same way that the Church, papacy, and episcopate are, even though church law would not easily concede this point. By this Rahner means that a parish is something more than an organization instituted by positive, human, church law to facilitate the pastoral care of people living in the same place. Rahner identifies the parish as "the representative actuality of the Church; the Church appears and manifests itself in the event of the central life of the parish."[20] Rahner argues that the Church is necessarily a local and localized community. This means that it achieves its highest degree of actuality where it *acts*, that is, where it teaches, prays, offers the Sacrifice of Christ, etc.[21] This is where the Church as institution becomes the Church as event in place and time and does this as a community. The parish is not a division of a larger segment of the Church, but "the concentration of the Church into its own event-fullness."[22] The parish is "the highest degree of actuality of the total church."[23]

At Vatican II the Dogmatic Constitution on the Church affirmed the presence of the Church in these local congregations:

> This church of Christ is really present in all legitimately organized local groups of the faithful which, united with their pastors, are also called churches in the New Testament. For these are in fact, in their own localities, the new people called by God, in the holy Spirit with full conviction (1 Thess I:5). In them the faithful are gathered together by the preaching of the Gospel of Christ, and the mystery of the Lord's Supper is cele-

brated, "so that, by means of the flesh and blood of the Lord the whole brotherhood and sisterhood of the body may be welded together..."

In these communities, though they may often be small and poor, or dispersed, Christ is present through whose power and influence the one, holy, catholic and apostolic church is constituted.[24]

Even though the document does not actually say that these groups are parishes, it does refer to them as congregations. Furthermore, it is difficult to identify a particular church as a community. Christ is present in congregations, and the congregation is truly Church.

Christifideles Laici, Pope John Paul II's Apostolic Exhortation on the Laity (1988), affirms the same point in signaling the pastor's role in the bond of communion between the parish and the particular church:

The ecclesial community, while always having a universal dimension, finds its most immediate and visible expression in the parish. It is there that the church is seen locally... It is necessary that in the light of faith all rediscover the true meaning of the parish, that is, the place where the very "mystery" of the church is present and at work... Plainly and simply, the parish is founded on a theological reality, because it is a eucharistic community. This means that the parish is a community properly suited for celebrating the eucharist, the living source for its upbuilding and the sacramental bond of its being in full communion with the whole church. Such suitableness is rooted in the fact that the parish is a community of faith and an organic community, that is, constituted by the ordained ministers and other Christians, in which the pastor—who represents the diocesan bishop—is the hierarchical bond with the entire particular church.[25]

This passage identifies the parish as a eucharistic community. Notably absent are any references to baptism. Also, identifying parishes solely in terms of the Eucharist does not distinguish them from other groups who regularly celebrate the Eucharist, but are not parishes.

In Rahner's theology the Church is also "most apprehensively and most intensively event in the celebration of the Eucharist."[26] This requires the specificity of place and a community gathered together in one and the same place. Rahner describes the difference in the "placeness" of the parish, saying that other types of Christian communities are united by factors other than purely geographical togetherness. Certainly the parish is identified as a face-to-face community, while a particular church under the ministry of a bishop does not have that same immediacy.

Rahner cites a number of limitations inherent in the parish. As noted above, if identified eucharistically, the parish is not the only form of local church in which the universal Church becomes event. There are many eucharistic celebrations which do not determine a parish community. For example, school groups, monastic communities, and youth groups may celebrate the Eucharist, but they are not necessarily parishes. Rahner has difficulty distinguishing the "placeness" of the Eucharist and the "placeness" of the parish, since they do not necessarily coincide in his analysis. He states that "the parish is still *de facto* and *de jure* the primary, normal, and original form of local community—and this simply because the parish exists by the principle of place alone."[27] He identifies place as the location in which Christians live together, have their homes, and come together as neighbors.[28] In our own time, when parish boundaries are sometimes more fluid and when monasteries identify the vow of stability as a "sense of place," this argument of geographical location is less than convincing.

I believe that this dilemma within Rahner's analysis of the parish can be resolved if a eucharistic theology of the parish is complemented with a baptismal theology of the parish. Rahner wrote his article well before the restoration of the catechumenate after Vatican II. What distinguishes the eucharistic community of the parish from the eucharistic community of a monastic community, school, hospital, or youth group is that the latter do not generally evangelize, prepare catechumens, baptize them, and continue to nurture them in the context of a stable faith community. Historically, baptismal churches were distinguished from other kinds of congregations. In the fourth and fifth centuries, when local congregations spread out from the cities into rural areas, major churches were distinguished from lesser churches by their right to baptize. A full-fledged parish in the system of baptismal churches formed new Christians in the catechumenate, received them into full communion, and oversaw their further formation in faith and witness.[29]

Within a theology of baptism, the parish is the contextualized and particular *place* of Christian formation. With reference to Karl Rahner's theology of the universal Church coming to *event* in the parish, we can add that it comes to *event* in a particular *place,* in particular circumstances and a particular culture and within a particular community. Even though baptism is ritualized in the sacramental rite of baptism, the ritual marks a number of stages within a process of initiation that encompasses the entire life of the parish community. The initiation of adults is the responsibility of all the baptized,[30] not only through their active participation as sponsors and catechists, but also through the witness of their lives and the welcome they extend to new members of a vibrant Christian community. As a baptismal community, the parish is a formation community in Christian living.

Baptism also entails mission. Just as Jesus' public mission followed directly after his baptism in the Jordan and anointing by the Holy Spirit, so are Christians sent to give witness to their faith and to live baptismal lives. A parish is apostolic not only because it reflects the apostolic faith, but also because it is sent on a mission. The Church by its very nature is missionary because "it has its origin in the mission of the Son and the Holy Spirit."[31] Too few parishes have a sense of mission, of being sent not only to serve their internal religious and educational needs, but also to extend the work of Christ into the larger community. Even though "mission statements" perhaps originate from secular corporate structures, nevertheless, it would be advantageous for parishes to formulate them in order to become more aware of their missionary identity.

A parish priest's mission is to the community of the parish. What *Ad Gentes,* the Decree on the Church's Missionary Activity, defines as the duty of missionaries describes as well the responsibility of a presbyter charged with the pastoral leadership of a parish:

> Therefore, missionaries, the fellow workers of God, should raise up communities of the faithful, so that walking worthy of the calling to which they have been called, they might carry out the priestly, prophetic and royal offices entrusted to them by

God. In this way the christian community will become a sign of
God's presence in the world. Through the eucharistic sacrifice
it goes continually to the Father with Christ, carefully nourished with the word of God it bears witness to Christ, it walks
in charity and is enlivened by an apostolic spirit.[32]

A presbyter's mission to his parish is to enable that parish to be apostolic, not only in the sense that it professes apostolic faith, but also in
the sense that the parish is sent to bear witness to Christ in charity.

A parish priest's identity flows from his mission to his parish community. Karl Rahner comments that "the New Testament usage never
designates the priest's office in terms of the language of cult, but always
that of apostolic and pastoral work."[33] Priests are servants. Even though
priestly service is associated with the Last Supper in John's Gospel, and
the liturgy is the source and summit not only of Christian life but of
priestly life, Rahner notes that what arises from the liturgy—the apostolic, prophetic, and pastoral aspect of the priestly vocation—is "the existentially determining factor in his life, the thing that sets a special
stamp upon his Christian life."[34] That work is the contextual and particular existential embodiment of what he celebrates sacramentally.

PRESBYTER AND ECCLESIAL COMMUNION

Within this baptismal context, a presbyter experiences his pastoral
identity through the pastoral care of his community. In Roman Catholicism we have developed an understanding of the priestly identity of the
priest, but we have not done as well in developing an understanding of
his pastoral identity because we have not attended to the particular community, the parish, where he exercises pastoral care.

Many baptized persons are called to give pastoral care in such roles
as parish administrators, catechists, liturgical ministers, and directors of
catechumenate programs. Many of them do so as professional ecclesial
lay ministers. What distinguishes them from the ordained pastor is that
in the case of the ordained minister the community elects this person for
ordination by prayer to the Holy Spirit and the laying on of hands by the
bishop to represent them in communions corresponding to the threefold

office: communion of churches within a pastoral office; communion with Christ's self-offering within a priestly office; and communion in apostolic faith within a prophetic office. The presbyter represents his people in the communion of churches through his participation in the priesthood of the bishop. He represents the ecclesial body of Christ in Christ's eucharistic prayer to the Father and is able to represent Christ to his people in the sacraments. He exercises a prophetic office in proclaiming the faith of the apostolic church to this community. Ultimately, a presbyter's identity is defined representationally rather than functionally. His representational role is not limited to his priestly role within the Eucharist, but extends to the rest of the threefold office. It is not simply a formal role, but entails particular pastoral responsibilities.

Perhaps the most important role of ordained ministry is to assure the communion of a local community both with the apostolic tradition and with other eucharistic communities so that the local church is a communion in communion with other communions. This is ministry to the apostolicity and communion of the Church. We do not generally speak of presbyters as being in apostolic succession. The college of bishops is in succession to the apostolic college.[35] Thus, the presbyter's claim as guarantor of apostolicity is tied to his relationship with his bishop. The presbyter extends the bishop's teaching role to the particular circumstances of the baptismal community that presbyter serves.

Consequently, there is both a synchronic communion of churches within the universal Church and a diachronic communion in history with the apostolic faith. Since each bishop is a member of the college of bishops by virtue of his episcopal ordination and communion with the bishop of Rome, he represents his particular church within the communion of particular churches. The communion of churches is mediated by the communion of bishops. Parishes are united within this communion because of the relationship between priests and their bishop. Each particular church is defined as an altar community under the sacred ministry of the bishop. There can be no Eucharist apart from communion with other eucharistic communities. A Eucharist in isolation or division is a self-contradiction. Hence, ordination is more than a sacred power to confect the Eucharist; it is also the authorization through the election of the community, prayer to the Holy Spirit, and the laying on of hands to represent the community within the communion of churches.

PRESBYTER AS PASTORAL LEADER

The pastoral identity of the presbyter as pastor of a baptismal community includes the pastoral care of a church. Even though Roman Catholicism identifies the basic unit of the Church as the particular church under the ministry of the bishop, the particular church comes to event through the baptismal community of the parish. However, the difference between a particular church (the diocese) and a parish is that a parish cannot exist apart from its relationship to its bishop, who in turn represents the particular church in the communion of churches of the universal Church. A church cannot exist as Church in isolation, but must be in communion with other parishes and particular churches. This communion is accomplished through the personal relationships of ordained presbyters to their bishops and of bishops to other bishops within the college of bishops. Ordination constitutes this network of relationships by authorizing a person to represent ecclesial communities in these relationships.[36]

A parish does not include everything within itself needed to constitute a church, since it is lacking the ministry to represent it in the communion of particular churches. However, as we have seen, it does have ecclesial identity as long as it is in relationship with the rest of the particular church through the relationship of the presbyter to the local bishop. Here a presbyter is defined not by what he does not represent, namely the particular church, but by what he does represent, namely the parish. As the parish has an ecclesial identity, so the presbyter finds his identity in relationship to this segment of the Church. He represents it and is the primary person responsible for its pastoral care. He has oversight of the various ministries within it.

As the person who is charged with the internal communion of the parish and its communion with the particular church, the presbyter presides over the sacrament of communion, the Eucharist. Presbyteral identity envisioned as a pastoral charge to a baptismal community is not in conflict with priestly identity within a eucharistic theology. Baptism and Eucharist celebrate the same mystery of Christ's dying and rising. What is celebrated once and for all in baptism is celebrated repeatedly in the Eucharist and in a sense is completed there, so there is a direct trajectory between the two sacraments. Conversely, what is celebrated in the Eucharist finds historical and particular expression in the everyday life of the baptismal community. This is the sense in which the Eucharist is the "source and summit" of the activity of the Church.[37] The unity between the presbyter's pastoral identity and his priestly identity reflects the unity of these two sacraments.

A presbyter's role of pastoral leadership encompasses his priestly and prophetic roles, but also includes the discernment and oversight of other ministries within the parish. A presbyter does not exercise pastoral leadership alone, but always collegially. This is not only the collegium of the presbyterium, but also the collegiality of shared ministry in a fully functioning baptismal community. A fully developed catechumenate implies a diversity and multiplicity of ministries and parish participation that extend far beyond liturgical ministries. Catechists, parish visitors, directors of faith formation, youth ministers, sponsors, those charged with sacramental preparation and hospitality—all need direction, inspiration, and orchestration. All are necessary for evangelization, sacramental preparation, mystagogia, and the ongoing pastoral care of a congregation. Parishioners are not just consumers of these services, but actively participate in ministry, whether informally or formally as ecclesial lay ministers. This is as it should be, for ministry and *diakonia* are attributes of the Church before they are attributes of an individual.

PRESBYTER AS PROPHET

A presbyter fulfills his prophetic function within a baptismal community by preaching the Gospel to awaken, nurture, and sustain the faith of the community. When the Scriptures are proclaimed, the community recognizes its faith in them and interprets its experience accordingly. The function of ordained ministry within the assembly is to guarantee both the apostolicity of what is read and to assure that the texts serve as an exemplar of the community's identity.[38] Ordination empowers a person not only to perform this function, but also to represent the community and so link the community to the text.

The succession with the apostolic tradition occurs through the ministry of the bishop, since the college of bishops is in succession to the apostolic college. This is ritualized in the Church by the succession of ministers ordained with the laying on of hands, although this succession cannot be documented for the period prior to the second century. The purpose of the succession is to assure that the faith of a present church is in continuity with the apostolic faith of the first century.

Louis-Marie Chauvet describes how continuity is assured through the preaching of an ordained minister in this way:

1. In the Liturgy of the Word, texts are read from the canonically received Bible.

2. These texts, which relate a past experience of the people of God, are proclaimed as the living Word of God for today.

3. The assembly recognizes them as an exemplar of its identity.

4. The assembly is under the leadership of an ordained minister who exercises the symbolic function of guarantor of this exemplarity and the apostolicity of what is read.[39]

Notice the interplay between the ordained minister and the rest of the assembly in this process. It is not just any text that is read to the community, but a text from a canonically received Bible. The Scriptures have been officially received in the Church. The ongoing reception of this canon occurs as the assembly recognizes the texts as an exemplar of its identity. In other words, the assembly recognizes itself and its faith in the proclamation of the Word. The ordained minister functions as a link between this assembly and the community that produced the text, because he witnesses to apostolicity. As a member of the assembly, the ordained minister also witnesses to the exemplarity of the text because he stands within the assembly and testifies that this text reflects the present life and faith of the community. Just as in the Eucharist the priest functions both *in persona Christi* and *in persona ecclesiae*, representing Christ to the community and the community to Christ, so in the liturgical proclamation of the Word, the ordained minister connects the community to the faith proclaimed in the text and represents the canonicity and apostolicity of the text to the community. The official proclamation of the Gospel in liturgical prayer belongs to an ordained minister, because it is not just a matter of reading a text from a book, a function that any literate person can perform, but an act of official witnessing on behalf of the community and in the name of the apostolic tradition.

Karl Rahner had a similar understanding of priestly identity with respect to the Word. His definition of priestly ministry is: "The priest is s/he who, related to an at least potential community, preaches the word of God by mandate of the church (more exactly: "on behalf of the church") as a whole and therefore officially and in such a way that s/he is entrusted with the highest levels of sacramental intensity of this word."[40] Perhaps we can say that the function of proclamation by an ordained minister is to stand *in persona Verbi*, that is, to witness to the canonicity of the text to the community.

A presbyter primarily but not exclusively exercises his prophetic role in his preaching. He also exercises prophetic leadership in giving direction to the parish council and in setting priorities. In addition to linking the community to its apostolic roots, the presbyter in his prophetic role calls the community into its future. This is facilitated by a certain "over-againstness" of the ordained to the community he serves. He is not simply a representative of the community who can only repeat back to the community its own prejudices and biases; he brings something new. Ordination is not just election, but also epiclesis, the invocation of the Spirit.

A baptismal community lives in the power of the Spirit. The prayer of the blessing of the baptismal water evokes the power of the Spirit of God hovering over the waters of chaos: "At the very dawn of creation your Spirit breathed on the waters, making them the wellspring of all holiness."[41] The epiclesis of the prayer of ordination for a presbyter also invokes the Spirit of holiness: "Almighty Father, grant, we pray, to these servants of yours the dignity of the priesthood, renew deep within them the Spirit of holiness."[42] This holiness is destined for the people of God, that they may be renewed in the waters of rebirth and nourished from the altar[43] so to be transformed into one people and be brought at last to the fulfillment of God's kingdom. This holiness, however, is lived in historical time within the concrete and particular circumstances of the event which is the parish.

This analysis of presbyteral identity within parish identity as a baptismal community does not address all instances of presbyteral identity. However, it does attempt to correlate an understanding of the Church as a communion at various levels with a theology of ordained ministry in service to those communions, thus contributing to an understanding of the historical and contextualized identity both of the parish and of the pastor.

NOTES

1. For a sampling of books from just the past ten years, see *Priests for a New Millennium: A Series of Essays on the Ministerial Priesthood by the Catholic Bishops of the United States* (Washington, D.C.: Secretariat for Priestly Life and Ministry, 2000); Congregation for the Clergy, *Concluding Message to All Priests in the World: International Symposium Celebrating the 30th Anniversary of the Promulgation of the Conciliar Decree* Presbyterorum ordinis (Washington, D.C.: United States Catholic Conference, 1996); Avery Dulles, *The Priestly Office: A Theological Reflection* (New York/Mahwah, N.J.: Paulist Press, 1997); Donald Goergan, *Being a Priest Today* (Collegeville, Minn.: The Liturgical Press, 1992); Donald B. Cozzens, *The Changing Face of the Priesthood* (Collegeville, Minn.: The Liturgical Press, 2000); Donald Goergan, ed., *The Theology of Priesthood* (Collegeville, Minn.: The Liturgical Press, 2000); Thomas Rausch, *Priesthood Today: An Appraisal* (New York/Mahwah, N.J.: Paulist Press, 1991); Susan K. Wood, *Sacramental Orders* (Collegeville, Minn.: The Liturgical Press, 2000).

2. Chapter 2 of *Lumen Gentium (LG)* attributes the threefold office to the people of God. Chapter 3 applies it to bishops and priests. Chapter 4 applies it to the laity.

3. *LG* 28.

4. In this article I am presupposing and further developing work I've already done on priestly identity. See Susan K. Wood, "Priestly Identity: Sacrament of the Ecclesial Community," *Worship* 69 (March 1995) 109–127; and *Sacramental Orders* (Collegeville, Minn.: The Liturgical Press, 2000) chapter 5.

5. James O'Malley argues that the documents *Presbyterorum Ordinis, Christus Dominus*, and *Optatam Totius* presuppose that presbyteral ministry serves a stable community composed of the faithful, a community in which a regular rhythm of liturgies of Word and sacrament will be celebrated. The documents also presuppose that a priest-minister is in hierarchical communion with his bishop. J. W. O'Malley, "Priesthood, Ministry and Religious Life: Some Historical and Historiographical Considerations," *Theological Studies* 49 (1988) 250; see also "One Priesthood: Two Traditions," in *Concert of Charisms: Ordained Ministry in Religious Life,* ed. Paul K. Hennessy (New York/Mahwah, N.J.: Paulist Press, 1997).

6. See, for example, Dennis Michael Ferrara, "Representation or Self-Effacement? The Axiom *In Persona Christi* in St. Thomas and the Magisterium," *Theological Studies* 55 (1994) 195–224; "In persona Christi: Towards a Second Naiveté,"

Theological Studies 57 (1996) 65–88; Sarah Butler, "'In Persona Christi': A Response to Dennis M. Ferraro," *Theological Studies* 55 (1994) 61–80; Sarah Butler, "Priestly Identity: 'Sacrament' of Christ the Head," *Worship* 70 (1996) 290–306; David Power, "Church Order: The Need for Redress," *Worship* 71 (1997) 296–309; Thomas Rausch, "Priestly Identity: Priority of Representation and the Iconic Argument," *Worship* 73 (1999) 169–179; Susan Wood, "Priestly Identity: Sacrament of the Ecclesial Community," *Worship* 69 (1995) 109–127.

7. *LG* 26.

8. Ibid.

9. I am indebted to Michael Root and to discussions of the U. S. Lutheran–Roman Catholic Dialogue for reflections on this relationship.

10. Karl Rahner, *Theology for Renewal: Bishops, Priests, Laity* (New York: Sheed and Ward, 1962) 42.

11. *LG* 19.

12. *LG* 18.

13. *Sacrosanctum Concilium (SC)* 41.

14. *LG* 28.

15. Ibid.

16. Mitered abbots were given jurisdiction to ordain in earlier periods.

17. *LG* 28.

18. *SC* 42.

19. Karl Rahner, "Theology of the Parish," in *The Parish: From Theology to Practice*, ed. Hugo Rahner (Westminster, Md.: The Newman Press, 1958) 23–35.

20. Ibid., 25. See also Jerry T. Farmer, *Ministry in Community: Rahner's Vision of Ministry,* Louvain Theological and Pastoral Monographs #13 (Louvain: Peeters Press and Grand Rapids, Mich.: W. B. Eerdmans, 1993) 134–136.

21. Rahner, "Theology of the Parish," 26.

22. Ibid., 30.

23. Ibid.

24. *LG* 26.

25. John Paul II, apostolic exhortation *Christifideles Laici* 26, *Origins* 18/35 (1989) 573.

26. Rahner, "Theology of the Parish," 28.

27. Ibid., 31. However, Rahner seems to mitigate this position somewhat in *Theology of Pastoral Action* (New York: Herder and Herder, 1958) 100-106, where he admits the possibility of a personal parish—of students, actors, lawyers—that can have as much justification as a territorial parish. He says that "it can be of far greater Christian significance than the more artificial society created by the neighborhood in which the parishioners happen to live" (p. 101).

28. Rahner, "Theology of the Parish," 31–32.

29. James A. Coriden, *The Parish in Catholic Tradition* (New York/Mahwah, N.J.: Paulist Press, 1997) 25.

30. Rite of the Christian Initiation of Adults, 9.

31. *Ad Gentes (AG)* 2.

32. *AG* 15.

33. Karl Rahner, *Theology for Renewal Bishops, Priests, Laity* (New York: Sheed and Ward, 1962) 41.

34. Ibid., 40.

35. *LG* 20.

36. Note that authorization is not the same thing as delegation. Authorization is accomplished through prayer to the Holy Spirit and the laying on of hands. It is not simply the act of the community, but includes both election by the community and empowerment by the Holy Spirit. Delegation is simply naming one person within the community to represent the rest.

37. *SC* 10.

38. Louis-Marie Chauvet, *Symbol and Sacrament: A Sacramental Reinterpretation of Christian Existence* (Collegeville, Minn.: The Liturgical Press, 1995) 21.

39. Ibid., chapter 6.

40. Karl Rahner, "The Point of Departure in Theology for Determining the Nature of the Priestly Office," *Theological Investigations* 12 (New York: Seabury Press, A Crossroad Book, 1974) 36. The English translation is from *Concilium* 43, p. 85. Cited by Farmer, *Ministry in Community*, 167.

41. The Rite of Christian Initiation of Adults, Prayer Over the Water, 354.

42. Second typical edition of the Rite of Ordination of Priests (1990) 131.

43. From the ordination prayer for presbyters, 131.

Envisioning a Theology of Ordained and Lay Ministry

Lay/Ordained Ministry—Current Issues of Ambiguity

Kenan B. Osborne, O.F.M.

At the beginning of the present millennium, the relationship between lay ministry and ordained ministry in the Roman Catholic Church
has, as yet, to be clarified. The essays in this volume attempt to envision
a theology of lay ministry that will provide some clarification. The following essay is a part of this endeavor and relies on the entries of David
Power, O.M.I. and Kevin Seasoltz, O.S.B. Both of these essays are historical in their focus, and my own contribution is also historical in its
focus.

My intent is to highlight several current issues of ambiguity found
even in official documents of the Church. The documents from Vatican
II contained many significant and groundbreaking sections on lay ministry today. Subsequent documents from the Roman Curia have ambi-
tiously strengthened the role of lay ecclesial ministers.

Excellent as these documents are, they have also presented mixed
signals, which are particularly evident in the presentations on the interrelationship of lay and clerical ministers. This interrelationship is a sensitive topic, since the theologies of baptismal ordination, presbyteral
ordination, and official institution into lay ecclesial ministries have had
lengthy theological histories. The mixed signals that are found in the official documents have engendered serious questions and disturbing fric-
tions, doubts, and insecurities.

The first section of this essay deals with the twentieth-century
legacy regarding the theology of sacrament. The second section deals in

detail with two major historical/theological themes stemming from this
twentieth-century legacy. The third section offers some conclusions and
implications regarding today's theologically unsettled status of lay/
cleric ministerial relationship.

I. THE LEGACY OF THE TWENTIETH CENTURY

Traditional forms of differentiation in the lay/cleric relationship
have been challenged by a number of factors that arose during the twentieth century. These challenges stem basically from twelve major theological events that occurred in the last century. In today's Catholic
Church, the relationship between cleric and lay cannot be understood
nor can ambiguities be resolved unless one takes into account this historical legacy.

1. Historical Research on All the Sacraments
Historical research on sacramental ritual and theology began in
earnest from 1900 onward.[1] This historical research indicates that the
differentiation of cleric and lay has never been uniform in the history
of the Church. Today, a theologically immutable understanding or definition of both priest and bishop cannot be maintained, nor is there a
theologically immutable divide between priest/bishop on the one hand
and lay Christian on the other. In the course of Christian history there
have been several distinct theologies and functions of both priest and
bishop which do not coincide with the positions of the Scholastics, of
the Tridentine documents, and of the manual theologies of the last two
centuries. For the first time in the entire history of Catholic scholarship, theologians have access to in-depth researched histories of all
seven sacraments. Historical data has challenged time-honored theological positions on all sacraments, and for our purposes on the sacrament of orders.

2. Jesus as the Primordial Sacrament
and the Church as the Foundational Sacrament
In the second half of the twentieth century, both Jesus and the
Church were presented as primordial and basic sacraments. This position
has had a major impact on the way one understands all of the Christian

sacraments. Today no theology of ministry is possible unless it is based on the ministry of Jesus. The theological relationship of ministry to the humanness of Jesus has been enriched by the view that Jesus is the primordial sacrament or analog of all ministries in the Church. The *Church itself* is a sacrament of Jesus and, therefore, the *ministering Church* is a foundational sacrament for all ecclesial ministries. It is remarkable that in the *Catechism of the Catholic Church* the section on the seven sacraments does not include this view of ecclesial sacramentality as one of its key operative factors.[2] Jesus as primordial sacrament and the Church as fundamental sacrament are treated briefly in the section on the Church and even more briefly if at all in the section on the sacraments.[3] Many books on the sacraments written during the second half of the twentieth century developed a christological and ecclesiological understanding of all sacraments in which Jesus and the Church were foundational sacraments. The sacramental studies of Otto Semmelroth, Karl Rahner, and Edward Schillebeeckx were highly influential throughout the latter part of the twentieth century and their ideas were influential during Vatican II. The documents of Vatican II clearly present the Church as a fundamental sacrament. Why this aspect of sacramental theology is downgraded in the Catechism remains problematic.

3. The Liturgical Renewal

Liturgical renewal began early in the nineteenth century and achieved a major status during Vatican II. Post-Vatican II official documents have also pressed for liturgical renewal. Renewal centers were set up in major European areas as well as in Canada and the United States. Long before Vatican II some churches had already relocated the main altars. Masses had been celebrated in the vernacular. General absolution had become standard in various European parishes. This renewal of liturgy refocused both the sacramental and the non-sacramental ministries of clerics and laypeople. In the United States, the renewal of liturgy spearheaded by Virgil Michel of St. John's University stressed the social dimension as essential to liturgical service. The conciliar and post-conciliar official changes in the liturgy reflect a new theology of the liturgy involving vernacular participation, lay ministerial participation, emphasis on the proclamation of the Word, ecumenical and social relationships, etc. The twenty-first century has inherited sacramental liturgies that have been radically—not superficially—revised.

4. La Nouvelle Théologie

The movement called *La Nouvelle Théologie* shifted theological thought from scholastic formulations to early patristic and early medieval thought forms which were not at all similar to the Aristotelian-based theology of high Scholasticism. The revival of patristic theology and practice influenced the theology of Church, of ritual, and of ministry. This movement also changed the understanding of revelation from a revelation of doctrines to a revelation of personal encounter. Primarily God does not reveal teachings. God reveals himself.

This change regarding the theology of revelation has seriously challenged key aspects of ministerial theology for which ecclesial leaders and theologians had claimed immutability. All Christian ministry and each Christian minister is meant to reflect both the ministry of Jesus and Jesus the minister. When Christian ministers and their ministries do reflect Jesus, we can see what is truly changeless. The structuring of ministry, however, is historical and temporal and therefore changeable. Even a given structure of Christian ministry may not image Jesus and, as a consequence, the ministerial structure itself needs to be changed.

5. Existential, Phenomenological, and Postmodern Philosophies

Contemporary philosophies developed in the twentieth century have produced a paradigm change in the ways that new generations of the Western world envision the universe, human life, and the very meaning of existence. These philosophies have had a subtle but strong influence on the ways in which clerical and lay ministries in the Church are understood. In most of these philosophies, the onto-theological temporality of being and an epistemological return to the subject are fundamental. As a result, there is a strong operative presence of relativity throughout all forms of reality. The linguistic movement started by F. de Saussure emphasized the relativity of all synchronic and diachronic language events, eliminating any unchangeable linguistic definitions of persons and things. Since Christian ministry in all its forms is historical and temporal, it is intrinsically changeable. Since language is intrinsically relative, ministerial language cannot be seen as absolute. Since Christian ministry in postmodern philosophical thought is understandable only through personal perception, it is therefore to some degree subjective. For example, two of Maurice Merleau-Ponty's studies on philosophical thought, *The Phenomenology of Perception* and *The Pri-*

macy of Perception,[4] maintain that our knowledge of the world derives only from our respective standpoints of perception. We see and interpret the world primarily through our own perception. Martin Heidegger in *Being and Time* focuses on the subjective understanding of being (*Dasein*) and relates being (*Dasein*) in an ontological way to temporality, i.e., historical relativity.[5] Both of these authors, as also Paul Ricoeur, have had enormous influence on contemporary Catholic theology.[6] These three authors are specifically mentioned, but their positions are shared with a vast majority of postmodern philosophers. Temporality, historicity, linguistic relativity, and a form of subjectivity have had serious impact on the theology of ministry.

6. The Documents of Vatican II

In the documents of Vatican II the bishops drew up a list of official criteria for liturgical worship. These criteria radically changed the role of the layperson in the Church. At the council, the bishops voted to change the definition of priesthood into a form radically different from traditional scholastic and neo-scholastic formulations. When the episcopacy was reinstated into the theology of holy orders, the definition of bishop was also radically changed. Subsequent official documents on ecumenical issues have taken into account the forms of ministry in the Anglican, Protestant, and Orthodox churches, in which one of the major ministries is episcopacy.

7. Liberation Theology

Liberation theology has raised serious ministerial issues. Three of them have particular meaning for ministry in the new millennium.

- The relationship between a kingdom-centered theology and a Church-centered theology continues to be a sensitive issue between curial direction on the one hand and local theological and pastoral work on the other.

- The lack of priestly ministry for the majority of Catholics today remains a major scandal. The issue is complicated by the inability of the current hierarchy to make any radical change in the canonical qualifications for priestly ordination.

- Inter-religious dialogues have raised serious questions on the issue of "salvation" and the role that both Jesus and the Church play in this matter. This issue has called into question the ministry of evangelization itself, whether the ministry is that of a cleric or a layperson.

8. Feminist Theology

The influence of feminist theology has presented Roman Catholic ministry with an issue that will not disappear in spite of papal statements to the contrary. Central to feminist theology is the role of women in all ministries in the Church. Already women's roles in church ministry have been profoundly changed. Nonetheless, there are glass ceilings that prevent women from entering into all forms of church ministry. The theological appeal to Jesus' selection of the Twelve as an unchangeable reason for the exclusion of women in the diaconate, priesthood, and episcopacy has been seriously questioned. Even in some church documentation since Vatican II, women in the Church are still placed below men in the Church. On the other hand, some official church documentation forcibly states the equality of all men and women. The full equality of women in the Church, however, remains in doubt.

9. The Renewal of the Permanent Diaconate

The renewal of the permanent diaconate has resurfaced many ministerial questions: e.g., ministry and celibacy, ministry and gender, collaborative forms of ministry. The self-identity of a deacon today remains unclear. Some church leaders would like deacons to be primarily liturgical ministers; others want deacons to be multi-focused in their ministries. Although in the discussions at Vatican II a renewal of the diaconate was strongly endorsed by bishops from developing countries, deacons in post-Vatican II church life are overwhelmingly present in developed countries and few, if any, deacons are currently present in the developing countries.

10. The Catechism of the Catholic Church

The appearance of the Catechism has seriously complicated the theology of priestly and lay ministry. Throughout the Catechism there is never an indication that there might be alternative theological positions beyond the theological positions presented in the Catechism. However, other equally viable and acceptable theologies are part of Roman Catholic thought.[7] In the theological sections of the Catechism the authors present only one theological view, giving the impression that this particular theological view is the "teaching of the Roman Catholic Church today." This lack of theological honesty creates serious problems. Many Catholics, including bishops, priests, and lay ministers, consider the Catechism in its entirety to be the only authentic teaching of the Church. Many other Catholics, including bishops, priests, theologians, and a number of laymen and laywomen, accept the Catechism as *the* statement of the Catholic faith. As a Franciscan theologian, I realize that almost all the theological parts of the Catechism are largely based on Thomistic and neo-Thomistic theologies. These theological parts of the Catechism do express *a theological interpretation* of our faith. The Franciscan tradition clearly offers a different but eminently acceptable theological framework. Both of these two theological traditions have offered papally approved yet distinct theologies of Church and ministry.

11. A Multicultural Church

The rise of a multicultural appreciation of the Roman Catholic Church presents a theology of ministry with many unanswered issues. In the Church is there an over-emphasis on multiculturalism and a de-emphasis on equiculturalism? Is the Roman-Western approach the benchmark for any and all cultural adaptations? All cultures have forms of religious leaders, sages, and wise people. Can these religious leaders be fully incorporated into both clerical and lay ministries, or does the Western-Roman canonical legislation remain unchangeable? Catholics worldwide are only at the beginning of a major theological multicultural or equicultural renewal of the teaching and practice of the Church. A radical reformulation of Catholic theology using Confucian, Daoist, Buddhist, and Hindu ways of thought rather than Western ways of thought has only just begun. A similar rethinking of Catholic theology using thought-patterns and symbols from the many cultures in Africa and the native populations in both North and South America is also just beginning. The future development of these revisionings will challenge the entire theological framework of Roman-Western Christian thought.

12. The Hermeneutics of Biblical Studies

In 1943 Pius XII's encyclical *Divino Afflante Spiritu* provided an endorsement of biblical criticism and the hermeneutics involved in this methodology for the Old Testament. John XXIII endorsed a similar hermeneutic for the New Testament. As this methodology of biblical interpretation became more and more a part of Catholic life, traditional Catholics became vocal and, at times, belligerently so. The new ways of interpreting key passages in the New Testament on both priesthood and episcopacy presented the Catholic Church with a rethinking of core elements in ecclesiology, namely, issues on ministry and hierarchy. The Dogmatic Constitution on Divine Revelation promulgated at Vatican II endorsed biblical criticism, but this does not mean that the document endorses everything that is stated in the name of biblical criticism. However, the tremors from these seismic hermeneutical changes remain with us as we begin the third millennium.

The above list highlights some of the major legacies which the twentieth century has given to the new millennium. There was and still is a struggle to bring all of these differing issues together into a clear theology of ministry. The theological disunity in these factors remains operative. As a result, it is difficult to project in any clear way how the relationship of ordained ecclesial ministry to lay ecclesial ministry will actually be construed and presented in, say, 2006 or 2010 or 20XX. This irresolution indicates that the periodic clashes between ordained and lay ecclesial ministries will not disappear. However, an analysis of current clashes is helpful, since the day-to-day major areas of ambiguity and friction between cleric and lay more often than not point to deeper causes. It is these deeper causes that I intend to analyze in the second part of this essay.

II. UNDERLYING CAUSES FOR TENSIONS

In the daily life of Christian ministry, clashes between clerical ministers —bishops, priests and deacons—and lay ecclesial ministers are fairly common. The reasons for these clashes are multiple. Generally, the clashes center on quite specific matters, such as:

– Personality conflicts between the ordained minister and the lay minister
– Lack of communication between the ordained minister and the lay minister

- Difference of age between the ordained minister and the lay minister
- Lack of a clear "job description"
- Gender, ethnic, and sexual orientation issues
- Financial inequalities

These conflictual issues and others similar to them are, in my opinion, symptomatic of much deeper dissensions. Most of the serious lay/cleric clashes exhibit symptoms of deeper theological problems. Efforts to assuage these clashes through conflict resolution or arbitration may help, but only for the short run. Assuredly, symptoms need to be treated, but if one remains only with the treatment of symptoms, the underlying causes of the symptoms will never be faced. Two systemic theological causes for these clashes are:

1. Insufficient understanding of the common ministry that belongs to all Christians through baptism and confirmation

2. Contemporary historical research on episcopacy, priesthood, and diaconate

1. Insufficient understanding of the common ministry that belongs to all Christians through baptism and confirmation

In the documents of Vatican II, the common ministry or common priesthood of all Christians is spelled out in great length, particularly in chapter 2 of *Lumen Gentium*. The theme of common ministry, however, is not limited to *Lumen Gentium*. It is a theme found in several conciliar documents. Indeed, one can say that the teaching on the common ministry of all Christians is one of the most consequential teachings of Vatican II.

After the council, other church documents on either ordained or lay ecclesial ministries were issued.[8] In most of them the common ministry of all believers is presented, if at all, in only a passing way as, for example, in the instruction on "Some Questions Regarding Collaboration of Nonordained Faithful in Priests' Sacred Ministry." This document contains a brief introductory section, entitled "Theological Principles," that includes: (1) seven paragraphs on the relationship of the "Common Priesthood of the Faithful and the Ministerial Priesthood"; (2) four paragraphs on the "Unity and Diversity of Ministerial Functions"; (3) four paragraphs on

the "Indispensability of the Ordained Ministry"; and (4) five paragraphs
on the "Collaboration of the Nonordained Faithful in Pastoral Ministry."
These four themes are presented as a statement of the "theological principles" underlying the remainder of the document. It is theologically
unbelievable that the authors of this document felt that this brief section
of the instruction could possibly resolve the serious questions on lay/or-
dained ministerial collaboration. Much less could this section establish
clear "theological principles" for an issue that remains profoundly unresolved. The bishops during Vatican II and the canonists in their formulation of the new code engaged in intensive discussions on these same
issues. In both sets of discussions, no resolution was attained. The theological resolution of this issue of the common priesthood of all believers and its relationship to the ministerial priesthood was left to future
investigation.

After this brief presentation, the instruction takes up at great length
the conflictual areas. However, the common ground of all ministries,
i.e., the "theological principles," does not play a major role in the material called "Practical Provisions." The authors go immediately to the
symptoms of conflict. The focus is clearly on the canonical reasons for
such conflicts. There is no probing of the more basic *systemic factors* in
the canonical areas of disputed ministerial boundaries and identities.

This official instruction represents simply one of many such documents that give only a brief mention of systemic factors and move immediately to symptomatic factors. Whenever there is no developed
grounding of clerical and lay ministry in the ministerial priesthood of
all believers, any and every conclusion on clerical and lay ministry will
remain unsatisfactory. In such instances the fundamental grounding of
either ordained and lay ministry is put to one side, with the result that a
theology of ordained ministry and lay ministry is seriously unbalanced.

In his volume *The Ecclesiology of Vatican II,* Bonaventure Kloppenburg, a *peritus* at the council and now a bishop in Brazil, culled the
conciliar documents and drew up a significant listing of shared ministries.[9] He spells out the exact wording of the documents with references to other related documentary statements.

1. All baptized and eucharistic Christians "enjoy a true equality
   with regard to the dignity and the activity which they share in the
   building up of the body of Christ" (*Lumen Gentium [LG]* 32).

2. All share in "carrying out the mission of the whole christian people in the church and in the world" (*LG* 31).

3. All "have an active part of their own in the life and activity of the church" (*Apostolicam Actuositatem [AA]* 10).

4. All are called upon by the Lord "to apply to the building up of the church and to its continual sanctification all the powers which they have received from the goodness of the Creator" (*LG* 32; cf. *AA* 2).

5. All "are appointed to this apostolate by the Lord himself" (*LG* 33).

6. All are "made sharers in their own way in the priestly, prophetic and kingly office of Christ" (*LG* 31; cf. *AA* 2).

7. "The supreme and eternal priest, Christ Jesus," wills to "continue his witness and his service through the laity also." He "gives them a share in his priestly office" (*LG* 34).

8. "Christ is the great prophet who... fulfils his prophetic office, not only through the hierarchy who teach in his name and by his power, but also through the laity" (*LG* 35).

9. "He establishes them [i.e., all baptized Christians] as witnesses and provides them with an appreciation of the faith and the grace of the word" (*LG* 35).

After assembling these passages from the documents of Vatican II, Kloppenburg immediately remarks: "What a fine doctrine this is, but it raises the question: why priesthood?"

Gérard Philips in his commentary on *Lumen Gentium* presents a detailed overview of the bishops' discussion on the same topic.[10] He notes that "the two types of priesthood are to be defined in the light of their relationship to Christ the high priest."[11] He stresses a triad for ministry: first and foundationally, Jesus; second, the priesthood of all believers; and third, presbyteral ministry. Let us consider to some degree the foundational basis for these relationships, namely, Jesus.

The title of the dogmatic constitution is *Lumen Gentium,* but the word "light" does not refer to the Church. Jesus himself is the light. The

entire ecclesiology presented in the document is based on Jesus. Whenever this light, Jesus, animates the Church, then the Church is truly
Church. Whenever this light, Jesus, is not reflected in church people,
structures, and regulations, then the Church itself is questionable. For
our understanding of ministry in the Church, not only is the common
priesthood of all believers a major cornerstone for its interpretation, but
Christology itself is even more fundamental. Jesus' own example of
ministering remains the key to ministry. It is the light that enlightens all
church ministry.

Two New Testament titles for Jesus, Jesus the servant (deacon—
διάκονος) and Jesus the high priest, shed light on all aspects of Christian ministry.[12] Service is key to the New Testament understanding of all
ministry. Ministry in the New Testament is based on the ministry of
Jesus, and *Lumen Gentium* enjoins this same approach to church ministry. Jesus is the model of the *tria munera*. How Jesus taught and
preached (prophet), how Jesus sanctified and made people holy (priest),
and how Jesus was a leader and guide (king)—these are what constitute
the foundational model for the ministry of bishops, priests, deacons, and
all other special ministries in the Church.[13]

Chapter 2 of *Lumen Gentium* gives a theological foundation to
every Christian involved in the teaching, sanctifying, and leading ministry of Jesus. The *tria munera* approach to ministry in the documents
of Vatican II makes no sense unless the primary analog of the *tria
munera* is Jesus himself. In the New Testament Jesus is indeed presented as a servant, διάκονος, and anyone who wishes to serve and minister in the community called Church must be a sacrament of Jesus the
deacon. In the apostolic Church every writer described the ministry of
Jesus as that of servant. Jesus came to serve, not to be served, and his
service made an enormous impression on all the communities represented in the New Testament.[14] The gospel passage, "I have not come to
be served but to serve," remains the heart of all ministry, and the towel
that Jesus used to wash the feet of his disciples remains the icon of all
ministry. Thomas Rausch stresses the early Church's use of the term
diakonia in reference to leadership and authority, as well as to Jesus
himself.[15]

Only once (Heb 5:10) does the New Testament calls Jesus priest,
(ιερευς). Jean Galot, bypassing momentarily this particular passage,
makes an argument that Jesus understood himself as a priest. He ex-

plores "the witness which Jesus himself bears concerning his own priest-hood."[16] His arguments are less than convincing, and contemporary scholars take issue with his interpretation.[17] The priestly dimension of Jesus is first related to what we call today the priesthood of all believers. Only then is it related to the ministerial priesthood. It is precisely these relationships which now need theological clarification. The current theo-logical inadequacy of these relationships is one of the primary systemic reasons why there are symptomatic clashes between ordained and nonor-dained ministries. There is today an insufficient theological understand-ing of the common ministry that belongs to all Christians. How does this common priestly ministry relate to Jesus as priest and how does it relate to the special priestly ministry in the Church? Until this is clarified, a solid theology of lay ecclesial ministry will remain a non-reality.

2. Contemporary historical research
on episcopacy, priesthood, and diaconate

Throughout the twentieth century a substantial group of Catholic scholars developed in-depth studies on the history of ordained ministry.[18] Nonetheless, key magisterial documents on episcopal, presbyteral, dia-conal, and lay ministries have presented ministry in ways which the find-ings from this historical research have seriously questioned.[19] The tension between historical research on early Christian ministry and certain magis-terial and episcopal statements which do not reflect this historical data has raised mixed signals. Today's lack of clarity in the understanding of or-dained ministry and lay ecclesial ministry has been exacerbated by this conflict of interpretations.

Research on sacramental history began in 1896, when a reputable Protestant scholar, Charles Lea, published a three-volume work: *A His-tory of Auricular Confession and Indulgences in the Latin Church.*[20] It contained a massive amount of scholarly research, but it was also heav-ily anti-Catholic. Nonetheless, Lea's study occasioned the beginning of contemporary Catholic research into the history of Christian sacra-ments. Prior to 1896 there had been few historical studies of the sacra-ments,[21] but after the publication of Lea's three volumes, historical and theological investigation on the sacraments took on a much more con-certed and deliberative form. In 1896, however, Catholic scholarship was not well equipped to address all the issues presented by Lea. In

fact, it was a French canonist, A. Boudinhon, who wrote the first
Catholic reply to Lea. He did this in a lengthy article on the history of
the sacrament of penance through the eighth century, *"Sur l'histoire de
la pénitence. À propos d'un livre récent."*[22] The article, however, was
not well substantiated. More scholarly and detailed studies followed,
with solid historical works on the sacrament of penance by F. X. Funk,
P. Battifol, E. F. Vacandard, and P. A. Kirsch.[23] To the chagrin of many
Catholic systematic theologians, these authors tended to agree with
some major positions in Lea's study. A few years later, another group of
Catholic theologians and historians began to write histories of sacramental penance, e.g., P. Galtier, B. Poschmann, A. D'Ales, K. Adam, J.
A. Jungmann, and K. Rahner.[24] These studies have presented the Catholic world with a solid historical view on the development of sacramental penance.[25]

Since penance is the sacrament of reconciliation after baptism,
Catholic and Protestant scholars subsequently studied the history of
baptism, and their research began to appear in the first half of the twentieth century. Baptismal studies raised the question of confirmation and,
as a result, historical research on the sacrament of confirmation took
place. Baptism is the door to the Eucharist, and so scholars, both
Protestant and Catholic, began in the same period of time to produce
excellent works on theological and liturgical eucharistic history. An understanding of Eucharist is clearly tied to the sacrament of holy orders,
and therefore scholars provided the Christian world with a number of
historical studies on ministry, both ordained and lay. Key studies on
the histories of marriage and last anointing appeared in the later part
of the twentieth century. As a result of this historical research, scholars today have at their fingertips a vision of the history of each sacrament that Thomas Aquinas, Bonaventure, Scotus, Luther, and Calvin
never had. Nor did the Tridentine bishops have any such knowledge of
this history.

I deliberately stress the subject of sacraments, since sacramental issues more often than not have occasioned contemporary clashes between ordained and lay ministers. Ministry, of course, is larger than
liturgy and sacrament. Clashes also occur over administrative situations
as well as over matters of teaching and preaching. Nevertheless, clashes
involving liturgy and sacrament seem to be the more sensitive. Aylward
Shorter pinpoints the liturgical stumbling block. He writes:

> The ardent desire for liturgical inculturation—a new
> liturgical creation—has to compete with liturgy as a
> field for the exercise of hierarchical power.[26]

Although Shorter's focus is on liturgical inculturation, the statement that liturgy has become a competitive field of power is key. In sacramental and liturgical lay/cleric clashes, the systemic source of the problem is generally not liturgical, the symptomatic expression, but ecclesiastical authority.

The individual histories of the seven sacraments indicate that the present role of bishop (*episkopos*—ἐπίσκοπος) and priest (*presbyteros*—πρεσβύτερος) in sacramental ritual has not always been the paradigm. These historical differences have serious theological implications. Over the centuries, the role of the *episkopos* has radically changed. So too, the role of the presbyter has radically changed. As a result, one can say with historical confidence that there has never been a theological model of either *episkopos* or *presbyteros* which has remained unchanged. Church history presents us with several variant descriptions of *episkopos* and *presbyteros*. Each major historical change in the roles of *episkopos* and *presbyteros* has produced a change in the theological definition of bishop and priest. If the historical and theological definitions of bishops and priests have changed, then their relationship to lay ministers has also changed. A clear boundary between what only a bishop or priest does in sacramental life and what a layperson might do is not that clear. In his revised *Theology of Ministry,* Thomas O'Meara presents a detailed and well-substantiated description of the developmental use and meaning of *episkopos* and *presbyteros* in early Church history.[27] The developmental changes can be identified in summary fashion in the following way.

BISHOP

1. Ἐπίσκοπος in the New Testament cannot be equated with an understanding of bishop today. "It is impossible to find in the NT a clear view and even a definition of the precise function of the persons designated as *episkopoi* (bishops). The word occurs only five times (Acts 20:28, Phil 1:1, 1 Tim 3:2, Tit 1:7, 1 Pet 5:1-3), and it seems to be interchangeable with the title of *presbyteroi* (elders) used for the same person."[28] In

spite of the lack of clarity with regard to the meaning of the term in New Testament writings, one can say that *episkopos* was the name for one of the major ministers in the Christian community; that *episkopos* and *presbyteros* were often interchangeable; and that many early Christian communities did not use the title *episkopos*. In the early Christian communities there was considerable flexibility and diversity regarding the meaning and usage of the term *episkopos* and the naming and extent of authority of a minister called *episkopos*. It would be very difficult to say that a bishop in today's Church substantially mirrors the New Testament's description of *episkopos*. The following table highlights some major characteristics of *episkopos* in the early Church.

NEW TESTAMENT

Episkopos = – a major minister in the New Testament Church but not exactly identifiable with bishop in later Church history

– term often used in the same way as the title *presbyteros*

– in the New Testament, *episkopos* not associated with the Twelve or the apostles

---

2. From apostolic times to roughly 350 C.E. the *episkopos* gradually became the main leader in a Christian community. However, during this period the *episkopos* was more similar to today's *pastor* than to today's *bishop*. Even after 350 an *episkopos* continued to resemble today's pastor. In 411, the emperor Honorius called for a meeting at Carthage involving all the bishops of that area in North Africa.[29] Honorius named a layman, Flavius Marcellinus, the imperial commissioner in Carthage, as coordinator. The gathering was called a *collatio,* not a council, and the

emperor mandated that the agenda should be completed within four months. Those attending included 268 Catholic *episkopoi* and 279 Donatist *episkopoi*.[30] This area of North Africa did not consist of 547 dioceses. Rather, there were 268 parish churches under the presidency of a "Catholic *episkopos*" and 279 parish churches under the presidency of a "Donatist *episkopos*."[31] Many small towns and villages had both a Catholic and a Donatist church. In some of the larger cities there were even two or three Donatist churches and a similar number of Catholic churches. Each Christian community, i.e., each particular church, seems to have had as its main leader an *episkopos*. The *episkopos* in many ways resembled contemporary pastors, not contemporary bishops.

APOSTOLIC TIMES TO CA. 411 C.E.

Episkopos =   – by and large appears as the main
                      leader of a local community

                 – resembles to some degree the
                      pastor in today's churches

---

3. Mission churches branching from main churches were gradually staffed. In some instances, the staffing official was called by the ill-defined term *chore-episkopos*.[32] In time it became more customary for a presbyter or in a few instances a deacon to oversee these smaller church communities. The *episkopos* remained the main ecclesial leader over the wider community, a central church and a number of satellite communities. This development occurred in different regions at different times. We begin to see the contours of later dioceses. The *episkopoi* also began meeting in regional councils. This move helped ground the collegial nature of *episkopoi*. The number of these regional chapters of bishops mushroomed in the succeeding centuries until around 1100 in the West, when the number of regional councils declined dramatically and the number of papal councils increased dramatically.

For the first five centuries of Church history, global generalizations on church developments are for the most part inexact. Historically speaking, the developmental process of episcopal positioning within a community occurred at various stages and within differing time-lines. Slowly, the beginnings of a diocesan structure, such as we experience it today with the bishop as the main minister of a diocese and priests as the main pastors of smaller communities, took place. Historical data indicates a diverse development regarding the role, function, and theological meaning of *episkopos*.

CA. 411 C.E. TO CA. 1100 C.E.

Episkopos =   – main leader of a regional church
                   community

               – regional *episkopoi* form
                 councils to settle church issues
                 involving wider boundaries of
                 ecclesiastical concern

---

4. The next theological change for *episkopos* took place in the West and only in the West. Peter Lombard (ca. 1100–1160) was influential in bringing about this change. In the twelfth century the number of seven sacraments was finally determined, with holy orders one of the seven. However, there was considerable discussion by theologians and canonists as regards the specific orders to be included in that sacrament. Scholars almost unanimously excluded minor orders. The inclusion/ exclusion of sub-diaconate was a more disputed issue. Gradually, however, sub-diaconate was excluded from the sacrament of holy orders. The majority of scholastic theologians held that episcopacy was not part of the sacrament of holy orders. Rather, it was an office and a dignity.

One of the persistent questions that one encounters in the theological discussion of this period is that of the distinction (or non-distinction) of episcopacy as an order. Contrary to the opinion of earlier periods and to the patristic overshadowing of presbyterate by episcopacy, the medieval theologians see the essence and loftiest powers of priesthood being conferred in presbyteral ordination.[33]

The inclusion of deacon and priest in holy orders and the exclusion of bishop, sub-deacon, and those in minor orders eventually became the standard teaching of major Catholic theologians. Jean Galot enumerates the following: Hugh of St. Victor, Peter Lombard, Albert the Great, Thomas Aquinas, John Capreolus, Sylvester of Ferrara, Dominic Soto. He also includes theologians of the twentieth century: C. B. Billuart, L. Billot, P. Battifol and E. Hugon.[34] The inclusion of episcopacy in holy orders remained an open question, but the majority of theologians until Trent were of the opinion that deacons and priests alone were to be included. The Council of Trent did not change this teaching. From the Council of Trent on, the custom of using the term "ordination" only for deacons and priests became standard. The term "installation" was used for bishops and for those in the lesser orders. In other words, the Western church from the time of Peter Lombard until Vatican II officially installed bishops. It did not ordain them.

CA. 1100 C.E. TO VATICAN II

Episkopos = – an office of ecclesiastical jurisdiction and an eminent dignity in the church hierarchy

 – episcopacy not included in the sacrament of orders

---

5. At Vatican II the bishops were presented with an early document prepared by Cardinal Ottaviani and his committee in which chapter 3 was entitled: "The Episcopate as the Highest Grade of the Sacrament of Orders." During the council the bishops accepted this approach without making any clarifying statement that the understanding of episcopacy was

being theologically changed.[35] From the twelfth to the twentieth centuries, a few theologians had argued that episcopacy was indeed a part of holy orders, but there was no magisterial statement that they could cite to authorize this view. The vast majority of theologians during this same period of time had presented as the common teaching of the Church a theology of holy orders that included only priests and deacons. At Vatican II something astounding happened. The bishops simply reinstated episcopacy into a theological understanding of holy orders while making no statement clarifying the reinclusion. They just presented their documentation in which episcopacy became, once again, not only a part of holy orders but also the fullness of priesthood. The manner in which the bishops acted raises several major questions: Can Catholic ministers simply be excluded from holy orders such as occurred in the twelfth century and then reincluded by bishops in the twentieth century? What kind of a revolving door exists in the sacrament of holy orders? Can other ministries today be added? Can other "ordered" ministries today be removed?[36]

These same bishops described the bishop as having the fullness of the priesthood, but did not explain this. Contemporary priests are evidently less priestly than bishops, but what does this mean? Is it a matter of power, a matter of function, or a matter of something ontological? In the documents of Vatican II, the bishops stated that there is an "essential" difference between ordained ministry and lay ministry. Is there some similar "essential" difference between bishop and priest? If the difference is not essential, then, using scholastic philosophy, is it accidental? An ontological hierarchy remains unclear and the mere use of ontological terms such as "essential" and "fullness" does not clarify the central problems.

VATICAN II

Episkopos =   – fullness of priesthood

– reinstated into holy orders

– is by nature collegial

– not vicar of the pope

The above discussion on historical issues concerning episcopacy is not presented in an in-depth manner. Nonetheless, the findings of the last century's historical research on the key steps in the historical development of *episkopos* cannot be disregarded. Paul Bernier summarizes the historical research as follows.

> During the first generation, no single pattern of leadership emerged as one "willed by Jesus," or which was normative for all the churches; rather, ministry and leadership were extremely diversified.[37]

> Nowhere in the New Testament does it say that the apostles, or the Twelve, were bishops. This equation was made by Cyprian at a much later date. There is no evidence for linking the "college of apostles" and the "college of bishops." To say that the apostles were the first bishops goes beyond New Testament evidence. The apostles were surely the first chief leaders of the Christian assembly, but they neither had the title bishop, nor did they function the way bishops function later in the church.[38]

Were the Twelve *episkopoi*? Were the apostles ordained? Were the early *episkopoi* from the beginning of the Jesus communities the highest leaders in all the communities? A century ago, almost all Catholic ecclesial leaders and theologians would have responded to these questions with an unequivocal affirmative. Today such an unequivocal affirmative has become strongly problematic. What seemed immutable a century ago appears to have become mutable.

These changes in the understanding of episcopal ministry have serious ramifications for lay ministry in the new millennium, since all Christian ministries are interconnected. When the theology of one ministry begins to change, the theology of all other ministries undergoes changes as well. The historical data on episcopal development cannot help but impact all other Christian ministries.

Before we focus on the impact this has on an understanding of lay ministry today, let us consider similar changes in the understanding of the role of presbyter.

PRIEST

1. The history of the understanding of priest parallels that of bishop. One cannot find in the New Testament's description of *presbyteros* a definition of the modern understanding of priest. *Presbyteros* and *episkopos* are at times interchangeable. This interchangeability of titles remained in the Church until roughly 200 C.E.

Presbyters or elders were men of the community who had enough life-experience and enough acceptance by the community to be regarded as main leaders in a Christian community. Any further description of the *presbyteros* is in some degree conjectural.[39] "How someone in the early Church is called to ecclesial ministry is not described in the New Testament, so that theories relative to ordination have in part a hypothetical quality about them."[40] We cannot say with certainty that during this period the *presbyteros* was ordained, nor can we say with certainty that the *presbyteros* celebrated the Eucharist or any other "sacrament." Until 200 C.E. the *presbyteros* was clearly one of the major ministers in some local churches.

EARLY CHURCH

Presbyteros = – main minister in some local
                   churches

              – at times equivalent to *episkopos*

---

2. The first extant ordination ritual we have appears in the *Apostolic Tradition* (ca. 215 C.E.).[41] In this ordination ritual, the *presbyteros* is ordained primarily to give advice and help to the *episkopos*. No mention is made of sacramental duties. Although the prayer over the *presbyteros* is brief and one cannot derive too much historical data from it, still the *presbyteros* of that time does not reflect the priest of today.

APOSTOLIC TRADITION (CA. **215** C.E.)

Presbyteros =   – advisor/aide to *episkopos*

        – ordained to this ministry in the Church

        – a major ecclesial minister

---

3. When presbyters began to be sent to the mission churches, they were the main celebrants at the community's Eucharist. They were allowed to give the homily, a task most often reserved to the *episkopos*. Eventually, they oversaw the catechumenate formation for those in their small communities, but at first the baptism itself took place in the central church. This restriction gradually disappeared. In these mission churches the presbyter, without any additional ordination, took over the sacramental activities of the *episkopos* and began to act as the pastor of a local church.

CA. **215** C.E. TO CA. **1100** C.E.

Presbyteros =   – parish pastor

        – gradually became the presider at baptism, Eucharist, reconciliation

        – delivered the homilies

---

4. The next change in understanding the concept of priest took place in the Middle Ages when Peter Lombard and other major theologians defined the

priest as the highest order within holy orders. These theologians also defined the priest as the ordained minister who alone had the power to consecrate the bread and wine into the body and blood of Jesus and the power to forgive sins. In this scholastic theology, only a priest could celebrate Eucharist and forgive sins in the sacrament of penance. This form of scholastic theology of priesthood became dominant throughout the Tridentine period and the post-Tridentine period. It was the dominant theology of priesthood in all seminaries down to Vatican II.

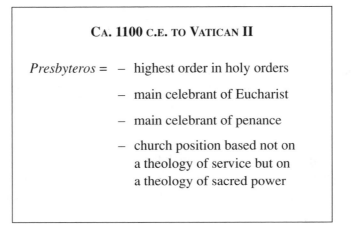

CA. 1100 C.E. TO VATICAN II

Presbyteros =   – highest order in holy orders

– main celebrant of Eucharist

– main celebrant of penance

– church position based not on
 a theology of service but on
 a theology of sacred power

5. The final radical change in an understanding of priesthood took place at Vatican II. In the documents of Vatican II the bishops clearly moved away from the then traditional scholastic understanding of priest, which centered on the power to celebrate Eucharist and the power to forgive sin in the sacrament of penance. It was precisely this definition which was set aside, changed, and modified. This did not mean that the scholastic definition was wrong; rather, it was deemed too narrow and needed to be enriched and enlarged. Archbishop Marty, in a plenary session at which all bishops were present, spoke quite clearly on this matter of change.

The commission cannot agree with those Fathers who think the position paper should have followed the scholastic definition of priesthood which is based on the power to consecrate the eucharist. According to the prevailing mind of this Council and the petition of many Fathers, the priesthood of presbyters must rather be connected with the priesthood of bishops, the latter being regarded as the high point and fullness of priesthood. The priesthood of presbyters must therefore be looked at, in this draft, as embracing not one function, but three, and must be linked to the Apostles and their mission.[42]

Thus, the final change to date with regard to the meaning of priesthood took place at the Second Vatican Council. The *tria munera* were presented as the framework for all ecclesial ministry, not merely priesthood or episcopacy. The *tria munera* are the framework for the common priesthood of all believers, episcopacy, priesthood, diaconate, and special ministries open to laymen and laywomen. The documents mention, however, that there is an essential difference between, on the one hand, bishop, priest, and deacon and, on the other, the laymen and laywomen who are in special ministries. No effort was made by the bishops to clarify this "essential difference." As a result, its precise meaning remains an open question for theologians.

Vatican II

Presbyteros =   – teacher (prophet)

– sanctifier (priest)

– leader (king)

– fullness of priesthood found in episcopacy

– ordained priesthood is related to priesthood of all the faithful

– ordained priesthood is related to Jesus, the one priest

One could argue that in the course of time there has been a development of dogma that has given divine approval to these changes in the concepts of episcopacy and priesthood. Several acceptable theories on the development of dogma, however, tend to place an *a priori* abstract restriction on what can and cannot be changed historically. In other words, these authors confront historical sacramental data within *a priori* limits. They review this same historical data on *episkopos* and *presbyteros* from an a priori and dogmatic stance, assuming that, from the beginning, there was a clear definition of both bishop and priest. They even maintain that from the very beginning there was ordination to these offices.[43]

This dogmatic stance, however, cannot be validated by historical data. It is not that historical data are mute on these issues. Rather, historical data indicate a quite different and varied interpretation of bishop, priest, and ordination. If a "development of doctrine" has taken place in past centuries, is it not logical that a "development of doctrine" can also be legitimately used in contemporary discussions, proposing further ministerial changes?

III. CONCLUSIONS AND IMPLICATIONS

The first section of this essay stressed the need to move from the symptomatic discussions of cleric/lay dissension to the underlying systemic factors which foment these clashes. I have argued that one of the most serious systemic issues for such dissension is, in theological terms, the as yet unresolved relationship between the priesthood of all believers or the baptismal "ordination" of the people of God and the special priesthood. Every acceptable theology of episcopal, presbyteral, diaconal, and lay ecclesial ministries today is intrinsically related to the priesthood of all believers. Until this relationship is more clearly and profoundly investigated, statements on all forms of church ministry today cannot help but be ineffective.

| INTERRELATED WITH: The special ministries of Bishop — Priest — Deacon — Layperson |

| FOUNDATIONAL: Priesthood of all believers and baptismal ordination |

| ORIGINAL: Jesus, the icon and source of all ministry |

In the second section of this essay I have argued that last century's massive historical research on all seven sacraments has to be seriously taken into account. Most official documents of the Catholic Church since Vatican II continue to speak of bishop and priest in ways that do not adequately reflect the historical process of episcopal and presbyteral development. In the essays of this volume, the authors have used the terms *episkope* (επισκοπή) and order (*ordo*). In these essays, *episkope* as oversight is not limited to episcopal or papal oversight, although both the pope and the bishops strongly share in this ecclesial oversight. It is the judgment of all the authors that baptismal ministry itself as well as all special ecclesial ministries share in some way the grace of *episkope*. The authors have also agreed that ecclesial ordering is far more comprehensive than the ordering within the sacrament of holy orders.

Ordering is an intrinsic reality in all ecclesial ministry. The theological understanding of both *episkope* and order cannot be confined to bishop, priest, and deacon. All the people of God share in *episkope* and in order. The first two sections of my own essay have been written in the light of this comprehensive theological understanding of *episkope* and order. It is on the basis of these two sections that I offer some specific conclusions and implications.

1. The legacy of the twentieth century on Christian ministry, both clerical and lay, has presented theologians and pastoral leaders with a serious number of as yet disunified factors. Because of this disunity, one finds in offical church documents mixed signals on the issue of lay ministry. For example, does the history of the seven sacraments, developed in the last century, play an operative role in sacramental theology? According to the *Catechism of the Catholic Church,* the answer is clearly no. The Catechism presents a few brief historical remarks on each sacrament, but the implications of these histories for the sacraments remain inoperative in the remainder of the texts on each sacrament. Had the sacramental histories been more operative in the Catechism's sacramental presentations, some of the unresolved issues troubling the pastoral and theological understanding of each sacrament would have been partially clarified.

2. Another mixed signal arises from the Catechism's use of the Church as a fundamental sacrament. The documents of Vatican II clearly state

that the Church is a sacrament. However, the Catechism simply states that "another" recent way of viewing the Church is the Church as sacrament. The Church as sacrament does not have a major operative role in either the Catechism's ecclesiology or its theology of sacraments. The teaching that the Church is a sacrament is important for lay ministry. Indeed, it is important for both clerical and lay ministry. Particular ministries in the Church have meaning only because all Christians, i.e., the entire people of God, are the fundamental sacrament of the Church. The distinction of lay ministry from clerical ministry is based on the common ministry of everyone, i.e., to be Church in a sacramental way.

3. From the Church as a sacrament stems the more basic position that Jesus, in his humanity, is the original or primordial sacrament. The human Jesus during his public life was a minister, and all ministry must reflect the ministry of Jesus himself. At this christological level of ministry, there is no distinction of cleric and lay. Both the spirituality of lay ministry (as well as that of clerical ministry) and the theology of lay ministry (as well as that of clerical ministry) must be rooted in Jesus the minister.

4. Liturgical renewal flourished in the decades following Vatican II. However, in more recent times, a renewal of liturgy in keeping with a multicultural church is almost non-existent. Today, any discussion on liturgical renewal is focused not on a liturgical renewal but on the issue of hierarchical authority. Even more, the Roman liturgical documents remain the benchmark for all other multicultural liturgical texts, and vernacular texts must adhere in a literal way to the Roman texts. These restrictions impact on multicultural ministry, since liturgical celebrations are experienced more and more as a "foreign" liturgy, and many lay ministers in non-European cultures do not want to be part of a "foreign liturgical invasion."

5. Human experience has become a major focus in contemporary theology. Revelation is not a revelation of doctrine; rather, God reveals his own self in a personal encounter. This encounter is at the heart of each sacrament, but the involvement of human experience in these sacramental moments means that sacramental events are to some degree subjective. Each existential moment of a sacramental event is unique, not

general, actual in a given space and time, not abstract in some timeless dimension. Sacramental celebrations are not cloned events. They are celebrations of very distinct individuals and communities. The existential depth of sacramental life changes the theology both of sacramental life and of ministry, whether clerical or lay.

6. Efforts to rethink sacramental life within the framework of postmodern philosophy have occasioned a radical change in the understanding of sacraments. The sacramental studies done by L. M. Chauvet and David Power as well as my own book on sacraments and postmodern philosophy present a form of sacramental theology which is clearly not scholastic. This postmodern attempt at a radical renewal of sacramental theology and its ministry is fundamentally a Western phenomenon. However, the postmodern model is indicative of what will happen when sacramental theology and ministry are rethought from the ground up using a Confucian basis, a Hindu basis, or an African basis. When such rethinking takes place, the theology of lay and clerical ministry will be presented in a radically new way. In my judgment, this rethinking has already begun as multicultural churches make use of their own diversity and integrity.

7. Although liberation theology might be associated with twentieth-century Latin America, there are similar movements today in Sri Lanka and India. African theologians continue to write and teach a form of liberation theology, although they do so with the real possibility of being silenced. Issues of justice within the Church remain explosive. These issues include the role of women in ministry; the role of married priests; the more compassionate inclusion of divorced and remarried Catholics; a more tolerant inclusion of Catholics who are gay and lesbian; and the subtle presence of ethnic racism in church polity. In all of these issues there is a need for some sort of liberation theology.

8. The permanent diaconate should be open also to women. Several dioceses and even conferences of local bishops have refused to establish the permanent diaconate in their dioceses precisely because it is not open to women. The present rumblings about establishing a ministry of deaconess are not an answer to the issues involved in an open and permanent diaconate.

9. Church leadership has as yet not accepted the historical data which indicates that there have been serious changes in the theological and historical development of the concepts of *episkopos* and *presbyteros*. Today there are still key Catholics in leadership positions who continue to maintain that episcopal and presbyteral roles have not substantially changed from the time of Jesus down to the present. They claim an immutable and untouchable theological core for this position. Historically, this cannot be demonstrated. Rather, history clearly indicates the changeability of both episcopal and presbyteral offices. The porosity of boundaries between lay and clerical ministries is evident. The envisioning of a theology of ordained and lay ministry will develop even more than it has already when the porosity and mutability of all ministry is better understood.

NOTES

1. Prior to 1900 there were a few important studies on the history of some sacraments, but these studies cannot compete with the twentieth century's thoroughgoing research on sacramental history.

2. *The Catechism of the Catholic Church* (Rome: Urbi et Orbi Communications, 1994) no. 1108 states: "The Spirit who is the Spirit of communion, abides indefectibly in the Church. For this reason the Church is the great sacrament of divine communion which gathers God's scattered children together." In no. 1118: "They [the sacraments] are 'by the Church' for she is the sacrament of Christ's action at work in her through the mission of the Holy Spirit. They are 'for the Church' in the sense that 'the sacraments make the Church.'" In the entire section on the sacraments, 1066–1690, these are the only times that the Church as sacrament is mentioned. Once mentioned, the theological insight of the Church as a fundamental sacrament plays no operative role. In the section on the Church, the Catechism, no. 849, restates the teaching of Vatican II that the Church is "the universal sacrament of salvation." In no. 738 the Catechism notes: "Thus the Church's mission is not an addition to that of Christ and the Holy Spirit, but is its sacrament." Cf. also 515, 774–776, 780. These few descriptions of the Church as a foundational sacrament do not reflect the theological position found in the documents of Vatican II. For a more thorough explanation of the place which the "Church as fundamental sacrament" plays in these documents, cf. Alois Grillmeier, "The Mystery of The Church," *Commentary on the Documents of Vatican II,* ed. Herbert Vorgrimler (New York: Herder and Herder, 1967) 138–140. Cf. also Gérard Philips, *La Chiesa e il suo Mistero nel Concilio Vaticano II* (Milan: Jaca Book, 1975) 69–72.

3. *The Catechism of the Catholic Church*, nos. 738, 1076.

4. Maurice Merleau-Ponty, *Phenomenology of Perception,* Eng. trans. Colin Smith (London: Routledge & Kegan Paul, 1962); *The Primacy of Perception and Other Essays,* Eng. trans. James Edie (Evanston, Ill.: Northwestern University Press, 1964).

5. Martin Heidegger, *Being and Time,* Eng. trans. J. Macquarrie and E. Robinson (New York: Harper & Row, 1962).

6. Cf. Paul Ricoeur, "Herméneutique et critique des idéologies," *Démythisation et idéologie,* ed. E. Castelli (Paris: Aubier Montaigne, 1973) 25–64.

7. In the apostolic constitution *Fidei Depositum,* which is the introduction for the Catechism, John Paul II states: "The *Catechism of the Catholic Church*...is a statement of the Church's faith...attested to or illumined by Sacred Scripture, the Apostolic Tradition, and the Church's Magisterium" (no. 3). If the Catechism is called *a statement* of the Church's faith, then there may be other statements of the same faith. Were the Catechism based on the theology of either Bonaventure or John Duns Scotus, the entire text would be crafted quite differently.

8. Cf. instruction "Some Questions Regarding Collaboration of Nonordained Faithful in Priests' Sacred Ministry," Eng. text in *Origins* 27/24 (November 27, 1997).

9. Bonaventure Kloppenburg, *The Ecclesiology of Vatican II* (Chicago: Franciscan Herald Press, 1974) 263–264.

10. Gérard Philips, "Dogmatic Constitution on the Church," *Commentary on the Documents of Vatican II,* 156–164.

11. Ibid., 158.

12. Kenan Osborne, *The Diaconate in the Christian Church: Its History and Theology* (Chicago: NADD, 1996).

13. Cf. John Risley, "The Minister: Lay and Ordained," *The Theology of Priesthood,* ed. Donald Goergen and Ann Garrido, (Collegeville, Minn.: The Liturgical Press, 2000) 121–137.

14. John N. Collins, *Diakonia: Reinterpreting the Ancient Sources* (Oxford: Oxford University Press, 1990).

15. Thomas Rausch, *Priesthood Today: An Appraisal* (New York/Mahwah, N.J.: Paulist Press, 1992) 22–24. Rausch refers in a detailed way to John N. Collins's book, *Diakonia: Reinterpreting the Ancient Sources.*

16. Jean Galot, *Theology of the Priesthood,* Eng. trans. Roger Balducelli (San Francisco: Ignatius Press, 1984) 31–54.

17. Cf. Kenan Osborne, *Priesthood: A History of the Ordained Ministry in the Roman Catholic Church* (New York/Mahwah, N.J.: Paulist Press, 1988) 36–37, 48, 56.

18. Cf. the excellent bibliography in James Puglisi, *The Process of Admission to Ordained Ministry,* vol. 1 (Collegeville, Minn.: The Liturgical Press, 1996) 228 ff.

19. Cf. e.g., the Lineamenta for the synod of bishops, *The Bishop: Servant of the Gospel of Jesus Christ for the Hope of the World* (Vatican City: 1998) 28–34, 43–44.

20. H. C. Lea, *A History of Auricular Confession and Indulgences in the Latin Church* (Philadelphia: Lea Bros. & Co., 1896).

21. Both Luther and Calvin had raised questions on the historical origins of the sacrament of penance, but at that time neither they nor the *periti* at Trent had any idea of its complicated historical past.

22. A. Boudinhon, "Sur l'histoire de la pénitence, à propos d'un livre récent (celui de Lea)," *Revue d'histoire et de littérature religieuse* 2 (1897) 306–344, 496–524.

23. For the bibliographical data concerning the authors mentioned in this paragraph, see Kenan Osborne, *Sacramental Theology: A General Introduction* (New York/Mahwah, N.J.: Paulist Press, 1988) 2–4; and *Christian Sacraments in a Postmodern World* (New York/Mahwah, N.J.: Paulist Press, 1999) 200–202.

24. Many authors other than those just mentioned could be included. See the bibliography in Kenan Osborne, *Reconciliation and Justification* (New York/ Mahwah, N.J.: Paulist Press, 1990) 285–296.

25. Liturgical studies, especially those on general absolution, raise serious theological questions which are still not resolved, e.g., if serious sins are taken away by general absolution, what theological reason can be brought forward to justify the regulation that such sins must be re-confessed privately to a priest?

26. Aylward Shorter, *Toward a Theology of Inculturation* (Maryknoll, N.Y.: Orbis Books, 1991) 194.

27. Thomas E. O'Meara, *Theology of Ministry* (New York/Mahwah, N.J.: Paulist Press, 1999) 74–79, 89–98, 151–157.

28. J. M. R. Tillard, "Bishop," *The New Dictionary of Theology* (Wilmington, Del.: Michael Glazier, 1987) 133.

29. For a historical discussion of this *collatio,* cf. Peter Brown, *Augustine of Hippo* (Berkeley: University of California Press, 2000) 330–335.

30. Scholars present a slight variance of the numbers for both the Donatist and the Catholic *episkopoi* attendees. Cf. Brown, *Augustine of Hippo,* 332 regarding the verbatim records of the *collatio.*

31. Perhaps some Donatist bishops were called in from other areas outside the Carthaginian area. The same might also be true for the Catholic bishops. The data is not clear on this matter. Still, such "outsiders" would not have significantly changed the totals for either group.

32. Bernard Cooke, *Ministry to Word and Sacrament* (Philadelphia: Fortress Press, 1976) 364.

33. Ibid., 581.

34. Galot, *Theology of the Priesthood,* 177–178.

35. Cf. O'Meara, *Theology of Ministry,* 129–138.

36. I firmly believe that bishops should be included within holy orders. I am questioning only the methods for such inclusion and exclusion.

37. Paul Bernier, *Ministry in the Church: A Historical and Pastoral Approach* (Mystic, Conn.: Twenty-Third Publications, 1996) 28.

38. Ibid., 40.

39. Cf. O'Meara, *Theology of Ministry,* 57–79; Osborne, *Priesthood,* 40–85.

40. D. Dupuis, "Theologie der kirchlichen Ämpter," *Mysterium Salutis* 4/2 (Einsieden: Benziger, 1973) 505.

41. Cf. Puglisi, *The Process of Admission to Ordained Ministry,* 10–85; Osborne, *Priesthood,* 119–129. Puglisi, in my view, uses the term "ordination" prior to the *Apostolic Tradition* in a facile way. It remains unclear whether ordination was part of the process for a community's induction of someone into leadership. Second, Puglisi accepts Botte's view that Hippolytus was the author of the *Apostolic Tradition.* Currently, authorship by Hippolytus of this document is seriously questioned.

42. The citation of Marty is found in Osborne, *Priesthood,* 316.

43. Osborne, "An Ecclesial Presupposition," *Priesthood,* 30–39. This chapter is pivotal for any interpretation of priestly ministry in the Church.

Institutes of Consecrated Life
Identity, Integrity, and Ministry

R. KEVIN SEASOLTZ, O.S.B.

Institutions are necessary in the life of the Catholic Church. There is, however, a widespread contemporary American distrust of institutions which often finds expression in a romanticized stress on individual initiative as opposed to formally organized action.[1] One of the functions of an institution is to give form and order to a social structure. Most people would certainly acknowledge that we need form and order in order to relate effectively to one another in any society. Many people, however, are uncomfortable with the adjective "institutional" because they feel that it implies a lack of individuality and vitality. Hence it is commonplace today, perhaps especially in the United States, to find many people who are suspicious of institutions. Pioneers, people who realize their dreams, and entrepreneurs are admired, whereas bureaucrats, company people, and institutional types are usually regarded as unimaginative and uncreative.[2] Contemporary distrust of institutions was set out as a marked characteristic of people in this country and often cited as a cause of the decline of American community life by Robert Bellah and his colleagues in their highly respected books *Habits of the Heart* and *The Good Society*.[3]

This mistrust of institutions is especially apparent in the contemporary American evaluation of religion. Many people in this country claim they are intensely concerned about their spiritual lives but not at all interested in organized religion. As Avery Dulles has remarked, "While people are willing to dedicate themselves to a cause or movement, they do not wish to bind themselves totally to any institution. Institutions are seen as self-serving and repressive and as needing to be kept under strong vigilance."[4] For many people, it seems that the word "religion" is opposed to any form of institutionalization, since religion is the realm of the deeply personal, whereas an institution is for them by definition impersonal. What is personal is often presumed to be private, certainly an equivalence that both the ancient and medieval world would not have recognized. Of course, religious institutions are not immune to the kind of corruption that often besets institutions. Nevertheless, the Catholic Church by its very nature is an institution and as such is always in need of ongoing conversion. The notion of the *ecclesia semper reformanda* is always applicable.[5]

Consecrated life in the Catholic Church, known more popularly as religious life, is made up of institutions that are described and governed by Book II of the Code of Canon Law in canons 573–746. The legislation is clear that members of a religious institute pronounce public vows and are to lead a life of brothers and sisters in common (c. 607, §2). Since the Second Vatican Council, the Church's magisterium has tried to deepen and enrich its vision of religious community life. Whereas the 1917 Code of Canon Law placed its emphasis on exterior elements and uniformity of lifestyle, the Second Vatican Council's document on religious life and the 1983 code both insist on the spiritual dimensions and the bonds of community which must unite all the members in charity. In canon 607, paragraph 2, the code has synthesized the two elements as it speaks of religious "living a fraternal life in common." Thus, in community life, the two elements of union and unity among the members are distinguished as follows: first of all, the more spiritual consists in brotherly or sisterly communion, which abides in the hearts of the members through charity. It underlies "communion of life" and interpersonal relationships. The other is much more visible. It consists of life in common or community life, described as "living in one's own lawfully constituted religious house," and "leading a common life" through fidelity to the same norms, taking part in common acts, and collaboration in common services.[6]

In the Catholic Church a religious institute differs from a secular institute as it is described in canon 710: "A secular institute is an institute of consecrated life in which the Christian faithful, living in the world, strive for the perfection of charity and seek to contribute to the sanctification of the world, especially from within." Canon 714 describes the

lifestyle of members of secular institutes: "Members are to lead their
lives in the ordinary conditions of the world according to the norm of
the constitutions, whether alone or in their own families, or in a group
living as brothers or sisters." In other words, common life or living together is an option.

In this paper I am concerned primarily with institutes of consecrated life or what are often simply called "religious institutes." Although they differ considerably one from another, in addition to a public
profession of the evangelical counsels, there are three basic characteristics of such religious institutes: a commitment to prayer, to community
or common life, and to ministry. The way in which these commitments
are prioritized differs from one institute to another. For example, Jesuits
are apt to place ministry in first place, whereas Benedictines are apt to
place an emphasis on prayer and community, with their ministry flowing out of the other two. There is little doubt that there is much confusion today, especially among American members of religious institutes,
concerning their commitments, their identity, and their ministry. In fact
many members, especially in regard to common life and institutional
witness, seem to be living lives that are more consonant with life in a
secular institute than with life in an institute of consecrated life. The
distinctive charism of many religious institutes seems to have been lost,
the vow of obedience has often been evacuated of its everyday meaning
and experience, and the supports and challenges for a life of poverty
and chaste celibacy have frequently given way to a highly individual-
ized ministry and life alone in an apartment.

In the pages that follow I want to scan the general history of so-
called religious life with the hope that some light might be shed on the
identity, integrity, and kinds of ministry that might be appropriate to institutes of consecrated life today. As Michael Himes has noted:

> Central to the Catholic Christian vision is the insistence that
> God relates to us and we to God through concrete communal
> experience in time and space. That is why institutionalization
> of the various aspects of the church's mission is necessary. We
> cannot collaborate, we cannot function as a community in time
> and space without some institutional forms. The shape of those
> institutions, the way they are administered, the distribution of
> authority within them and among them, the struggle to prevent

them from becoming obsessed with their own continuance rather than the furtherance of the mission, all these are absolutely essential concerns... All things human are ambiguous, and what can serve the greatest good can wreak the greatest harm. But that is the way of things in a world of creatures marked by sin and redeemed by grace.[7]

ROOTS OF RELIGIOUS LIFE

The origins of Christian religious life are disputed by contemporary scholars, who nonetheless agree that, in its Christian institutionalized form, religious life has existed almost as long as Christianity itself. All the institutes of consecrated life in the Church derive, in one way or another, from the first monks and nuns. Thus, the roots of the international and highly centralized Society of Jesus and the simple monastic communities founded in Africa, Asia, and India since the Second Vatican Council can be traced to the Egyptian hermits. Contemporary authors, however, point out earlier roots in the tradition of the Old Testament prophets.[8] They look upon the Old Testament prophets as prototypical for the vowed life within the Christian tradition.[9] In the Old Testament the prophet and the king are juxtaposed, with the priest closely aligned with the king.[10] The prophet serves to remind the community of a free and creative God under whom no humanly devised institutions can be perpetually validated. The prophetic movement seeks to develop and nurture the creative dimensions of religious life and to inspire the hope and dreams of the community that the institutional structures are meant to preserve and mediate but that are often stifled when the structures become ends in themselves.[11] The tension between the prophet and the priest in the Old Testament anticipates the future tension between religious life as prophetic and ordained ministry as institutional and, more specifically, between prophetic priesthood within religious institutes and the hierarchically structured church.[12]

The role of the prophet is to be counter-cultural in the sense that it emphasizes alternative values and ways of living, maintains a larger view of reality than the institution itself, and challenges those structures that repress or deny divine-human co-creativity. Institutional structures have a tendency to turn into idols; the prophet's role is to denounce all false idols while pointing continuously to God, who can never be confined, formalized, or limited to any set of institutions.[13] In the Old Testament, prophetic ministry appears to be contemplative, political, and inclusive. Prophets perceive in depth and struggle to see life as God sees it, while striving to discern the unfolding of the divine plan within the whole of creation.[14]

Although the Old Testament prophets elicit admiration, they also evoke hostility, for to the mainstream culture the prophet is a puzzle, a maverick, and often a pest. Above all, the prophet is a threat to the stability and security of the status quo: the institution tends to remove that challenge rather than engage it because it involves the risk of exposing vulnerability or possible corruption.[15] The prophetic ministry is precisely one of the ministries that has been picked up and developed in the Christian era by religious institutes, beginning with monasticism.

In the Old Testament, the prophetic tradition is confined to a number of outstanding individuals, such as Jeremiah, Hosea, Isaiah, and Amos. In the New Testament, however, apart from Jesus himself, only a few individuals are affirmed to have prophetic gifts, John the Baptist being the most significant. This does not mean, however, that the Old Testament prophetic tradition disappeared. As biblical scholars note, the Old Testament prophets pointed to Jesus, whose ministry fulfilled the promises of old.[16] But after the death and resurrection of Jesus, the prophetic vocation shifted from individuals to the Christian community as a whole. The twelve apostles are important not primarily as individuals but rather as the Twelve, representing communally the twelve tribes of Israel.[17] This emphasis on community witness has bearing on the appropriate lifestyle and ministry of contemporary members of institutes of consecrated life.

Jesus proclaimed that he had come to establish the reign of God in the midst of the human community, a reign that may be described as establishing a new order of life, marked by right relationships of justice, love, peace, and freedom, characteristics that reflect God's own relationship with the human community. The old ways of domineering control, often characteristic of patriarchal societies, are declared inappropriate. Jesus' disciples, then, are meant to be attuned to the inspiration of the Holy Spirit, leading the Church into the future. The Spirit invited the disciples of the Lord Jesus to allow God to reign in their hearts so they might proclaim the word of God to others; herein lies the

prophetic challenge that institutes of consecrated life are meant to es-
pouse today.[18]

BEGINNINGS AND DEVELOPMENT
OF INSTITUTIONALIZED RELIGIOUS LIFE

The observations that have just been made also have important implications for the emerging theology and practice of what came to be
known as religious life. They challenge the claim that the origins of
Christian religious life are to be found primarily in the eremitical life,
understood as an individualistic experience of God, rather than in individuals basically rooted in the Christian community though usually living at a distance from the important centers of the hierarchically
structured church. As Graham Gould has pointed out, the Desert Fathers
were deeply concerned with the nature of the monastic communities
that they formed and with the issues that regularly affected relationships
between individuals and their communities.[19]

Early Christian monastic men and women responded above all to a
call to discipleship, not to a call to *diakonia*, to service or ministry within
the Church. The call to be a disciple of the Lord Jesus, however, was
also a call to an ascetical way of life. The Desert Fathers and Mothers
did in fact renounce life in secular society because they often experienced that society as corrupt, but their withdrawal led to the creation of
new monastic communities in Nitria and Scetis that, although they were
more loosely organized than the cenobitic communities later established
by Pachomius, were definitely not collections of individuals living mutually unrelated lives. Their lifestyle was a very flexible one, not burdened
by complex institutional structures.[20] Their ministry was primarily one of
supporting and challenging one another.[21]

As these monastic groups moved to the frontiers or margins of the
Church and society, they certainly became centers radiating counter-
cultural values. In that sense they exercised a liminal, prophetic role.
Their primary commitment was to the reign of God in their lives rather
than to the institutional structures of the hierarchical church.[22]

Early Christian women were sometimes able to overcome gender
biases and to some extent claim an active role in ministry by embracing
a life of virginity. Chastity was their way to achieve some degree of

freedom in the Church. By removing women from the constraints of sexuality and marriage, virginity allowed them to achieve a religious identity that was somewhat independent of the prescribed social roles and conventions of femaleness. Certainly among the followers of Jesus and in the early Christian communities, women had prominent places as patrons and evangelizers. Chaste partnerships like those of Paula and Jerome and Rufinus and Melania testify to the important role that women played in the development of early monasticism.[23] One must, however, be careful not to overestimate the degree of gender equality in the early Church and thereby produce an overly idealized view of the collaboration of women and men in ministry.[24]

For centuries the dominant frame of reference for institutes of consecrated life has been the Church as an institution. They were to provide a model of holiness that the whole Church could imitate, one that would guarantee salvation in the next world. In this ecclesiastical culture, the primacy of the reign of God was more or less subverted as it gave way to a Church that was often more and more idolized.[25]

If institutes of consecrated life are to reclaim their prophetic role, they must once more become liminal or marginal communities, but they must also retrieve their own proper institutional or communal identity and forms of witness. It is useful to recall that many founders of institutes of consecrated life had to confront the institutional church, often to the point of open conflict, in order to be faithful to their prophetic charism and to bring about creative changes in the Church. If the primary allegiance of religious is to the reign of God rather than to the institutional church, they must often confront, and at times denounce, those systems and institutional structures that militate against the reign of God.

Unfortunately in the past, religious, both as individuals and as communities, have sometimes colluded with systems that oppress people; their lifestyles and value systems have often emulated the dominant culture of secular society and have failed to be prophetic in challenging and denouncing oppressively sinful structures. They have lost the subversive vision of the Old Testament prophets and have betrayed their liminal calling to be catalysts for establishing the reign of God.[26]

The development of a well-defined cenobitic or communitarian way of monastic life was the work of the Egyptian Pachomius (ca. 287–346). Under his direction, eremitical asceticism underwent an important shift in emphasis. All excesses and bizarre feats occasionally found in earlier monks and nuns were excluded, because Pachomius's ordered community based its life on the norm of the average. Obedience became an essential component; the rule and above all the superior of the community were the authorities that both set monastic requirements and gave encouragement to the members in their ascetical efforts. Obedience to the monastic superior increasingly withdrew the communities and their members from the control of the local bishops.[27]

The ideal of cenobitism spread to Cappadocia, where St. Basil wrote a long and short rule for his monks and insisted that monasteries remain small so that solitude could be assured for the members and the relationship between superior and subject would remain on a personal basis.[28]

In the early period, religious life in the East remained basically a lay movement even in its Basilian form in which it was integrated into the social and apostolic life of the larger Church. In the West, however, it was increasingly clericalized. For example, Eusebius of Vercelli, shortly after 363, organized the clerics of his cathedral into a clerical monastery. A similar arrangement was made by St. Ambrose of Milan and by St. Paulinus of Nola. It was St. Augustine, however, who had the most influence in this regard. In 396 as the bishop of Hippo he organized the life of his clergy around himself with a common life, renunciation of property, and obedience, all directed toward effective pastoral ministry.[29]

Side by side with this clerical monasticism there were also in the West proponents of monasticism as it was lived in the East. This older type was exemplified by the monasteries founded by St. Martin of Tours at Marmoutier, John Cassian at Marseilles, and St. Caesarius at Lérins and later at Arles. It was in the rule of Caesarius (ca. 470–542) that the notion of stability was introduced into Western monasticism.

Of primary importance in the history of Western monasticism is the rule of Benedict, which extolls the call to seek God within the framework of the monastic community. Caesarius's idea of stability was strengthened from the point of view of the abbot, who was to be the spiritual father of the entire community for life, and from the point of view of the monks, who were to remain attached to the monastery of their profession. The monastery itself was to form, as far as possible, an autonomous community independent of the outside world. Although the monks were primarily responsible for one another in community, hospitality toward guests was an important form of ministry, which meant that the monks shared with their guests not only their material goods but also their religious values.[30] Their ministry and service to others flowed out of their cenobitic life.

With the spread of the rule of Benedict, the founding period of religious life came to an end. However, it should be noted that there were women counterparts for the monks of Egypt; their communities gradually grew in both number and importance. Toward the end of the fourth century, both St. Ambrose and St. Augustine established monasteries for women and gave these foundations important attention. In his Letter 211 Augustine gave them the basic framework for their life, which was later developed into the rule of St. Augustine.[31] Caesarius of Arles also wrote a rule for nuns based on the work of Augustine but strongly emphasizing enclosure.[32] Benedict did not envisage his rule as one for women religious but it was applied to women in England and by the middle of the eighth century was the most common rule for women religious and remained so until the twelfth century.[33]

After the frontiers of the Roman empire collapsed in the face of the Germanic migrations, the monasteries became havens of stability and security as well as sources of leadership for missionary activity among the Germanic peoples. In the case of women, chastity and the freedom for ministry it once entailed took second place to the value of monastic enclosure as women entered monasteries for various non-religious reasons. It was commonly asserted that a woman had to have *aut murus aut maritus*—either a wall of monastic enclosure or a husband. Women's monasteries became refuges for widows, undowried and consequently unmarriageable daughters, wives of priests and bishops, captives who had been abused by conquering soldiers, women seeking sanctuary after refusing to marry, and even children.[34]

During the Carolingian period, Benedictinism came to dominate the religious life of the West. The monasteries were not only numerous but were also deeply involved in missionary activity, in cultural pursuits, in education, in scholarship, and in the administration of extensive landholdings. These activities often distracted them from Benedict's original purpose for a monastery. Hence Benedict of Aniane in the ninth century proposed what he thought were the two essential aspects of monastic life: uniformity of practice and fidelity to prayer through a faithful observance of the liturgy.[35]

Benedict's monastery was envisioned as a community of laymen, although he did allow for priests in his monastery and even permitted his own monks to be ordained. Nevertheless, in the centuries after Benedict, monasticism in the West became increasingly clericalized due to a number of complex developments both within and outside the monasteries. It has been suggested that the need for the monks to provide the Eucharist as part of their parochial responsibility, their desire to bring the Eucharist to missionary lands, and the growing commitment to the Eucharist as the center of their spiritual lives were strong influences. Subjective eucharistic piety and the multiplication of Masses, especially for the dead, along with the custom of offering Mass stipends would have also come into play. Likewise the development of the conventual Mass and various social and cultural factors affected the increasing importance of the Eucharist in the daily horarium of monastic communities.[36]

Along with the increased clericalization of monasticism went a shift in the relationship between monasteries and the hierarchical church. In the Middle Ages, monasteries were often very vulnerable to influence by local ecclesiastical and secular authorities, with the result that monks had little control over their personal or communal life. This was the situation when the abbey of Cluny was founded in France in the early tenth century with a commitment to return to basic Benedictine principles. From its small beginnings, Cluny developed into a great monastic order that was to dominate Western monasticism for years. These Cluniac communities were in fact worlds unto themselves. Instead of political or public activity, scholarly work, or traditional manual labor, it was an elaborate liturgy that filled the life of a Cluniac monk. However, this one-sided approach disturbed Benedict's wise balance of prayer, holy reading, and manual labor. Cluny understood its primary ministry as celebration of the liturgy and prayerful intercession for the entire world. Although Cluny dominated monastic reform throughout the tenth and eleventh centuries, it gradually became devitalized, thus inspiring other minor reform efforts which eventually gave rise in the eleventh and twelfth centuries to several important new orders.[37]

In the eleventh century a movement strongly committed to eremitism developed and gained much ground. Numerous monks became hermits so they might separate themselves from the wider world and be independent of the secular demands of society. This strict separation from the secular sphere led to an important new development in monasteries, namely, the institution of the *conversi*, laymen who served the monastery as brothers. Their ministry was simply servile work for the fully professed monks. While there were economic reasons for this development, it also showed that the reform movement affected the laypeople who wanted to follow to some extent this widely publicized way of Christian life. The hermit's life of simplicity was thought to be the only authentic realization of life according to the Gospel. This observation, together with a critical attitude toward both the Church and the diocesan clergy, gave the eremitic life broad sympathy among the laity and consequently attracted many recruits.[38]

In 1089 Robert of Molesmes and several other Benedictines laid the foundation for the Cistercian order. They sought to establish a form of Benedictinism stricter and more primitive than any existing at the time by emphasizing the ascetical elements in the rule of Benedict, insisting on silence, eliminating liturgical splendor as well as architectural and artistic extravagance, and downplaying communal interrelations. The clerics in the order continued to carry a heavy burden of liturgy while the lay brothers managed the farms. It was St. Bernard (1090–1153) who introduced quite harsh severity into the order's legislation, but he balanced the asceticism with a deep mystical piety that spread far beyond the Cistercian order. His extensive ecclesiastical and political activities, however, meant that the order got involved in preaching, writing, and ministry outside the cloister. Bernard even assisted in the foundation of military orders to support both colonization and missionary activity, with the result that the Cistercians' field of influence went far beyond the walls of their own monasteries.[39]

Several new orders developed out of a combination of eremitism and itinerant preaching. For example, Blessed Robert of Arbrissel (ca. 1055–1114) first lived as a hermit but then set out to be an itinerant, thus giving the apostolic life a new emphasis by reviving the life of the apostles and their mission of preaching.[40]

Among the new orders were those of canons regular, clerical religious who modeled their lives after the groups of diocesan clergy who had gathered around Eusebius and Augustine in the fourth and fifth centuries. The Lateran synods of 1059 and 1063 gave full religious status to priests living in common, so that by the beginning of the twelfth century canons living in accordance with the norms of the Lateran synods were generally called canons regular. Their ministry was priestly but their life was in community according to prescribed vows. Probably the most important of these canons regular were the Premonstratensians founded by St. Norbert of Xanten (ca. 1082–1132).[41]

With the proliferation of religious orders of men in the late Middle Ages, women with great determination emulated the new male communities such as the Cistercians and the Premonstratensians; they adopted their rule, followed their way of life, and claimed their name. Most of the male orders, however, did not want to be involved in providing sacramental services or pastoral care for these communities of women.[42]

MENDICANT ORDERS

The most important medieval development in religious life was the founding of the mendicant orders which began in the early thirteenth century with the Dominicans and Franciscans. They represented a radical departure from the past monastic tradition. By adopting a rule of community poverty and refusing to accept endowments or to own property, they left behind impediments that had long been regarded as indispensable to any institutionalized community of monks. While maintaining a strong commitment to common life, they abandoned the seclusion and withdrawal of the cloister in order to engage wholeheartedly in pastoral ministry. Preaching and service to the people were their major concerns. They preached a message that was often different from that of monks and canons, namely, that salvation need not be sought by flight from the world but could be found by faithfully fulfilling one's normal obligations in the secular world. The earlier monastic communities had settled in rural areas where they cultivated the land and to some extent ministered to their neighbors. In the late Middle Ages, the city, the bourgeoisie, and the merchant class characterized much of European society;[43] hence the mendicants went where the people were and tried to minister to them in terms of their concrete needs.

The oldest mendicant order demonstrates quite clearly the respect for tradition and the need to adapt ministry to the cultural conditions of the times. The Order of Friars Preachers, founded by St. Dominic (1170–1221), was the first religious order to incorporate as an integral part of its religious life a ministry that shared the bishop's fundamental responsibility to preach the Word of God. Dominic had been trained in the tradition of the canons regular; hence he committed his friars to observe the same rule that governed the canons, namely, the rule of St. Augustine with its strong emphasis on community. In the traditional monastic and canonical communities, the monastery as a geographical location was the basic unit possessing economic power and juridical authority. By profession monks and canons became members of a specific community located in a particular place.

The Dominicans emphasized community life but not location in a specific place. The order assigned the friar to a residence which was called a *conventus*, a place of assembly. In these houses the friars simply lived together as a community and placed themselves at the service of the entire Church. Although the order quite quickly came to be widely dispersed, unity was preserved because of the carefully structured constitutions that clearly established a firm bond among the friars. In this way the Order of Preachers was distinguished from the bourgeoisie and from monastic communities.[44]

From their early days, the Dominicans were known not simply as preachers but as friar preachers, preachers who were brothers, for they were vowed to a *vita communis*. Although not all the friars in fact preached, they were all members of a preaching community, a *praedicatio*. It was because the order was established on a sound institutional basis with a clearly defined ministry that the Dominicans have been singularly blessed with a sure sense of identity throughout their long history. Strongly committed to a life of prayer in community, they have passed on to the larger Church the fruits of their contemplation through preaching.[45] Dominic died in 1221, but his death caused neither a catastrophe nor a rupture in his order because he had successfully translated his special charism into an institution which faithfully carried on his work.[46]

In the early years of the order, the Dominicans assumed pastoral care of women converts. They carefully maintained this ministry and thereby helped to integrate women more successfully into the life of the Church. Dominic also founded a second order, this one for women; it eventually became a model for other institutes of women religious. Likewise, the Dominicans reached out to Christians living in the secular world and thus laid the foundations for a third Dominican order, the Order of Penance of Saint Dominic.[47]

Contemporary with the foundation of the Dominicans was the foundation of the Order of Friars Minor. One of the great gifts that Dominic had, namely, the gift for organization, was a charism sadly lacking in the founder of the Franciscans, for Francis of Assisi (1181/2–1226) failed to establish a stable religious institute. In the beginning, Francis and his disciples were an intimate fraternity of nomadic preachers, some clerics but most of them laymen, who moved from town to town preaching in the market squares. They were committed to a life of absolute poverty. In 1210 Francis took his companions to Rome, where he persuaded the Pope to authorize their activities. Because of their lack of structure, their early history was extremely turbulent. It was left to Saint Bonaventure, who was general of the order from 1257 to 1273, to translate Francis of Assisi's brilliant originality into a permanent institution that could survive.[48]

Like Dominic, Francis and his disciples also ministered to women. In fact, one of Francis's earliest and most distinguished converts was Clare of Assisi, the daughter of an aristocratic family who vowed to follow him in the practice of absolute poverty and imitation of Christ. The rule that was provided for the women, however, insisted on strict enclosure based on the rule of Saint Benedict, for female mendicancy was unthinkable at the time. Hence the Poor Clares, though strongly committed to evangelical poverty, became an enclosed monastic order of the traditional type.[49]

After the foundation of the Dominicans and Franciscans, the Hermits of St. Augustine, the Carmelites, the Servites, and the Minims all modeled themselves and their way of life on the example of the first orders of friars.[50]

Mention should also be made of the Beguines, an anomalous movement of urban women who did not take vows and who followed no specific rule but lived together in small communities and supported themselves by working in textiles or other crafts. Because they lacked firm clerical supervision and did not live within an enclosure, the Beguines were often held in suspicion, but they survived those who persecuted them and provided a model for later institutes of women religious that would surface in the seventeenth and later centuries. In a real sense, the Beguines represented an early movement of women's liberation.[51]

In the period between the high Middle Ages and the Reformation, there were newly founded religious orders which demonstrated a strong commitment to an active pastoral or charitable ministry. Among male religious these groups constituted a new type of religious order, namely, the clerks regular. They were modeled after the Dominicans and other mendicant orders which had become clericalized. As ordained priests they lived in community, generally following the rule of Augustine with their own constitutions, and practiced the evangelical counsels.

MODERN RELIGIOUS INSTITUTES

The most important new foundation in the sixteenth century was that established by Ignatius of Loyola (1491–1556).[52] Following a deep religious conversion, he and six companions took vows on August 15, 1534, committing themselves to a life of poverty and chastity, to make a pilgrimage to Jerusalem, and to work for the salvation of souls. From the beginning their community was a clerical society, even though some of the members were lay brothers. In 1549 Pope Paul III confirmed the community under the title "Society of Jesus." Their ministry was divided into preaching, teaching, and works of mercy. A fourth vow was added to the usual three religious vows of poverty, chastity, and obedience—the members were to obey without any hesitation all commands of the pope concerning the salvation of souls and the spread of the Gospel.[53]

The early constitutions of the Society were modeled on those of the medieval mendicant orders but excluded their democratic elements. The principle of central authority was strongly emphasized. Ignatius also went much further than the mendicants in abandoning monastic practices. He and his community wore no distinctive habit, nor did they pray the divine office together as a community. Another distinguishing characteristic was the strict classification of the members. The professed members took solemn vows but only priests were admitted to that rank. Furthermore, the higher offices in the Society were open only to the professed. The Jesuits were committed above all to continue the mission of Jesus Christ in the world; they understood that obedience was at the heart of Jesus' mission. Hence a strong bond of obedience bound the individual Jesuit to his superior, and the whole society was committed to fidelity to the pope. In monastic communities the vow of stability bound the individual to live his entire life in the monastery where he would seek his salvation. By contrast, the Jesuit's fourth vow was in essence a vow of mobility, committing the Jesuit to travel anywhere in the world to "save souls." This fourth vow constituted one of the clearest indications that the new society sought to break firmly with the older monastic traditions.[54]

In the sixteenth century a momentous innovation took place in the history of women's religious orders with the foundation of a new way of religious life by St. Angela Merici (1464–1540). In 1525 in Italy she founded a society for the education of orphaned girls and the care of the sick and named the group after the martyr St. Ursula. Until that time women's religious orders had been established in close relationship to orders of religious men; nuns were generally strictly enclosed and usually had very limited contact with the secular world. In the case of Angela Merici's order, there was no bond with a community of men; she likewise abandoned common life. In the latter regard, her group resembled a modern secular institute, but as such it was far ahead of its time. The virgins who joined her community continued to live with their parents and siblings. They were united by a common rule of life, common prayer, worship, regular community meetings, and a common ministry. They were essentially a society of devout women committed to charitable work. Their uniform clothing, however, and their custom of taking private vows moved them in the direction of traditional orders of women religious.[55]

The Company of St. Ursula took on a more formal shape after 1530. The rule, approved in 1534, divided the members into two tiers: virgins and widows, each with their own superiors. Angela was the mistress-general in charge of finances and legacies under direct papal jurisdiction, though provision was made for corporate ownership.[56]

Angela's death in 1540 coincided with preparations for the Council of Trent. On December 3, 1563, at the end of the final session, the council fathers hastily decreed that all nuns were to observe strict enclosure and were forbidden to go out of the monastery without episcopal approval. In 1566 Pope Pius V decreed that the law applied to all professed nuns. As the Ursulines spread from Italy to France in the early seventeenth century, they became an order of nuns under strict enclosure.[57]

No less daring than St. Angela to found a new type of religious life for women was the attempt made by the English woman Mary Ward (1585–1645).[58] She came from an old English Catholic family. Inspired to found a new religious community for English women, she sought first to strengthen the Catholic faith in England by providing women with a religious education so that they could take part in the re-conversion of England to Catholicism. Besides the work of education, the sisters were to assist the Catholic priests with their apostolic activities. The sisters were to live in community but without a distinctive habit and with no strict enclosure. In developing her order, Mary Ward was obviously inspired by Ignatius of Loyola; she wanted a similarly mobile order of women to work together with the Jesuits. In fact, when she drew up the constitutions for her order, she carefully followed the constitutions of the Society of Jesus. The Jesuits were not at all interested in collaborating with a female branch of the Society and the papal curia could not tolerate abandonment of enclosure. Mary Ward was misunderstood everywhere; consequently, her plans received no approval in Rome. In 1631 Pope Urban VIII suppressed her institute. A number of her foundations, however, survived, especially through support from secular authorities. Eventually the so-called "English Ladies" were domesticated in that they became an order within the traditional framework of religious life, but an order which earned special recognition because of its work in education.[59]

In the same period there were foundations of women's orders devoted specifically to charitable work. Under the direction of St. Vincent de Paul (ca. 1580–1660) and St. Louise de Marillac (1591–1660), various local groups of devout women were united into a community and called the Daughters of Charity. In 1654 Pope Innocent X confirmed the congregation; however, they were not religious in the strict sense. Common life under a superior, in the monastic tradition, was prescribed for these women, but their life was committed to social and charitable ministries outside the convent.[60] After the founding of the Daughters of Charity with their freedom for apostolic work because of their lack of cloister, various societies of women were founded for education, nursing, and missionary work.[61]

The Jesuits had introduced the practice of simple vows for some of their members, thus breaking the long tradition that solemn vows were the only vows permitted in religious orders. Their lead in this matter was followed by many religious congregations after the Council of Trent. Some new communities took only simple vows, others took no public vows at all; the former were called religious congregations, the latter societies of common life without vows. Many of these groups were clerical groups, such as the Sulpicians, Redemptorists, Passionists, Oblates of Mary Immaculate, Marists, Marianists, and Oratorians.

The nineteenth and twentieth centuries in the history of religious institutes were characterized by a clear process of consolidation and stabilization. In 1917 a major turning point in the history of religious life occurred with the promulgation of the Code of Canon Law. In the years after 1917 all religious orders and congregations had to adapt their particular legislation to the general ecclesiastical laws of the Church. The highest authority for all questions about religious life was the Congregation for Religious which had existed since 1586. Canon 487 of the 1917 code defined religious life as "a stable manner of living in community, by which the faithful, in addition to the common commandments, also undertake to observe the evangelical counsels through vows of obedience, chastity, and poverty." That definition was drawn from history and current practice, but it soon lagged behind further developments in religious life. The change was characterized by the twentieth-century development of secular institutes, defined by Pope Pius XII as "clerical or lay societies whose members profess the evangelical counsels in the world for the sake of attaining Christian perfection and fully exercising the apostolate."[62]

At first glance, secular institutes appeared to be new ecclesiastical structures. In their own writings, the members often described themselves as living out a radically new vocation in contrast to the vocation of brothers and sisters in traditional religious institutes. Their goal remained Christian perfection, often described in both the older and more recent religious institutes as "the salvation of one's soul." The members of the secular institutes were to engage in the apostolate, which traditionally meant pastoral, social, charitable, or educational work undertaken either in a religious community's own institutions or those of the wider church. Secular institutes, however, did not originally own and staff their own institutions, such as hospitals supported by the community or schools staffed by members. The members of secular institutes tended to work primarily in secular, professional areas and carried out their professions in places and situations that had nothing to do with the secular institute itself or the wider church. They professed the evangelical counsels like religious, but they lacked the other essential component of religious life, namely, permanent community life in the form of an authentic common life. Some of the members did and still do in fact live in small communities. For the members of secular institutes, external signs of their way of life and openly manifested membership in the group are merely incidentals. Above all they are distinguished from traditional religious institutes by their general abandonment of common life and their work in secular professions. They often manifest little or no institutional witness.[63]

This cursory review of the history of institutes of consecrated life yields a number of basic characteristics of religious life which developed over the centuries and which are vital on both theoretical and practical levels for the identity, integrity, and ministry of such institutes today. First of all, in keeping with the prophetic tradition of the Old Testament, institutes of consecrated life should be made up of persons who are profound hearers of the Word of God and who, as men and women committed to a life of prayer, are able, as counter-cultural people, to proclaim that Word effectively while emphasizing values and ways of living that stand in opposition to the contemporary stress on consumerism, success, and individualism. This prophetic stance not only should be manifested in the lives of the individual members but should find expression in the community structures and corporate life style. Like the Old Testament prophets, men and women religious should be men and women of God.

Second, institutes of consecrated life should be expressions of the charismatic rather than the hierarchical dimension of the Church. Living in accord with the spirit of the charism of their founder, the members should manifest a spirituality that is clearly in keeping with their own tradition and their approved constitutions. Although they have a right to the legitimate autonomy provided for institutes of consecrated life in the Code of Canon Law, they also have a responsibility to be in respectful dialogue with diocesan authorities, especially concerning their ministries, and to be faithful to the directives from the Holy See concerning all institutes of consecrated life.

Third, the members of institutes of consecrated life normally take public vows in the Church. Over the centuries the vow patterns have undergone considerable change. Since the late medieval ages most non-monastic communities have taken vows of poverty, chastity, and obedience. The members of the older religious orders have taken solemn vows while the members of modern religious institutes have taken simple vows. Each institute, attentive to its own proper character and purpose, defines in its constitutions the manner in which the vows are to be observed. The juridical effects of the vows are regularly spelled out in approved constitutions. In any case, the vows are usually public rather than private, though some institutes do not require vows of any sort. These communities are called societies of apostolic life.

Fourth, the members of institutes of consecrated life are expected to live in community in one of their own religious houses. They may for a just cause live outside a house of the institute, but not for more than a year, except for the purpose of caring for ill health, of studies, or of exercising an apostolate in the name of the institute (c. 665, §1).

Finally, the work or ministry of an institute of consecrated life is usually specified in its constitutions; however, that work or ministry should always proceed from a member's intimate union with God and should be carried out in communion with the larger Church. The dominant motive for such work or ministry should be service rather than the development of a career or profession.

RELIGIOUS INSTITUTES TODAY

The tendency to create their own educational, healthcare, and social service institutions has been one of the most distinctive and enduring characteristics of religious institutes in the United States.[64] Thousands of hospitals, clinics, Catholic schools, colleges, seminaries, and orphanages have borne effective witness to the Catholic Church's concern for the well-being of its own members and its desire to serve others as well.[65]

Every religious congregation has been founded to respond to some specific need in the Church or in society; hence, each has had its own proper mission—for example, education, healthcare, care of orphans or prisoners, religious education, etc.—which has been spelled out in its own constitutions or charter. In the vast majority of cases, religious institutes have in turn founded institutions or committed themselves to staffing institutions established by parishes or dioceses. The history of religious congregations and orders mirrors and provides insight into the development of Catholic institutions in this country. Ministry in their own institutions or those of a diocese or parish traditionally implied that religious live together in a house of the institute and observe life in common. It was not, however, uncommon for priests in a religious institute to live alone in a parish and to identify much more closely with the diocesan clergy than with their own proper religious institute.

In a carefully crafted document released on February 19, 1994, entitled "Fraternal Life in Community," the Vatican Congregation for Institutes of Consecrated Life and Societies of Apostolic Life raised hard questions for many, if not most, institutes of consecrated life and their members.[66] The document analyzed factors that have influenced community life in religious institutes in recent times, noting, for example, that "the tendency in some institutes to emphasize mission over community and to favor diversity over unity has had a profound impact on fraternal life in common to the point that this has become at times almost an option rather than an integral part of religious life." The document observes that "the sincere desire to serve the church" sometimes leads a religious "to take on too much work, thus leaving less time for common life" and concludes that a religious man or woman living alone is never an ideal, and that religious institutes in which the majority of members no longer live in community would no longer be able to be considered true religious institutes.

Since the Second Vatican Council, there have been several developments in the Church which have something in common with life in religious institutes but are distinctly different. First of all, there has been a renewed interest among laymen and laywomen in associating themselves with religious communities as oblates or members of secular third orders. The term "oblate" has traditionally been applied to adults who do not take vows but choose to live in close connection to a monastery, while integrating the spirit of the monastic rule into their daily lives. Groups of such "secular oblates" have in fact multiplied today in various forms. The term "third order" generally has been a category for laity who seek to follow a way of life in the world but under the inspiration and spiritual guidance of a canonically approved religious institute. Various religious institutes founded since the Reformation, especially institutes of women, have begun to accept associates into their communities; such associates are in fact very similar to members of secular third orders. Canonically, secular oblates, secular members of third orders, and religious associates would seem to have more in common with people in secular institutes than with those in religious institutes, since they do not take public vows nor do they normally live a common life with members of the religious institute.

In an address to the National Religious Vocation Conference on September 5, 1996, Doris Gottemoeller stressed the importance of clear boundaries between those within and without, between members and non-members of religious institutes. She noted that, while in some sense boundaries are in fact limiting, they also promote organizational health, creativity, and prophetic witness. Sociologists have pointed out that the maintenance of boundaries requires specific commitment mechanisms, that is, practices, rituals, and obligations that reinforce common identity and differentiate members from non-members. Although many religious institutes have rightly discarded various commitment mechanisms that are no longer appropriate, many communities have been left with scarcely any public commitment mechanisms. Religious institutes must identify those mechanisms both for their own proper sense of identity and for effective community life and community witness.[67]

The other significant development in recent decades has been that of so-called ecclesial movements. In May 1998 a World Congress of Ecclesial Movements and Communities was held in Rome, drawing members from approximately fifty movements and new forms of community. Although priests are sometimes associated with these groups, the members are predominantly lay. Pope John Paul II sent an encouraging message to the assembly, enthusiastically supporting their commitment to the Christian faith and their lives of impressive witness. The following year, a seminar on movements and new communities in the Church was organized by the Pontifical Council for the Laity. Although tensions have sometimes developed between the members of these groups and diocesan and parochial authorities, such movements do in fact seem to fill a need in the Church and to respond to the desire for spiritual nourishment, direction, and leadership that the laity are not finding in traditional church structures or in religious institutes. Some of the movements are primarily interested in developing the spiritual lives of the members, while others also have a strong ministerial component and often are involved in justice and peace issues on a political level.

As the study on ordained ministry in religious life sponsored by the Conference of Major Superiors of Men pointed out several years ago, the parochialization of the Church in the documents of the Second Vatican

Council resulted in the parish being viewed as the center of the local church. This development has become increasingly pronounced in recent years and has had a major impact on religious institutes, especially those with ordained members. As the number of diocesan clergy has decreased and the number of Roman Catholics has increased in this country, not only ordained but also nonordained members, both men and women, have been increasingly called upon to staff parishes and even chanceries in a variety of ministries. This has happened despite the fact that for centuries religious institutes have maintained a strong independence from diocesan structures.[68] What has regularly happened is that the religious who serve in diocesan structures of one kind or another almost inevitably tend to function simply as diocesan ministers; consequently, they lose a sense of their own distinctive charism. Doris Gottemoeller has noted that one effect of the ministerial reorientation of women religious after Vatican II has been that many women religious, who had previously been involved in education or healthcare ministry, entered parish and chancery work in catechetical or administrative positions. As a result of their almost total investment in the ministerial demands of their parishes and dioceses, many of them have invested less and less time and energy in their own religious institutes.[69]

One of the sad outcomes of the reforms in institutes of consecrated life after Vatican II is that the strong witness of institutions owned and operated by religious has largely disappeared from the American scene. Many communities no longer have what might be described as a common work consonant with the charism of the institute. There is no doubt that a common work can be a valuable unifying factor in a community.[70]

The reasons behind the demise of Catholic institutions are extremely complicated, many of them linked to financial exigencies and lack of adequate personnel. Employment opportunities have often been a determining factor in instances of religious seeking work outside of their own communities. At the same time, however, one must ask whether many individual religious living alone—and their number seems to be legion —could not in fact pursue worthwhile ministries while living in their own communities. Has careerism or professionalism or independence been a decisive factor in establishing the widespread phenomenon of religious living in their own apartments? Have religious superiors and their councils thought out sufficiently the implications of their decisions to allow religious to live outside of their communities for extended periods of time? It is unlikely that those who might be tempted to consider a religious vocation will be attracted to such a diaspora situation. In fact, it seems that those communities that have a clearly defined ministry, spirituality, and common life are the very ones that are attracting new members. It is presumptuous to say that they are getting new members simply because they are "conservative."

The ultimate basis of unity in a religious institute lies not primarily in its work or ministry but rather in the religious ideals, the prayer, and the Christian community to which it is committed. Some institutes of consecrated life have in fact asked whether they should not seek to change their canonical status because they are no longer living as members of institutes of consecrated life but rather as members of secular institutes. For some members of religious institutes and for some communities, the task of beginning once again to rebuild community life in common may appear daunting, perhaps utopian. In the face of past wounds and present difficulties, the task may appear impossible. It is basically a question of taking up in faith a serious reflection on the theological sense of community life in common and of being convinced that through it the primary witness of religious consecration flows. In this way, institutes of consecrated life might once again achieve a strong sense of identity, a life of integrity that is in keeping with their approved constitutions, and a variety of ministries that flow out of community but are at the same time subordinated to authentic community life.

NOTES

1. Michael J. Himes, "Church Institutions: A Theological Note," *New Theology Review* 14 (May 2001) 7.

2. Ibid.

3. Robert N. Bellah, Richard Madsen, William M. Sullivan, Ann Swidler, and Steven M. Tipton, *Habits of the Heart: Individualism and Commitment in American Life* (Berkeley: University of California Press, 1985); *The Good Society* (New York: Alfred A. Knopf, 1991).

4. Avery Dulles, *Models of the Church* (Garden City, N.Y.: Image Books/Doubleday and Company, 1974) 49–59.

5. Himes, "Church Institutions," 8–9.

6. See cc. 602, 608, and 665, §1.

7. Himes, "Church Institutions," 14–15.

8. Vincent Desprez, "The Roots of Christian Monasticism: The Jewish Bible and Ancient Religions," *The American Benedictine Review* 41 (1990) 348–356; Diarmuid O'Murchú, *Reforming Religious Life: An Expanded Vision for the Future* (Slough, England: St Paul's, 1995) 30–43; and idem, *Religious Life: A Prophetic Vision: Hope and Promise for Tomorrow* (Notre Dame, Ind.: Ave Maria Press, 1991) 14–41; Sandra M. Schneiders, *Finding the Treasure: Locating Catholic Religious Life in a New Ecclesial and Cultural Context* (New York/Mahwah, N.J.: Paulist Press, 2000) 5–18.

9. Evelyn Woodward, *Poets, Prophets and Pragmatics: A New Challenge to Religious Life* (Notre Dame, Ind.: Ave Maria Press, 1987); O'Murchú, *Reforming Religious Life;* R. Arbesmann, "Fasting and Prophecy in Pagan and Christian Antiquity," *Traditio* 7 (1949) 1–71; Schneiders, *Finding the Treasure,* 315–335.

10. Walter Brueggemann, *The Prophetic Imagination* (Philadelphia: Fortress Press, 1986); idem, *The Hopeful Imagination* (Philadelphia: Fortress Press, 1986); Joseph Blenkinsopp, *Sage, Priest, Prophet: Religious and Intellectual Leadership in Ancient Israel* (Louisville: Westminster Knox Press, 1995).

11. O'Murchú, *Reforming Religious Life,* 34; Blenkinsopp, *Sage, Priest, Prophet,* 115–165.

12. See Paul K. Hennessy, *A Concert of Charisms: Ordained Ministry in Religious Life* (New York/Mahwah, N.J.: Paulist Press, 1997).

13. O'Murchú, *Reforming Religious Life,* 34.

14. Joan Chittister, *Womanstrength* (Kansas City: Sheed and Ward, 1990) 52.

15. See Anne Wilson Shaef, *When Society Becomes an Addict* (San Francisco: Harper and Row, 1987).

16. O'Murchú, *Reforming Religious Life,* 36–38.

17. Leonardo Boff, *Ecclesiogenesis* (Louisville: Westminster Knox Press, 1986) 51.

18. See Judith Merkel, *Committed by Choice: Religious Life Today* (Collegeville, Minn.: The Liturgical Press, 1992); Sandra Schneiders, *New Wineskins: Re-imagining Religious Life Today* (New York/Mahwah, N.J.: Paulist Press, 1986); idem, *Finding the Treasure,* 42–119; Barbara Fiand, *Refocusing the Vision: Religious Life into the Future* (New York: Crossroad, 2001); Duncan Fisher, "Liminality: The Vocation of the Church," *Cistercian Studies* 24 (1989) 181–205; 25 (1990) 188–218.

19. Graham Gould, *The Desert Fathers on Monastic Community* (Oxford: Clarendon Press, 1993) 1–17, 183–187.

20. Ibid., 19–35.

21. *Apophthegmata Patrum: The Sayings of the Desert Fathers. The Alphabetical Collection,* trans. Benedicta Ward (Kalamazoo, Mich.: Cistercian Publications, 1975); *The Wisdom of the Desert Fathers: Apophthegmata Patrum,* trans. Benedicta Ward (Oxford: Fairacres Press, 1975). See also *The Harlots of the Desert,* trans. Benedicta Ward (Kalamazoo, Mich.: Cistercian Publications, 1987); *The Lives of the Desert Fathers: The Historia Monachorum in Aegypto,* trans. Norman Russell (Kalamazoo, Mich.: Cistercian Publications, 1980).

22. O'Murchú, *Reforming Religious Life,* 70–71.

23. Jo Ann Kay McNamara, *Sisters in Arms: Catholic Nuns through Two Millennia* (Cambridge: Harvard University Press, 1996) 9–88.

24. Francine Cardman, "The Long History of Catholic Sisterhood," *Harvard Divinity Bulletin* 26 (1997) 12.

25. O'Murchú, *Reforming Religious Life,* 70–72.

26. Ibid., 71–76.

27. Karl Suso Frank, O.F.M., *With Greater Liberty: A Short History of Christian Monasticism and Religious Orders,* trans. Joseph T. Lienhard, S.J. (Kalamazoo, Mich.: Cistercian Publications, 1993) 42.

28. *Basil Regula: A Rufino Latine Versa,* ed. Klaus Zelger (Vindobonae: Hoelder-Pichler-Tempsky, 1986).

29. F. van der Meer, *Augustine the Bishop,* trans. B. Buthershaw and C. R. Lamb (New York: Sheed and Ward, 1961) 199–217.

30. Ibid., 69–84.

31. George Lawless, *Augustine of Hippo and his Monastic Rule* (Oxford: Clarendon Press, 1987).

32. *The Rule for Nuns of St. Caesarius of Arles,* trans. Maria Caritas McCarthy (Washington, D.C.: Catholic University of America Press, 1960).

33. McNamara, *Sisters in Arms,* 209–214.

34. Ibid., 91–119; Cardman, "The Long History of Catholic Sisterhood," 12.

35. See *Benedicti Anianensis Concordia Regularum,* ed. Pierre Bonnerue (Turnhout: Brepols, 1999).

36. See Otto Nussbaum, *Kloster, Priestermönch und Privatmesse* (Bonn: Peter Hansteln Verlag, 1961) 66–69; Angelus Häussling, *Mönchskonvent und Eucharistiefeier* (Münster: Aschendorffsche Verlagbuchhandlung, 1973) 298–374.

37. Frank, *With Greater Liberty,* 79–84; C. H. Lawrence, *Medieval Monasticism: Forms of Religious Life in Western Europe in the Middle Ages* (London: Longman, 1984) 76–96.

38. Frank, *With Greater Liberty,* 88–90.

39. Lawrence, *Medieval Monasticism,* 146–175.

40. Frank, *With Greater Liberty,* 98.

41. Lawrence, *Medieval Monasticism,* 146–175.

42. McNamara, *Sisters in Arms,* 260–288.

43. Lawrence, *Medieval Monasticism,* 142–145.

44. Simon Tugwell, *The Way of the Preacher* (Springfield: Templegate Publishers, 1979) 1–96; William A. Hinnebusch, *The Dominicans: A Short History* (New York: Alba House, 1975) 3–18; Lawrence, *Medieval Monasticism,* 203–207; Frank, *With Greater Liberty,* 109–115; *Early Dominicans: Selected Writings,* edited with an introduction by Simon Tugwell (New York/Mahwah, N.J.: Paulist Press, 1982) 1–35.

45. Tugwell, *The Way of the Preacher,* 82–110.

46. Frank, *With Greater Liberty,* 115.

47. Ibid., 114–115.

48. William J. Short, *The Franciscans* (Collegeville, Minn.: The Liturgical Press/Michael Glazier, 1989); *Francis and Clare: The Complete Works,* translated and introduced by Regis Armstrong and Ignatius Brady (New York/Mahwah, N.J.: Paulist Press, 1982).

49. Lawrence, *Medieval Monasticism,* 214–215.

50. Ibid., 216–218.

51. Ibid., 186-190; Cardman, "The Long History of Catholic Sisterhood," 13; McNamara, *Sisters in Arms,* 239–242; Saskia Murk-Jansen, *Brides in the Desert: The Spirituality of the Beguines* (Maryknoll, N.Y.: Orbis Books, 1998).

52. See John W. O'Malley, *The First Jesuits* (Cambridge: Harvard University Press, 1993).

53. Frank, *With Greater Liberty,* 153–156.

54. Ibid.

55. Ibid., 158.

56. McNamara, *Sisters in Arms,* 460–461.

57. Frank, *With Greater Liberty,* 158.

58. See Mary Wright, *Mary Ward's Institute: The Struggle for Identity* (Sydney: Crossing Press, 1997).

59. Frank, *With Greater Liberty,* 158–159.

60. Ibid., 159–160.

61. McNamara, *Sisters in Arms,* 526–530.

62. Apostolic constitution *Provida Mater,* February 2, 1947, *Acta Apostolicae Sedis* 39 (1947) 120.

63. Frank, *With Greater Liberty,* 204–208.

64. See Clyde F. Crew, "American Catholics: 1965-95," in *The Encyclopedia of American Catholic History,* ed. Michael Glazier and Thomas J. Shelley (Collegeville, Minn.: The Liturgical Press, 1997) 83–86. Also in *The Encyclopedia of American Catholic History,* see Gerald P. Fogerty, "American Catholics: 1865–1908," 73–78; Philip Gleason, "Catholic Education, Higher," 249–254; James O'Toole, "American Catholics: 1908–1965," 78–83; Michael Perko, "Catholic Education, Parochial," 254–259; Thomas Shelley, "American Catholics: 1815–1865," 69–73. See also Jay Dolan, *The American Catholic Experience* (New York: Doubleday and Co., 1985); James Hennesey, *American Catholics: A History of the Roman Catholic Community in the United States* (New York: Oxford University Press, 1981).

65. Doris Gottemoeller, "History of Catholic Institutions in the United States," *New Theology Review,* 14/2 (May 2001) 16.

66. *Origins* 23/49 (March 24, 1994) 694–712.

67. *Origins* 26/17 (October 10, 1996) 265–269; see also Doris Gottemoeller, "Religious Life in Crisis," *Origins* 28/35 (February 18, 1999) 634–638.

68. Hennessy, "Introduction: The Parochialization of the Church and Consecrated Life," *A Concert of Charisms,* 1.

69. Doris Gottemoeller, "The Priesthood: Implications in Consecrated Life for Women," in *A Concert of Charisms,* 127–128.

70. Daniel Rees et al., *Consider Your Call* (Kalamazoo, Mich.: Cistercian Publications, 1978) 301–312.

Conclusion

Convergence Points
toward a Theology of Ordered Ministries

Susan K. Wood, S.C.L.

The Collegeville Ministry Seminar proposed these convergence points as principles to shape a theology of ordered ministries. The convergence points emerged out of the participants' discussion of their working papers and represent a summary of the consensus of the results of the seminar.

1. Theologies of ministry must begin with an experiential description of ministry today.

Today a wide variety of lay ministers serve as catechists, directors of RCIA programs, youth ministers, liturgists, and directors of faith formation, to name just a few of the expanding roles for the laity in the life of parishes. At the same time, ordained ministry is expanding with the adoption of the permanent diaconate. Priestly ministry is also undergoing momentous change. Parishes without a resident pastor increased from 549 in 1965 to 2,393 in 1997. This has resulted in the practice of pairing and clustering parishes. Meanwhile, some suburban parishes register as many as ten thousand families. New demographics in the Church as well as the accessibility of ministerial education and formation for the laity have influenced the shape of ministry today and who ministers. Much of this change precedes theological reflection and arises out of necessity. Theologies of ministry must reflect this diversity and change, for ministry arises from the Church and reflects the life of the Church in all its particularity.

2. Baptism is an initiation into the life of Christ and the way of discipleship in the Church by which all participate in the mission of the Church. It is the ground for all discussion of ministry.

Pre-conciliar theology identified ministry with the sacrament of orders and distinguished the various degrees of orders by the sacramental powers proper to each. The seminar proposes a broadening of the understanding of ministry to include the laity and to view ministry in terms of distinct ecclesial relations that further specify the exercise of discipleship grounded in baptism.

Baptism initiates a person as member of the community, and ministry arises from the community. Through baptism we participate in the threefold office of Christ as priest, prophet, and king. Thus, all the baptized share in the priesthood of Christ in diverse ways within the royal priesthood of the baptized. The primary priesthood is that of Christ, followed by that of the baptized. Baptism is the primary sacrament of ministry. Ordained ministry does not have a different source, but finds its source in baptism, as does lay ministry. All ordained ministry, as all discipleship, proceeds from baptism. Priests "are disciples of the Lord along with all the faithful" and "in common with all who have been reborn in the font of Baptism, are brothers among brothers and sisters as members of the same body of Christ which all are commanded to build."[1] The priesthood of the sacrament of orders serves the priesthood of the people of God.

Baptism configures us to Christ, incorporates us into the Body of Christ, and initiates us into ecclesial relations. A working principle of the seminar has been that the life and structures of the Church can be understood only relationally. All are "ordained" in baptism, as the Greek Orthodox bishop and theologian John Zizioulas puts it.[2] This means that the most fundamental ordering of the Church occurs in baptism. We assume our place in the order of the Church according to our state in life and the charisms we bring for the upbuilding of the community and Christian discipleship.

3. Mission is grounded in the divine missions of Word and Spirit, which flow from God's love for the world.

The communitarian and personal nature of the Church finds its source in God, who is a communion of Father, Son, and Spirit. The missionary

character of the Church flows out of Word and Spirit, the two missions of
the Trinity. The Father sends the Son to give the Spirit and thus is present
in the world. Thanks to this presence, the world becomes the *oikonomia,*
the household of God.[3] In Jesus' baptism in the Jordan, the Father revealed
him as his beloved Son and anointed him with the Spirit. Jesus' baptism
inaugurated his mission. Jesus, filled with the power of the Spirit, was
tried in the wilderness and then returned to Galilee proclaiming the advent
of the kingdom of God (Mark 1:9-15; Luke 3:21–4:14). His message was
the transformation foretold by Isaiah 61:1-2: good news brought to the
poor, captives released, the blind given sight, and the oppressed freed. This
is the transformation of the world achieved in the person of Jesus, Son of
the Father and empowered by the Spirit.

The missionary Church flows out of this baptism of Jesus. It is missionary in its very identity. Members are baptized into the mission of
the Church. The Decree on the Ministry and Life of Priests, *Presbyterorum Ordinis,* affirms that, since within the mystical body all the faithful
are a holy and kingly priesthood, "there is no such thing as a member
who does not have a share in the mission of the whole body."[4] This mission of the Church is prior to our individual missions, which serve the
mission of the Church and the coming reign of God. Thanks to its mission to the world, the entire Church has a secular dimension, namely the
mission for the transformation of the world.[5] The mission of the Church
is identical with its sacramental nature, to serve this communion as sign
and instrument of universal salvation and the unity of humankind.

4. Ministry, grounded in baptism, is the building up of the Body of Christ for the mission of the Church. Ministry not only serves the internal needs of the Church but enables the Church to pursue its mission for the transformation of the world.

A division of labor between the "sacred" and the "temporal" has traditionally divided ordained ministry from lay ministry. According to this
view, clerics exercise ministry within the Church and the laity through
their work and witness seek to infuse the world with Christian values.
The documents of Vatican II stress the renewal of the temporal order[6] by
the engagement of the laity in temporal affairs.[7] The strength of this
teaching lies in the preservation of the mission of the Church to transform the world. It has proved problematic, however, in the effort to de-

termine what might be appropriate lay ministry in the Church. Too often lay ministry that serves the internal life of the Church has been seen as a stopgap measure that can be dispensed with once the priest shortage has been reversed.[8] Assigning ordained ministry to a "sacred" sphere and lay ministry to a "temporal" or secular sphere constitutes a division of labor that reduces the term "lay ecclesial minister" to an oxymoron.

The term "lay ecclesial minister" has encountered two major problems. At the time of the council there was an attempt to restrict the use of the term "ministry" to priests.[9] In the years preceding the council the activity of the laity was referred to as the "apostolate" of the laity rather than the "ministry" of the laity. Second, the arena of the laity was the world rather than the Church. Ecclesial ministers were ordained. Lay involvement in the work of the Church was usually described as "collaboration in the mission of the hierarchy."[10]

Nevertheless, the Decree on the Apostolate of the Laity, *Apostolicam Actuositatem,* affirms the role of the laity in both the temporal and spiritual orders: "The laity, carrying out this mission of the church, exercise their apostolate therefore in the world as well as in the church, in the temporal order as well as in the spiritual."[11]

The challenge today is multiple. First, we must find a way to locate all ministry as the ministry of the Church before it is the ministry of an individual, whether that person be ordained or nonordained. We have largely avoided seeing the ministry of the ordained individualistically, because an ordained person is seen as a public person, a representative of the Church. This has been more difficult for lay ministry. We must find a way to recognize this work of the laity in the Church as ecclesial, that is, the ministry of the entire Church and not just that of an individual baptized Christian. Finally, as ministerial functions pass from presbyter to deacon, or from presbyter to lay person, we are challenged to articulate a theology of orders and lay ministry that respects the distinction as well as the autonomy of the two states while at the same time rooting both in baptism and acknowledging their rightful roles in the Church.

5. *Within the diversity of the Spirit's gifts, the life, communion, and mission of the Church have been served by ordered ministries.*

The seminar proposes "ordered ministry" as a way of thinking through the question of ministry, lay and ordained, in the Church today. In the language of Richard Gaillardetz, an ordered ministry constitutes a "repositioning" within the Church whereby a person assumes a new relationship with the Church as a particular kind of minister. Such a ministry represents a significant and distinguishing role within the Church, a role characterized by a certain stability of function as contrasted with occasional service to the Church, which would not be considered an ordered ministry. Finally, the repositioning is recognized ritually through some sort of commissioning, installation, or ordination. Thus, the components of repositioning include (1) a personal call, (2) ecclesial discernment and recognition of a genuine charism, (3) formation appropriate to the demands of the ministry, which may require significant education, (4) ecclesial authorization by community leadership, and (5) some liturgical ritualization of assuming this ministry. Official authorization of ministry signifies that ministry is the work of the Church through an individual acting on behalf of the Christian community.

The concept of "ordered ministries" preserves the unity of the community served by a variety of ministries, takes us away from the term "lay ecclesial ministry," and minimizes the dichotomy between lay and ordained. Such a dichotomy fails to acknowledge that both forms of ministry are essentially grounded in baptism and that all the baptized share a common mission and common identity as the *Christifideles* before they are further specified by state in life and particular ministry. One seminar participant recalled the intervention of one of the bishops at Vatican II who commented that the sacramental character of orders does not erase the sacramental character of baptism.[12]

The concept of "ordered ministries" may also be a way of acknowledging that a person is entrusted with an ecclesiastical office.[13] An office "is a function established in a stable manner by divine or ecclesiastical ordinance, to be carried out for a spiritual purpose by one who has been legitimately named to the office (cc.145-146)."[14] Historically, only clergy could be named to church offices. Vatican II made it possible for laypeople to be named to church offices[15] and to perform functions constituted as offices.[16] The Code of Canon Law stipulates that only those who have received sacred orders are qualified for the power of governance (c. 274, §1), although the question concerning the exercise of the power of governance by the laity is still being debated. The work of a layperson in charge of a parish (c. 517, §2) would certainly imply governance. It would be to the individual's and the Church's benefit to recognize it as an "ordered ministry." Similarly, in some circumstances, the task of catechist might also be an "ordered ministry."

"Ordered ministries" are similar to offices in that they are functions constituted in a stable manner through divine or ecclesiastical ordinance to be carried out for a spiritual purpose.[17] Offices ensure continuity in a particular function in the name of the Church even when the initial office holder is no longer available. Thus, the emphasis is not on the person who holds the office, but on the ministry in the name of the Church which the office represents. There is an unresolved question today as to whether some of the current positions in the Church are in reality ecclesiastical offices, particularly when a layperson is entrusted with the pastoral care of a parish in the absence of a resident pastor.[18] "Ordered ministries," with their emphasis on vocation, discernment, formation, ecclesial authorization, and liturgical ritualization, include elements proper to an office, but place them in a larger vocational and liturgical framework. The category is more theological than juridical.

The sacrament of orders constitutes a specific instance of ordering within the Church and is also an "ecclesial repositioning." Although much more work remains to be done to clearly identify what distinguishes sacramental orders from other ordered ministries, ministry associated with apostolic office clearly includes a responsibility for judging, in one's own time and place, the authenticity of the ways in which the founding message of Christianity contained in the word of God is handed on in the Church today. It also includes the preservation of church order through the supervision of the exercise of charisms.[19] These are essentially episcopal activities that historically have been delegated in various ways to presbyters and deacons. Such activities may be helpful in sorting out the distinction between sacramental and non-sacramental ordered ministries, even though it is more difficult to envision how they are entrusted to deacons.

Among the ordered ministries, there is a particular need for an apostolic *episcope*, which is fulfilled in the sacramental order of bishop. Bishops exercise this apostolic office by virtue of their membership in the episcopal college, which is the successor of the college of the apostles.[20] Through their mission for the apostolicity of their church, they keep their particular church in communion with its apostolic past. They are designated "high priests" in the ordination prayer.[21] "Invested with the fullness of the sacrament of Orders," they are stewards of the grace of the "supreme priesthood" above all in the Eucharist.[22] In actualizing this priesthood, they enable the Church as the mystical Body of Christ to be in communion with its head and to actualize the communion of its members sacramentally through the communion in the Body of Christ (1 Cor 10:16-17). They represent their particular church in the communion of particular churches, sacramentalizing the communion of these churches within the college of bishops.[23]

Bishops entrust "in varying degrees various members of the church with the office of their ministry."[24] Presbyters and deacons also receive the sacramental character of orders because they share the office of the bishop in varying degrees. Presbyters are associated with the bishop because they are ordained to the priesthood.[25] They, too, are consecrated in the image of Christ to preach the Gospel, shepherd the faithful, and celebrate divine worship.[26] They depend on the bishop for the exercise of their ministry and through their ministry they make the bishop present in each local assembly of the faithful.[27] Presbyters have a responsibility to keep the portion of the people of God for whom they have responsibility in communion with the larger particular church to which they belong.

The sacramentality of the diaconate is likewise associated with the deacon's relationship to the bishop. The bishop is the principal person responsible for *diakonia* in his diocese. Since the bishop possesses the fullness of the sacrament of orders, he possesses in full what is only partial in the other two orders. The bishop promises to "show compassion and kindness for the sake of the Lord's name to the poor, to strangers, and to all who are in need."[28] Presbyters and bishops have responsibilities to serve God's people. This service is essentially a diaconal service. However, they didn't "pick up" empowerment to serve because they were ordained as transitional deacons on their way to being ordained presbyter and bishop. When viewed from the perspective of the bishop's ordination to the fullness of the sacrament of orders, the bishop is the one who first and foremost bears responsibility for the diaconal service in his diocese. The deacon in his ordination to the diaconate actually shares in the diaconal responsibility which is first the bishop's responsibility. The 1990 *Editio Typica Altera* of the rite of ordination makes this clear by eliminating the *cursus honorum*, the ascending steps of ordination, and beginning with the rite of ordination of a bishop. Thus sacramental orders are distinguished by their relationship to the bishop, their responsibility for the *episcope* of the Church, or their role in keeping the Church in apostolic communion.

6. What is constant historically is the principle of sacramental order. What changes is how ministries evolve and are ordered.

A variety of offices including bishop-presbyters, deacons, traveling prophets, and teachers existed well into the late first century. In the early Church, when the offices of leadership and oversight were evolving, there was little distinction between a bishop and a presbyter. The earliest writings witnessing to a clearly delineated threefold office of bishop, presbyter, and deacon are the letters of Ignatius of Antioch and Polycarp of Smyrna at the turn of the first century. The bishop was the original minister of baptism, post-baptismal anointing, Eucharist, and penance. Presbyters, originally counselors to the bishop, gradually took on sacerdotal functions as the Church expanded.

The role of deacon has likewise evolved, with the permanent diaconate even disappearing for centuries. The view articulated within the *Apostolic Tradition* (ca. 215) that a deacon is ordained to serve the bishop, but is not ordained to the priesthood and does not share in the counsel of the presbyterate, was not universal. Optatus of Miletus (ca. 370) considered deacons the third rank of priesthood, and fourth-century conciliar prohibitions against deacons exercising priestly functions like celebrating the Eucharist also indicate that this position was held by others.[29] Although deacons became a very powerful group in the Church during the first three centuries, the decision at the Council of Nicaea (325) to limit the powers of deacons because of their attempts to usurp the position of the presbyters contributed to the decline of the diaconate in the West.[30] By the tenth century, the diaconate was a preliminary step to the priesthood almost everywhere in the West, and the diaconate as a separate permanent order disappeared in the Middle Ages and reappeared only in *Lumen Gentium*.

Fairly recent changes in the ordering of ministries include the restoration of the permanent diaconate in the Latin Church by Paul VI in 1967. He suppressed tonsure, minor orders, and the sub-diaconate in his 1972 *motu proprio, Ministeria Quaedam*. At the same time, he established the installed ministries of reader and acolyte for laymen and opened the possibility for episcopal conferences to establish other installed ministries. Installed ministries have not developed in the Church, largely because those of reader and acolyte were reserved to lay*men* and because they are required for men who are being ordained to the diaconate or presbyterate. This latter requirement has had the effect of retaining the *cursus honorum*, the steps to ordination, despite the elimination of minor orders.

Given the change that has already occurred in the ministerial life of the Church, it is reasonable to expect ministries to continue to evolve. A concept of ordered ministries, including an expansion of installed ministries, envisions ministries as specific vocations with their own particularity. Ministry is no longer a more or less homogeneous gradation, but truly diverse, contextualized, and particular according to specific ecclesial relationships. For example, in many countries catechists often exercise a particular leadership role in relationship to a faith community, a role that is even more pronounced for communities that do not have a resident pastor. The same is true in the U.S. context for lay parish administrators. It may be appropriate for these to be recognized, installed ministries in the Church today.

> **7. These principles call us to an ongoing ecclesial discernment and a fresh articulation of an ordering of ministries (e.g., installation, commissioning) in the Church in order to recognize emerging ministries and changes in church practice.**

These principles result in a diversity of ministries participating in the order of the Church. They may be ordained ministries, installed ministries, or commissioned ministries. The distinction between ordained, installed, and commissioned ministries does not lie primarily in what each does, for a particular function may be performed by more than one kind of minister, but in the stability and ecclesial validation that accompanies the ministry, the vocation from which each arises, and how radically the ministry orients a person's core self. "Ministries" are services that exceed occasional services, engage a person at a vocational level, and have a certain stability. They are recognized or validated within a community, integrated into its life, and associated with a charism received from the Holy Spirit. Sacramental ordination gives a sacramental character, permanently conforming the ordinand to a certain aspect of imitation of Christ and creating a particular relationship with the Church. For example, a bishop imitates Christ the Shepherd, a presbyter, Christ the Priest, and a deacon, Christ the Servant.

"Installed ministries" are ministries bestowed by installation, both a juridical act and a liturgical act, by the bishop or his representative. Acolyte and lector are presently installed ministries replacing the former minor orders. The seminar's proposal for "ordered ministries" presupposes that these installed ministries be expanded in the Church, a possibility within current church law.

"Commissioned ministries" involve ecclesial recognition of a ministry, but in a less formal manner than installation. These ministries may be less permanent. Possibly someone other than a bishop could do the commissioning. Since "commissioned ministry" is not a formal category of ministry within the Church today, the details of who would be included in this category and how they would be commissioned would have to be worked out within the episcopal conference. A commissioned ministry would indicate that the ministry is more than the service of one baptized person to another, but represents the ministry of the Church.

The seminar has been able only to sketch out with broad strokes this vision of ordered ministries. Many issues remain to be developed further, such as the difference between installed ministries and commissioned ministries, why ordained ministry is sacramental and installed ministries are not, the difference between deacons and installed ministers, and the difference between ministry and office. Nevertheless, the recognition that all ministries are grounded in baptism, constitute a repositioning in the Church, and serve the mission and communion of the Church provides a way forward in articulating a contemporary theology of ministry. Such a theology respects the role of the laity in both the spiritual and temporal orders.[31] Furthermore, it offers a way to account for more stable ministry on the part of the laity who have prepared themselves formationally and professionally for service to the Church. It officially positions their contributions among recognized ministries in the name of the Church. Finally, it heals the divide that too often separates the lay and the ordained by allowing for a diversity of ordered ministries within the official ministry of the Church.

NOTES

1. *Presbyterorum Ordinis* 9.

2. John Zizioulas, *Being as Communion* (Crestwood, N.Y.: St. Vladimir's Seminary Press, 1985) 215–217.

3. Catherine Mowry LaCugna, *God For Us* (New York: HarperSanFrancisco, 1991) 21–52.

4. *Presbyterorum Ordinis* 2.

5. *Apostolicam Actuositatem (AA)* 5.

6. *AA* 7.

7. *Lumen Gentium (LG)* 31.

8. For example, see "Some Questions Regarding Collaboration of Nonordained Faithful in Priests' Sacred Ministry," issued by eight dicasteries of the Vatican, August 15, 1997, in *Origins* 27/24 (November 27, 1997) 397–410.

9. Kenan Osborne observes that Vatican II reserved the word "ministry" to the three offices of the ordained ministry. "In the case of the lay minister, the documents of Vatican II consistently employ the term 'apostolate.' This distinction of terms—'ministry' = ordained; 'apostolate' = nonordained—was deliberately done to indicate the 'essential difference' between the ordained and unordained ministries in the Church. However, after the council closed, this distinction in naming has not been followed, even by documents which have come from the Roman curia itself." *Priesthood: A History of the Ordained Ministry in the Roman Catholic Church* (New York/Mahwah, N.J.: Paulist Press, 1988) 324.

10. John Ford, "Ministries in the Church," in *The Gift of the Church*, ed. Peter Phan (Collegeville, Minn.: The Liturgical Press, 2001) 300.

11. *AA* 5.

12. Bishop Franjo Seper, *Acta Synodalia* II/3, 202.

13. See the discussion by Diane L. Barr on c. 230 and by John E. Lynch on c. 274, §1 in *New Commentary on the Code of Canon Law* (hereafter, *Commentary*) ed. John P. Beal et al. (New York/Mahwah, N.J.: Paulist Press, 2000) 299–301, 347–350.

14. James H. Provost, "Introduction to Canons 145–196," in *Commentary,* 195. See also *Presbyterorum ordinis*, 20.

15. *LG* 37.

16. *AA* 24.

17. Provost, "Introduction to Canons 145–196," 198.

18. C. 517, §2.

19. Brian Daley identifies these activities with the exercise of office in "The Ministry of Disciples: Historical Reflections on the Role of Religious Priests," *Theological Studies* 48/4 (1987) 621–629.

20. *LG* 20.

21. *Pontificale Romanum, "De Ordinatione Episcopi, Presbyterorum et Diaconorum," Editio Typica Altera*, 1990, 83.

22. *LG* 26.

23. Susan K. Wood, *Sacramental Orders* (Collegeville, Minn.: The Liturgical Press, 2000) 75–77.

24. *LG* 28.

25. *Pontificale Romanum*, 131.

26. *LG* 28.

27. Ibid.

28. *Pontificale Romanum*, 40.

29. See Council of Arles, c. 15; Council of Nicaea, c. 18. Texts in Hermann T. Bruns, ed., *Canones Apostolorum et Conciliorum Saeculorum VI-VII* (2 vols. Bibliotheca Ecclesiastica, Berlin: G. Reimeri, 1839; repr., Turin: Bottega d'Erasmo, 1959), II, p. 109 (Arles); I, p. 19 (Nicaea). Cited by Nathan Mitchell, *Mission and Ministry: History and Theology in the Sacrament of Order* (Collegeville, Minn.: The Liturgical Press, 1982) 206.

30. Council of Nicaea, c. 18.

31. *AA* 5.

Contributors

Michael Downey is Professor of Systematic Theology and Spirituality and the Cardinal's Theologian, Archdiocese of Los Angeles. He is the author of nine books and editor of the award-winning *The New Dictionary of Spirituality* (The Liturgical Press, 1993). His most recent books are *Altogether Gift: A Trinitarian Spirituality* (Orbis Books, 2000) and *The Cathedral: At the Heart of Los Angeles* (The Liturgical Press, 2003). Two Catholic colleges in his home Archdiocese of Philadelphia awarded him honorary doctorates.

Zeni Fox is Associate Professor at Immaculate Conception Seminary, Seton Hall, New Jersey. She is the author of *New Ecclesial Ministry: Lay Professionals Serving the Church* (Sheed and Ward, revised and expanded edition, 2002) and *Laity in Leadership Roles in the United States Today: A Theological and Pastoral Overview* (FADICA, 2000). She received the Gaudium et Spes Award from the National Association for Lay Ministry in 1998 and has been an advisor to the American Bishops' Subcommittee on Lay Ministry since its inception in 1994.

Aurelie Hagstrom is Associate Professor of Theology at Providence College in Rhode Island. She is a faculty member in the Diocesan Permanent Deaconate Program and the Lay Ministry Formation Program and a former theological advisor to the NCCB Committee on the Laity. Her publications include *The Vocation and Mission of the Laity* (Catholic Scholars Press, 1994).

Richard R. Gaillardetz is the Margaret and Thomas Murray and James J. Bacik Professor of Catholic Studies at the University of Toledo in Toledo, Ohio. He has published numerous articles and authored or edited six books, including *By What Authority? A Primer on Scripture, the Magisterium and the Sense of the Faithful* (The Liturgical Press, 2003). He has served as a theological consultant for several committees of the U.S. Conference of Catholic Bishops. In 2000 he received the Sophia Award from the faculty of the Washington Theological Union in recognition of "theological excellence in service to ministry."

Kenan B. Osborne, O.F.M., is Emeritus Professor of Systematic Theology at the Franciscan School of Theology/Graduate Theological Union, Berkeley, Calif., where he served as president and dean of the Franciscan School for eighteen years. He is a past president of the Catholic Theological Society of America and received the John Courtney Murray Award in 2002. The author of numerous books and articles on sacramental theology and ministry, his most recent book is *Christian Sacraments in a Postmodern World* (Paulist Press, 1999).

David N. Power, O.M.I., is Professor Emeritus at The Catholic University of America, where he previously held the Shakespeare Caldwell Chair in theology. Recipient of the Berakah Award of the North American Academy of Liturgy and the John Courtney Murray Award of the Catholic Theological Society of America, he is the author of ten books, of which the most recent are *Sacrament: The Language of God's Giving* and *Word of the Lord: The Uses of Scripture in Liturgy.* He has contributed many articles to journals and chapters to books and encyclopedias.

Thomas P. Rausch, S.J., is the T. Marie Chilton Professor of Catholic Theology at Loyola Marymount University in Los Angeles. A specialist in ecclesiology, ecumenism, and the theology of the priesthood, he has published ten books and over 160 articles and reviews, including the award-winning *Catholicism at the Dawn of the Third Millennium* (The Liturgical Press, 1996). His latest book is *Who Is Jesus? An Introduction to Christology* (The Liturgical Press, 2003).

Elissa Rinere, C.P., has worked as a canonist since 1981 in diocesan offices and in several lay ministry education programs. Currently, she is Assistant Professor of the Canon Law Faculty at The Catholic University of America in Washington, D.C.

R. Kevin Seasoltz, O.S.B., a Benedictine monk of Saint John's Abbey in Collegeville, is a professor in the School of Theology-Seminary at Collegeville. For the past seventeen years he has been the editor of *Worship.* As a canon lawyer, he has written extensively on the theology, history, and canon law of religious life.

Susan K. Wood, S.C.L., is Professor of Theology and Associate Dean at Saint John's University, Collegeville, Minn. She is the author of numerous articles on ecclesiology, ecumenism, sacramental theology, and priesthood as well as *Spiritual Exegesis and the Church in the Theology of Henri de Lubac* (Eerdmans, 1998) and *Sacramental Orders* (The Liturgical Press, 2000).

Index